Adventures
on the margins of
a wasteful society

FREE

KATHARINE HIBBERT

EBURY
PRESS

3 5 7 9 10 8 6 4 2

Published in 2010 by Ebury Press, an imprint of Ebury Publishing
A Random House Group Company

The Random House Group Limited Reg. No. 954009

Addresses for companies within the Random House Group can be
found at www.randomhouse.co.uk

A CIP catalogue record for this book is available
from the British Library

The Random House Group Limited supports The Forest
Stewardship Council (FSC), the leading international forest
certification organisation. All our titles that are printed on
Greenpeace approved FSC certified paper carry the FSC logo.
Our paper procurement policy can be found at
www.rbooks.co.uk/environment

Mixed Sources
Product group from well-managed
forests and other controlled sources
www.fsc.org Cert no. TT-COC-2139
© 1996 Forest Stewardship Council

Printed in the UK by CPI Mackays, Chatham, ME5 8TD

ISBN 9780091932732

To buy books by your favourite authors and register for offers visit
www.rbooks.co.uk

chapter one

I was sitting in a park, feeling sick. I'd left my job, packed my possessions away and given up my rented flat; it had been three hours since I'd locked myself out of it for the last time. My plan when I set out had been to find a squat to stay at and some food dumped by a shop or a café to eat, and to see how long I could survive without spending money, living off what would otherwise go to waste. Now I just wanted to go home. But it was too late.

Earlier, I'd wavered on the doorstep in the chill of the spring morning before making myself post the key back through the letterbox and walk away. I'd trudged around for hours, searching for a place to stay. All I had with me was a couple of changes of clothes, a sleeping bag and a wash kit – less than I'd taken for weekend breaks in the past and all I had for the indefinite future. My pockets were empty. There was a £20 note buried in my bag but that was the only money I had.

I was hungry. It was only lunchtime so everywhere was still open for business – far too early for them to have thrown out anything worth eating, I reckoned. For the last few weeks I'd been looking for newspaper cuttings and web pages mentioning squats and keeping my eyes open for possible places. I'd thought I might be able to knock at a squat's front door and ask if the residents or anyone they knew had any space for a new person. I doubted that anyone would let me in when they didn't know me, had no reason to trust me and didn't owe me anything. But if that failed I'd have to start my own squat and that idea seemed even more difficult and terrifying.

I had spotted a couple of derelict buildings that looked as if people might be living there, or had once squatted there. In the backyard of one, a former nightclub, there was a sea of junk – furniture, crockery, electronics, rubbish. The squatters and all their possessions had clearly been thrown out fairly recently and all that was left was the pile of trash. At another squatted-looking building, a disused pub, there were sheets at the windows as curtains and peace flags flying from the eaves but no answer to my knock on the door. I couldn't find the guts to knock again more loudly. As I was walking towards an old warehouse, its walls covered with layers of graffiti, a girl with lank hair and bad skin, wearing clothes that looked like she'd slept in them, had opened the door to three hard-faced men. A mongrel dog trotted out. I walked towards them but they'd already turned to go inside. The girl leaned out to shout, 'Fucking get inside now, Dolly!' to the dog and the door slammed shut. I almost knocked but I couldn't do it. It felt too dangerous. Sitting on that park bench, I couldn't stop myself from crying. What had I been thinking?

But I did know what I had been thinking when, in the comfort of my safe, warm flat, I had decided to walk away from it all. I was 26, and on paper my life was pretty good. I had a decent job as a journalist and shared a flat in a pretty but slightly shabby Victorian building with my sister. Work brought me invitations to parties and paid for nights out, clothes and drinks. I had a wide circle of friends and a boyfriend who liked the things I liked and knew how to make me laugh. I had the money for music festivals, holidays and treats. But life had become faintly tedious. I was tired of dragging myself out of bed in the morning to get to the office and disappointed that I could rarely muster much excitement about going out in the evening. I had begun to take it all for granted – my clothes, my record collection, my travel pass, my gig and theatre tickets. I was falling into a cosy, domesticated rut, increasingly committed to debts, responsibilities and possessions, and I could see a time coming when making any changes to my life would cause chaos for myself and everyone around me. I could feel myself becoming so accustomed to a steady wage and a comfortable life that I couldn't break out of it to do anything more interesting, challenging or worthwhile. Call it a quarter-life crisis or call it a failure to count my blessings, but I missed the enthusiasm and idealism I knew I'd felt more strongly in the past. I'd had one too many conversations with friends about office politics, supermarket home deliveries and the pros and cons of different makes of juicer, and I didn't want to feel faint gloom on a Sunday night at the prospect of another week.

I'd read articles and books highlighting the social and environmental problems with consumerism, and I felt guilty about my lifestyle while simultaneously being tired of green nagging. Of course I disliked huge supermarkets – disliked going shopping in their endless, brightly lit aisles as well as objecting to their stranglehold on the market. I knew perfectly well that they applied huge pressure to their suppliers to provide them with ever-cheaper stock. I knew they minimised their tax bills by any means possible. I knew that by shopping in them I was fuelling their expansion and therefore undermining the owner-run shops and the cheerfully raucous market on my local high street. But I went at least once a week to stock up on everything in one handy swoop. Although I felt guilty about flying anywhere or eating air-freighted fruit and vegetables, I liked going on holiday and I liked to be able to eat lettuce and grapes all year round. I was concerned that the disposable fashion touted on the high streets was produced in sweatshops while poisoning cotton farmers and I bought the argument that advertising and fashion magazines encourage debt, poor self-image and maybe even depression by encouraging shoppers to max out their credit cards in pursuit of an impossibly airbrushed ideal. But I owned piles of clothes bought on a whim, worn once or twice then pushed to the back of the wardrobe.

So far, so much over-privileged whinging. But then the papers filled with stories about crunching credit, banks in crisis, crashing house prices and a coming wave of job losses. The system I'd resented while relying on seemed to be crumbling. My boss at the newspaper where I'd worked part-time as a reporter called me into his office: 'We're going to have to make some redundancies and I'm afraid it's going to be you.' The freelance work with which I'd filled the other three days of my week seemed to be drying up as the shrinking advertising market pushed many magazines and papers into the red. The landlord phoned: 'I've been forced to reassess the rents on my properties now my mortgage costs have increased – I'm afraid yours is going to have to go up.'

Perhaps I could have found another job and a cheaper flat, and relied on debt and government allowances in the meantime. But I'd had enough. A couple of years before, I'd met several people who claimed to live on next to nothing in the centre of Britain's cities. They knew where to find food that had been thrown away by shops and cafés and where to scavenge for clothes and household goods. If they wanted to go somewhere, they walked, cycled or hitch-hiked. They knew how to spot buildings that had been left empty for months or years, and how to get inside and live in them for free.

They seemed to be showing that Britain's households and businesses are wasting enough food, clothes and businesses to support a hidden army of people. I already knew that we recycle only a small proportion of the 400 million-plus tonnes of waste we produce every year, that we've already covered more than 100 square miles of our own country with landfill sites and that we pollute the developing world by shipping our waste there for them to dispose of. But they showed me that much of the stuff that goes into the wastebins doesn't even need to be recycled, let alone burned or buried. It can be reused or even used for the first time. Fresh food and undamaged furniture and clothes are going into dustcarts. Still-functioning electronic goods containing arsenic, lead and mercury are going into landfill. Easily habitable buildings are standing empty, falling into dereliction and dragging down neighbourhoods.

Many of the people who were living out of the bins and skips seemed to be doing all right on it – most of those I met were opinionated and eloquent, healthy and fairly happy. Theirs were not the intolerably uncomfortable, chaotic lives of the most visibly homeless people who sleep rough or stay in night shelters. But I wasn't sure if I could do it myself. Of course I knew I could sometimes do without a cup of coffee in the morning and a couple of drinks in the evening. I knew I ought to be able to face the world without make-up and a wardrobe full of clothes. I wouldn't die of boredom if I couldn't buy cinema tickets. But I'd never done without those things for more than a couple of weeks and I didn't know how I would feel if I couldn't sleep in a proper bed, have a hot shower or hop on public transport. Would I lose touch with my friends if I couldn't pay to join them for gigs or theatre trips? Would my boyfriend, Colin, get tired of me if I didn't spend money on myself?

I wanted to know, though. I wanted to find out what I would really miss and what I only thought I couldn't do without. If my relationships couldn't survive without money, it would be better to know that now rather than later. And perhaps I would see what I really wanted and needed rather than taking my way of life for granted and letting it irk me.

After I'd boxed up my clutter and said goodbye to my friends at work I'd felt liberated. My mum had offered to help me sort my things out and to stash what I wanted to keep in her garage. 'Thanks! It shouldn't take too long,' I'd said, blithely. She had raised an eyebrow very slightly. Around midnight, after two trips between my flat and her garage, we still hadn't finished. Three years of living in the same place had allowed me to accumulate an unbelievable amount of junk: packets of barely used make-up, books I'd half-read, disliked, but still hung on to, elaborate kitchen equipment I'd received as presents, tried out once then packed away in the back of the cupboard. Mum and I filled several bin bags with clothes and carted them round to a charity shop. After hours of walking up and down the stairs carrying boxes I couldn't even muster much affection for the possessions I did want to hang on to.

Mum was doing her best to suppress her anxiety about what I was about to do, but I could see that she was worried and if anything that made me more determined not to admit any doubts. If I didn't take this opportunity to cast off the moss I had gathered, I felt, it might not come again. My job had gone and my sister had found a nice new person to take my room in the flat who could afford the increased rent. I didn't have kids or a mortgage. Even my expensive phone contract had expired.

Sitting on that bench, though, I ached to have it all back again, missing the certainty about what I'd be doing and where I'd be living tomorrow, next week and next month, which I'd found oppressive just days before. But there were always going to be withdrawal symptoms, I told myself. If this was cold turkey, I would have to get through it. I had reckoned that I'd need to give it all up for a year to find out what I could adapt to doing without. If I could find a way to get through four seasons without my possessions and without working, borrowing or signing on for benefits, I'd know I could do it indefinitely and I'd be able to decide whether or not I wanted to.

There had been no way to find out what I would be letting myself in for. I wanted to join an invisible group of people who live outside normal society and who don't want to be found. Although homelessness charity Crisis estimates that around 10,000 people are squatting in the UK, most squatters keep a deliberately low profile. No census data exists on them, and Crisis points out that many squatters are self-sufficient and undisruptive and therefore off their radar and that of the police, government agencies and other charities. Newspaper reports about squatting usually focus on particularly chaotic or attention-seeking cases – the crack dens and murder scenes, or the activists or artists squatting to gain publicity for their work or political agenda. Most squatters and scavengers coordinate by word of mouth or by noticeboards – an open online discussion forum is too easily read by the owners of disused properties or rubbish bins.

The only way to find out whether it was a way of life that might work for me was by doing it. I decided to stop spending, to become what some might call a scrounger, a freeloader, a bum. I wasn't going to take anything that wasn't going spare and I wasn't going to claim charity, steal or beg. I wouldn't accept favours from friends that I couldn't repay. If I wanted to see Colin, I'd have to make sure I had a safe, comfortable-enough place that he could come and stay with me. If I was going to be a parasite, I would be a benign one.

'How am I going to know if you're all right?' my mum had asked me quietly and tearfully. 'What if you get attacked, beaten up, raped, murdered in some crack den? Even if you aren't taking anything with you, you might still be worth robbing to someone even more desperate.'

I hadn't known what to say, and I hadn't known what to say when Colin wanted to talk about what this would mean for our relationship which, as well as bringing me a partner in crime for drunken nights out, hung-over Sundays of Scrabble and newspapers, and daytrips to faded English seaside resorts, had brought me deep, secure happiness in the year and a half since we had met. Sitting on that bench I couldn't help wishing one of them had tried harder to persuade me not to go, rather than accepting my reasoning and my assurances that I'd be careful. But I'd done it now and I had to choose: I could either give up straight away or keep walking. I mopped my face on my sleeve and plodded on.

Another couple of hours of wandering and the afternoon

was running out. I'd tramped a wide circle that had brought me back towards central London, having seen nowhere I could possibly stay that night along the way. I headed to Whitechapel where, down a dingy alley and up three narrow, rickety flights of stairs, I knew I'd find the office of the Advisory Service for Squatters, known as ASS.

It's a tiny attic room, rented cheaply from an anarchist group which owns the building, crammed from floor to ceiling with filing cabinets and shelves laden with papers, books and folders. One or two people volunteer there every day, offering legal advice on everything from getting the electricity and water switched on legitimately in an abandoned house to helping squatters put up a fight in court when they're being evicted.

The volunteer staffing the office seemed used to would-be squatters coming in for advice on getting started, but the small room was already crowded with people waiting for help and there wasn't very much he could do for me, he said. I waited until he was free, keeping myself to myself in the corner of the room, too overwrought to be sure I was capable of conversation. When the office quietened down, he introduced himself as Greg and gave me a cup of incredibly strong coffee and a basic outline of the laws on squatting and how to start a squat of my own. I knew some of it already because I had a copy of the *Squatters Handbook* produced by the ASS – a slim, stapled booklet in print since 1976 which costs, as I was told, 'A pound fifty if you've got it, nothing if you don't.'

Living in someone else's building without their permission is legal for two reasons. First, trespass isn't a crime under English and Welsh law – it's a civil matter, a dispute between two parties like a debt or a breach of contract which has to be dealt with in a civil court, not by the police. Signs in England warning that 'trespassers will be prosecuted' are a con – being on someone else's land is not, in itself, illegal. By contrast, squatting is outlawed in Scotland, where an act passed in 1865 after the Highland Clearances displaced farmers from their land made it an offence for them to go back. North of the border it is a crime punishable by jail or a fine to 'lodge in any premises or encamp on any land which is private property without the consent or permission of the owner or legal occupier'.

Second, squatters rely on the protection brought by a 1381 law forbidding forcible entry to any building that is someone's home. The rule, which was introduced after the Peasants' Revolt to bring order into land disputes by forbidding owners from taking matters into their own hands, one of the causes of the rebellion, states that entry can be made 'not with strong hand nor with multitude of people, but only in a peaceable and easy manner'. The upshot of the law is that an Englishman's home really is his castle, even if it's a squatted castle. It is illegal for anyone – even the owner – to break into a squat without a court order, as long as at least one squatter is inside and the building is not someone else's home. Police can come in only for the same reasons as they can break into a normal house: if they suspect that a crime is under way inside, to prevent harm to property or people or if they have a search warrant. Not that owners always observe the law – less scrupulous ones sometimes send round the heavies, risking the £5,000 fine or six-month prison sentence threatened by the 'Legal Warning' that most squatters hang on their doors, which sets out section six of the Criminal Law Act 1977, the modern version of the 1381 law.

The most dangerous bit, at least from the point of view of trouble with the police, is actually getting into a building, Greg warned me. Trespassing may not be a crime but breaking and entering is, and so is criminal damage and going equipped for burglary. I'd have to assemble a group of other would-be squatters then hunt for a building we could get into without causing damage, or without causing visible damage, or without getting caught causing visible damage. Perhaps we could climb through a badly secured window, skylight or coal hole. Perhaps an already-broken pane of glass would let us hook open the latch on a door. However we did it, once we were inside and locked in with our own locks we'd be on safer ground. It was imperative to squat in a group because someone would have to stay at home all the time to keep the protection of the 1381 law. But if we did that and got our utilities connected legally so that the police couldn't hassle us for stealing electricity or gas, didn't do anything criminal in the building, and as long as the building genuinely was lying unused, then we couldn't legally be evicted until the owners took us to court.

I didn't want to admit to Greg how overwhelmingly impossible that all seemed. He pointed to a noticeboard where, he said, there were occasional messages pinned up offering spaces in under-populated squats. My stomach was tense as I scanned the notices, hoping that an existing squat would need an extra person to help them keep the place occupied or to help with the DIY needed to get a derelict house working as a home.

But that day, as on most days Greg said, offers of places to stay were vastly outnumbered by notices about empty buildings others had spotted and people asking for empty rooms or hoping to form groups to open a squat together. There were a couple of spare rooms listed, but I noted them down without much optimism; the dates on the ads were all a week or more old and I was sure they'd already have gone. After all, a rent-free room in a place where the other people have already done all the work by finding and getting into an empty building sounded too good to be true. So I busied myself writing down phone numbers of people who had put up messages seeking other people to start squats with, and a few addresses of supposedly empty places – though Greg warned me that they might not be up to date.

Greg turned his attention to the next squatters in line, a pair who had brought in court papers issued by the owner of the building to evict them. They were hoping that Greg would spot an inaccuracy or incompleteness in the owner's case so that it got adjourned in court, buying them a little more time in the building, a disused nursing home. The nursing home had closed down several years ago and the building had been empty since. They were pretty sure it was going to stay empty, as they had looked at applications for planning permission submitted to the local council and seen that it was owned by a property developer who wanted to level it and replace it with flats. Because the building was listed, planning permission had been denied so it remained disused, with smashed windows and filthy floors.

When Greg turned away to start writing them a defence, one of the squatters, a scarecrow in his early twenties with a lopsided grin, hacked-around hair and calf-length checked trousers over stripy knee-high socks, passed the time by asking me what I was up to.

'Looking for a place to stay,' I replied.

'Oh well, that's easy – there's loads of empties around.'

He started reeling off squattable places he'd seen near their own. But I'm alone, I told him, and a beginner. He and the girl he came in with looked at each other for a moment. 'Well, if you just need a place to crash for a little while to get yourself sorted out, why don't you come to ours?'

It was huge, he said, with loads of spare rooms. They wouldn't be there for much longer, but – as long as everyone else who lived there was OK with it – he saw no reason why I shouldn't sleep there for a few nights.

The relief was like exhaling after holding my breath. Pete and Marie were smiley and likeable. After a few minutes chatting to them, I was as sure as I could be that they were harmless. Meeting them and Greg made my plan to find a way to live like this seem more realistic and less terrifying than it had all day. Pete and Marie set off to cycle home, but I had to follow them on foot. The walk took more than an hour and the sun was low in the sky when I found the lane their house was on. It was easy to spot – Pete had told me it would be, because someone had spray-painted their door number in digits a metre high on the fence nearby. The house was big, as they had said – a chunky two-storey Victorian building in red brick, sprawl-ing in a long rectangle on the edge of acres of churned-up land, where the rest of the hospital it was once attached to had already been demolished and a 'luxury development of one-, two- and three-bedroom contemporary apartments' was set to spring up. Most of the ground-floor windows of the squat were boarded up. Black bin bags of rubbish were piled by the front door. Two men with spanners were working on an engine outside the front door.

'Is Pete or Marie around?' I asked.

'Probably – inside somewhere, upstairs most likely,' one replied. 'Go and have a look if you want.'

The hallway was dim behind the boards on the windows and smelled of dogs and damp. On both floors, dozens of rooms opened off the corridors that formed the spine of the building. Although the group had only been inside the building for three weeks, they had made it fairly homely. Some rooms had been turned into bedrooms with mattresses and bedding on the floors, possessions stacked up and spray-paint or posters on the walls. Others were empty. Someone found Pete for me and he introduced me to everyone else – more than a dozen people of a mixture of

European nationalities – Spanish, Italian and Portuguese as well as British – most of them pierced, dreadlocked and in their twenties. People shook my hand, told me their names, asked me a question or two about myself then shrugged when I asked if I could stay for a few days. 'Don't see why not, really – plenty of space.'

'You hungry?' asked a small, perky-looking girl called Kelly. 'We're just about to cook up some dinner – want some?'

Yes! I really did want some! I'd barely eaten all day and I'd been too tense to notice how hungry I had become, but when I thought about it I realised my stomach was painfully empty. So walking into their kitchen, which was piled high with food, a jumbled selection of bread, vegetables, dips, ready-meals and cake rescued from local supermarket bins, was almost overwhelming. The big room was raucous, with some people trying to cook while others shooed out the dogs or horsed around, starting arguments and play-fights. Kelly coordinated the preparation of tomato and olive pasta and a vegetable pie, in huge, catering-size pans and dishes. It was ready just after midnight and we ate it sitting round a huge table built on trestles in the living room. It was delicious, and not only because I was famished.

After we'd all eaten, a meeting was called to discuss the court date and where the group should move to when they lost in court – as they knew they would sooner or later, because owners are always entitled to a possession order against squatters who have been in a building for less than ten years. Even if the ASS succeeds in finding a few legal inaccuracies in their claim, it only delays the inevitable eviction. Marco, a Spaniard and slightly older than the rest of the group, was elected to chair the meeting, so he wrote an agenda on the 'whiteboard' – the door of the fridge: 'WHO? WHERE? HOW? WHEN? WHY?'

Marco decided to take the agenda in reverse order, easiest first. 'Why are we squatting?' A chorus of answers, backed up by whoops from the others. 'Because otherwise our dogs would have to live on their own.'

'To redress the balance between rich and poor.'

'To prove there's an alternative to consumerism.'

'Cos we've got no money.'

'To organise events – to have a place where we can make stuff happen.'

Where, when and how to look for a new building came next. A rota was drawn up of people to go and scout for possible 'empties', properties that seemed to have been uninhabited for months or years and which looked ripe for squatting. They discussed what they needed – a big place with lots of rooms and some spacious communal areas where gigs and parties could be held. And ideally not too close to any neighbours so the parties could go on unhindered. Then there was discussion about which night they should aim to actually 'open' one – get inside and immediately secure the doors and windows so that the owner couldn't break in and kick them out.

Marco tried to prevent the meeting from descending into quarrelling but Tom, an Englishman in his mid-twenties who made money as a street performer, seemed to consider every issue under discussion to be deeply personal. It was clear to him that he was working harder than anyone in the group, and that the fact that they hadn't yet found a new home and that the current one was messy and dirty was everyone's fault except his and, possibly, his ghostly quiet girlfriend's.

At around two in the morning, the discussion had reached 'who' – who should be allowed to move into the new squat, the trickiest item on the agenda. After a long row, it was put to the vote whether Ernesto, a peaceful-looking Portuguese man with a mane of dreadlocks, should move out. He didn't make enough contribution to the household, some said, spending too much time out, not bringing in any food and only coming home to sleep. 'This is horrible,' said an Italian girl called Monica. 'How come we get to decide who gets to stay or go? It's a squat – it doesn't belong to any of us. I thought we believed that things should be used by whoever needs them. Who are we to tell people they can't stay when there's room for them?'

'But the group has to work as a group,' said Tom. 'People have got to be in or out, and Ernesto's never here.'

Narrowly, it was voted that he should leave. He had managed to keep calm during the discussion but now he stopped restraining himself and his handsome face filled with hurt and anger. 'Fuck you all,' he muttered as he stormed out of the room. 'I was leaving anyway – I don't want to be in a place where you can't put a finger down without getting filth on it, where there's dog piss all over the floor. But I'm going because I'm going, not because you vote that I go.'

Now it was my turn to be discussed and everyone was tired and riled. Was it OK for me to stay for a few nights? I asked cautiously. Just until I sorted myself out elsewhere, not to move into the new place with them, not to join their group. Everyone seemed to think I could, except for Tom. He didn't know me, didn't trust me and didn't want to live in an open house. A few people nodded. But as he wound himself up into a rant about why I shouldn't have been invited round in the first place, people started to turn against him. A guy called Juan took my part even though I'd exchanged no more than a couple of sentences with him. 'We've got the space – why on earth shouldn't she stay a few nights? Hasn't anyone ever done the same for you, Tom?'

I kept quiet, except to say that I'd leave without argument if it was decided that I shouldn't be there. There was a vote. Tom raised his hand alone when Marco the chair asked for votes against my staying for a night or two. So I had a roof for tonight and maybe a little longer. It was a start.

The meeting continued with increasingly heated discussions about who should be allowed to remain with the group and who should be made to find another gang when they moved house. By three in the morning I was completely past it. The room was full of shouting and, when I stood up, my knees visibly shook with nerves, cold and exhaustion. Monica and Paula, Tom's silent girlfriend who had abstained from the vote on whether I could stay, showed me an empty room I could sleep in. The windows were boarded up so the only light was from an unshaded neon tube in the ceiling. It was full of junk with bits of wood and metal stacked on the gritty floor. The girls apologised that it wasn't very nice. But it was more than good enough for me – I'd barely dared to hope for a place to unroll my sleeping bag tonight. I piled the debris against the wall. Monica helped me carry in a spare mattress and lent me a quilt, a pillow and a broom to sweep the floor.

When she'd gone, I perched on the edge of the bed, too shaken to think sensibly but unable to stop my mind from racing. I was deeply grateful to have found a bed and a few people who were friendly and kind. Still, I didn't feel at home at all and it had been made abundantly clear to me by Tom that I shouldn't. I shoved two five-kilo bags of coal that were in my room up against the door. It wasn't going to stop anyone from opening it but at least I'd hear them. I zipped myself into my sleeping bag and tried to relax but my mind carried on circling, trying to work out how I could sort myself out, where I could go from here, what I ought to do tomorrow.

Eventually I must have drifted off because suddenly I found myself jolted out of sleep and sitting bolt upright in the pitch dark yelping, 'Who is it? Who is it?' before I could work out where I was, let alone what was happening and why the bags of coal were being pushed noisily across the floor as the door opened. A light shone in and a tall, skinny man with tangled hair peered at me. 'What do you want?' I asked, trying not to sound terrified.

'Sorry, sorry – I thought this room was empty. Looking for a screwdriver,' he replied as he backed out of the room.

False alarm. But the adrenalin that had flooded my bloodstream kept me awake and jumpy.

chapter two

The next few days passed in a haze. My boarded-up room was always dark, making it easy to sleep until mid-morning and hard to tell what time it was when I did wake. That first night, I managed to sleep for a few hours after dawn must have broken outside. When I was woken by children yelling and fighting as they walked past on their way to school, I lay in the gloom, wondering what to do with myself. There was no hot water and I didn't feel up to a cold shower. The house had the guinea-pig hutch smell of unwashed skin, hair, clothes and bedding, so I guessed I wasn't the only one to make that decision. I was sure I didn't smell yet, but I felt grimy in yesterday's clothes.

I was aware of how much I had to do – I had no means of transport other than my exhausted legs, no allies, no food to contribute and nowhere to stay beyond the next couple of days. But I couldn't leave the squat until someone else woke up because the door would have to be locked behind me. I was too agitated to sit still. I didn't feel like breakfast but knew I'd need energy and might not find any food for myself later. I'd been told to help myself to whatever I wanted in the kitchen. I took a glass of out-of-date but still fresh milk and some shop-made summer pudding and, feeling steadier, started doing the washing-up from last night's meal to keep myself occupied.

Around midday, Monica stumbled out of bed and let me out. Standing in the street, I knew I should be doing something to get myself more sorted but I couldn't think where to start. I wandered towards central London, my eyes open for empty buildings or other squats to go to. No joy. I went into a branch of Starbucks and asked for some tap water. I sat down but suspected the mums and nannies sipping their coffees were watching me, though I never caught them looking when I glanced up. At Oxford Street, I went into Selfridges and asked for a makeover at a beauty counter. The free treat left me feeling slightly more human.

By early evening I was walking through the streets looking for something to eat. It was closing time, and the cafés and sandwich shops were putting sacks of rubbish onto the pavement. I opened bag after bag but found them filled with real rubbish – empty packaging, used paper cups, coffee grounds and floor sweepings. After a dozen or so sacks of trash I got lucky and found a black bin bag full of sandwiches. Wrapped in cardboard and plastic, they were completely untouched and, the packaging promised, they had been freshly made from the finest ingredients that very morning. Sounded good to me. There were more than I could carry, let alone eat. Triumphant, I filled my bag then sat on a bench to eat a BLT baguette ahead of the long walk back to the squat.

Dark began to fall before I was halfway home. Walking was like dragging my legs through mud and my brain had fogged up. Although I wasn't hungry, I'd eaten what felt like the wrong things at the wrong times of day. My head ached – whether from tiredness, anxiety, lack of caffeine or all three, I couldn't tell. I didn't want to go back to the squat, to the late-night arguments, the dark room, the bare mattress, the sense of being on other people's turf and the uncertainty about whether I was going to be allowed to stay for another day or, maybe, another week.

As I walked, I thought back to my old teacher, Mrs Cartwright, who had been the first person to get me interested in history and to make me wonder whether squatting could – in some circumstances at least – be morally justifiable. Decidedly eccentric and with Marxist sympathies she made no effort to hide, she had taught us about the seventeenth century 'Diggers', the first squatters to achieve notoriety when they took over a patch of disused land near Walton-on-Thames in Surrey in 1649, when she probably should have been teaching us about Charles I's religious reforms. But it had captured my imagination and I'd taught myself more about it since.

The Diggers had aimed to cultivate the land communally in protest against the Acts of Enclosure, which allowed fields that had been commons to be fenced off and sold to private owners. The group's leader, Gerrard Winstanley, decried the system of private ownership, whereby 'Some are lifted up in the chair of tyranny, and others trod under the footstool of misery, as if the Earth was made for a few, and not for all men', and hoped to create an uprising that would force property owners to surrender their estates. But landowners began to hound the rebels within days of their occupation. The group clung on for months, despite beatings and an arson attack on their communal houses. By the beginning of 1650, almost a dozen other Digger colonies had been established across the country, from Cox Hall in Kent to Wellingborough in Northamptonshire. But by the end of 1651, after the military intervened to support the landowners, the settlements had been abandoned and the movement had collapsed.

Unlike most of the things I was taught at school, I could still remember 'The Diggers' Song', the seventeenth-century folk song Mrs Cartwright had insisted that my class learned. I hummed it as I walked, thinking of chubby little Mrs Cartwright leading a class of surly comprehensive-school teenagers through the chorus ('But the gentry must come down, and the poor shall wear the crown / Stand up now, Diggers all'), enjoying it despite themselves.

Mrs Cartwright hadn't missed the opportunity to teach us about the squatting that followed the Second World War either, although I doubt it featured on the National Curriculum. Returning soldiers had come home to an acute housing crisis. Britain had entered the war with a shortage of decent homes, which was compounded by the impossibility of building new houses during the six years of fighting, while bombing destroyed 110,000 homes and nearly 850,000 had to be evacuated because of structural damage. Demobbed veterans got home to find themselves expected to cram their families into a single room in a squalid slum house while other buildings stood empty.

In the spring of 1945, a Brighton-based group of ex-servicemen began moving their families into holiday houses that were left unused out of season. Copycat squatting spread along the coast to other resorts and to Birmingham, Liverpool and London. Calling themselves the Vigilantes, the squatters demanded that empty property in the private sector be requisitioned for immediate use by the homeless – and although Churchill sent a memorandum to the police asking them to consider 'all means of putting an end to these pranks', he introduced powers for local authorities to requisition buildings for civilian purposes. The hopes raised by this move and by the election of a Labour govern-ment, along with increased police action, defused the Vigilante-style squatting.

But as demobilisation gathered pace, overcrowding grew, waiting lists for housing got longer, prosecutions for vagrancy became more frequent and desperation became more widespread. At the same time, army camps, depots and prisoner-of-war camps were emptying. To the home-less families looking in through the barbed wire, the solution was obvious. The first family moved into the offi-cers' mess of an unoccupied anti-aircraft camp outside Scunthorpe on 8 May 1946. By the evening, they had been joined by several more. Word spread and the pattern was repeated at other camps as families broke in, chalked their names on the doors of their chosen hut, then set off to bring in their possessions.

The War Office issued a statement saying that the squatters were trespassers but that no immediate action would be taken against them. By October 1946 the House of Commons was told that 46,335 people were occupying 1,181 camps. The squatters had huge popular support. Even the *Daily Mail* was on their side, applauding their 'robust common sense' and their ability, when the government had failed them, 'to take matters quietly but firmly into their own hands'. It was 'a refreshing example of what ordinary people can do when they have a mind to do it'. *The Economist* agreed, saying: 'In a country so law-abiding as Great Britain, it is always refreshing when the people take the law into their own hands on an issue in which the spirit of justice, if not its letter, is so evidently on their side.' Eventually the government announced that almost all the squatters would be allowed to stay where they were until better housing could be provided, and many camps remained in use for social housing until the end of the fifties.

Less sympathy was directed towards Mrs Cartwright's favourite post-war squatters who targeted empty blocks of luxury flats and disused hotels in London. On Monday 9 September 1946, around 400 homeless families, carrying their bedding, gathered in Kensington High Street. Tubby Rosen, a councillor from Stepney, climbed into Duchess of Bedford House, an empty seven-storey block of flats, through a side window, then let the waiting families in through the tradesman's entrance. Similar scenes occurred across the capital over the following days, with groups occupying Fountain Court in Pimlico, the 630-room

Ivanhoe Hotel in Bloomsbury, and Abbey Lodge near Regent's Park – a building which has been converted into flats that now sell for upwards of £3 million. These occupations were more carefully planned than those at the barracks, with Communist Party members, who may have targeted posh buildings to score political points rather than to provide people with long-term accommodation, playing prominent organising roles.

Police resorted to siege tactics against the squatters at Abbey Lodge and the Ivanhoe, standing in ranks outside, allowing squatters out but not letting anyone back in. Food and bedding were thrown over the rows of police to the squatters waiting inside. But when the government started civil action to evict some of those staying at Duchess of Bedford House and arrested and charged four Communist councillors with 'conspiracy to incite and direct trespass' (a crime although simply trespassing is not), the squatters began to leave voluntarily, and by the end of September, the buildings had been vacated.

I continued the hike back to my own, temporary, squatted home. However uplifting the history, I was still exhausted and lonely and did not want to socialise with my housemates when I got there. I took myself to my room as quickly as I could. I realised, when I woke in the early hours, that I'd fallen asleep in my clothes and my sleeping bag was full of grit from the floor of my room.

I got used to evenings in the squat over the next couple of days. It was usually warm indoors, with a lidless pot of tea on the go in the living room and everyone gathered round eating and chatting – sometimes philosophy and politics, sometimes just dirty jokes. Someone with a few quid would usually go out to buy cans of beer, and fags were cadged with the promise of payback next time the cadger had some cash. Some of the squatters were art or drama students and most busked or worked a day or two a week in a bar, café or shop to get a bit of cash, but no one had a full-time job. The idea of sleep tended not to enter anyone's head until the early hours.

In the mornings, I still tried to go out as soon as someone else woke to lock the door behind me, returning in the evenings to hang out and share whatever food I had managed to find. When I couldn't summon the energy to wander around looking for food or possible new homes, I would enjoy the reassuring torpor of the British Library, taking my mind off my own worries by reading up on the more recent history of squatting. I passed a couple of days flicking through the library's extraordinary collection of squatters' magazines, many of them typewritten and mimeographed in purplish ink, distributed by hand, and somehow acquired for the collection by an assiduous librarian.

In 1968, I learned, the incendiary combination of home-lessness alongside empty houses had sparked yet another surge of squatting. On 8 February of that year, four houses in Ilford, east London, were occupied by local families who had spent years on waiting lists for council housing. The houses were among scores owned by Redbridge Council that had been left empty for several years in preparation for plans to redevelop the area. Dozens more families soon moved in to them.

After several failed attempts to evict the squatters through the courts, the council sent bailiffs without court orders to chuck the families out and gut the houses to make them uninhabitable. The evictions were brutal. One squatter was left with a broken jaw and a pregnant woman was struck in the stomach with an iron bar. Outraged headlines over the wasteful use of housing, the policy of wrecking perfectly sound homes to make them uninhabitable and the violence of the evictions forced the council to negotiate with the squatters. Some were given permanent council housing and the council agreed to bring some empty housing back into use.

From then on many families banded together into groups, inspired by the Ilford campaign, to occupy houses across the capital and the country. By the seventies tens of thousands of individuals and families had become squatters, taking over whole streets of disused houses, mostly owned by local councils, across the country, from Poole to York, Ipswich to Grimsby. Squatting had become part of the social and cultural landscape.

I read about the hotel on Eel Pie Island in the middle of the Thames in west London, which was squatted and used as a music venue in 1969, hosting gigs by bands including Black Sabbath and Hawkwind. I read about the group of squatters who, in 1974, occupied London's Centre Point tower to highlight the wastefulness of leaving buildings empty when people lacked homes – the 35-storey tower had been empty since it was completed in 1966. In 1977, the residents of an entirely squatted street, Freston Road, west London, had declared themselves the independent country of Frestonia in an attempt to prevent the Greater London Council from evicting them and redeveloping the area. The squatters wrote to the United Nations to demand recognition as a sovereign state and also warned that peacekeeping forces might be needed to keep the GLC at bay. Eventually, I read, the residents formed a housing cooperative and negotiated their continued habitation of the buildings with the local council. The Clash recorded their 1982 album *Combat Rock* in a studio on the street and the co-op continues to manage the properties there today.

But the reality of life in the nursing home was less fun than reading the old squatting zines, and I would feel myself growing anxious as I walked back there every evening. I had to avoid being alone with Tom. If he cornered me in the kitchen or the corridor he'd tell me off for invading his squat, splitting up his group and causing rows. He tried to fuel suspicion behind my back: 'What if she's a cop? What if she's bugged the place?' Other housemates told me of his accusations, laughed at them, and told me to ignore him. 'He's got delusions of grandeur – what would an undercover cop find here? A couple of joints of hash and a nicked supermarket trolley.' It was true that my presence was causing rows. Even though it was Tom who was initiating them, the squatters who had voted in my favour had only agreed that I could stay for a few days while

I found something else. A few days were up. It was time to stop faffing around in the library and get going.

Another meeting was called to discuss the court date, which was now only a day away. After the rows in the last meeting, Marco refused to be chairman so Pete took charge. The ASS had provided the group with a fairly flimsy defence but there was a slight chance it would buy the squatters an extra week or two in the house, which they badly needed because the hunt for suitable empties big enough to accommodate the whole group had so far been a failure. Someone – ideally two people – would have to stand up in court to put the case across and everyone seemed relieved when Tom said he'd do it. Pete, Marie and Monica were happy to go along as support but they didn't want to be the back-up speaker or be responsible for taking notes during the hearing.

Perhaps feeling that he had the group on his side, Tom raised the 'who' question once again. I had said I would leave in a day or two, he pointed out, and I was still here. What was going on?

'I'm really sorry,' I said. 'I'm looking for other places but it's not going very well.'

'Well, we're not a night shelter,' said Tom. 'Maybe you should go and check yourself in at one of those.'

'Sorry,' I said. 'Sorry, sorry.'

Then Juan, who was rarely at home but was a long-standing member of the group and seemed to have the respect of the others, spoke up for me once again. 'Of course you can't become a member of the group just by hanging around here. But we're in a difficult situation and so are you, so maybe we can help each other. You're English and you're a girl. You're the only person in this room without any dreadlocks or tattoos. You're exactly the kind of person judges like. Why don't you go to court and speak with Tom?'

The next morning we all got dressed as smartly as we could. I wore the same clothes I'd been wearing when I left my house – black trousers, black top, black cardigan, black plimsolls, all washed as well as possible with washing-up liquid in a bucket of lukewarm water. Pete toned down his normal multicoloured look, putting on a pair of jeans that were the right length and only slightly torn. Tom, however, had decided that court demanded a suit. Like virtually all the clothes in the house, his suit had come out of a skip. Shiny, blue and loudly pinstriped, it was about six inches too big for his skinny waist and its shoulders extended far beyond his own. He wore a brown shirt, tied his dreadlocks back in a bunch and clinched in the waistband of his trousers with a studded belt. On his feet he wore his only alternative to trainers: a skipped pair of purple patent loafers.

Sitting in the court waiting room I was sure that all the others were as nervous as me. Our too-loud laughter at the bad jokes Pete made about the adverts in the out-of-date magazines on the tables was more a way to relieve the tension and show a bit of defiance than a response to Pete's humour. Eventually, it was our turn to go into court. Looking bored, the judge asked the solicitor who had come on behalf of the nursing home owners for the certificate that would prove that they had served the court documents on us correctly, a formality. She didn't have it. The case had to be adjourned. Neither Tom nor I had said a word.

Walking out, Tom turned to speak to the solicitor and the woman from the property development company that owned the nursing home almost before they had got out of the court room. 'We're not doing any harm being in the building, and you can't use it yet – why don't you let us stay?'

His naturally aggressive tone wasn't helped by his nervousness. The two women looked scared too, cornered by a bunch of oddly dressed squatters. 'That's not something we want to discuss,' said the solicitor.

I'd been hanging back as we walked out, not wanting to antagonise Tom by seeming to worm my way into the little gang. I found myself in the corridor just behind the women. 'Seriously,' I said, 'you can see that we're not addicts or sociopaths. If there is any chance of coming to an agreement about the fact that we're in the building without having to come back to court, we'd be really happy to work around what you need.'

They barely nodded. Outside the court the others had to stop giving each other high fives in celebration of having won a couple more days' grace in the building when the two women walked over to us. 'Here's the phone number of our head office,' the woman from the company said to me, handing over a piece of paper. 'Call tomorrow and ask to speak to Sylvia, and maybe we can sort something out.'

When they'd walked away, the high fives and whooping really started.

'I've decided that it would be best if I made the phone call,' Tom quietly told me when we got back to the squat.

'That's not fair!' I wanted to say. 'They gave the number to me! Why should you get the glory?'

But although the squatters' chances of remaining in the house depended on that phone call, my own depended on Tom's goodwill before anything else. I handed the piece of paper over and tried to smile.

The topic of whether or not I should be allowed to stay didn't come up again. Although I carried on pushing the sacks of coal against my door at night, I began to get used to the night-time noises of the house and the street outside. I slept less fitfully, and started to take a freezing cold shower every couple of days – painful at the time but I'd feel cleanish afterwards. Better was the day when I walked into a health club and told the staff I was looking for a new gym. They showed me the exercise machines and the yoga studio. 'This might sound a bit odd,' I said, 'but the thing I really care about at a gym is the showers. Is there any chance I could try yours out?'

'Of course, madam.'

Banana sandwiches became a staple – healthy, tasty and easy to come by. Bruised, ripe bananas could be found every day, left by street markets when they packed up. And it wasn't hard to gather a few loaves of bread in the evening – every bakery seemed to throw out at least one or two, and most chucked out sacks filled with the remains of that day's stock. Every couple of days a few people from the house would go out in a van for a major food-hunting expedition. Each time, they'd come home with boxes and boxes of food – fruit, vegetables, bread, ready-meals, desserts – anything and everything you might buy in the supermarket rescued from the bins. Huge vegetarian meals were cooked up – peppers, tomatoes and mushrooms stuffed with bread-crumbs made from stale bread, dishes of steamed asparagus, mashed potato, huge saucepans of soup. I tidied and swept my own room and hid the junk under some dust-sheets that had been dumped in there.

Even if Tom was putting up with me, I still felt like an outsider in the house. I wanted to leave, but I didn't want to stop squatting. I had spent my days in the library reading about the current housing situation as well as the history of squatting, and it had strengthened my determination not to give up. Squatters today may have lost the sympathy of the *Daily Mail*, but houses are still being left empty – almost 800,000 of them in England in 2009, more than 3 per cent of the total housing stock, according to campaigning charity the Empty Homes Agency, with half those homes empty for more than six months. And the country's empty commercial property, if converted into housing, could create almost half a million more dwellings, according to the National Land Use Database.

And people are still badly housed. The government acknowledges the current housing shortage, pledging three million new homes by 2020. Almost two million families are on waiting lists for council housing, and homelessness charity Crisis estimates that 400,000 people are living in temporary accommodation – crashing at friends' or family's houses or in government-run hostels and B&Bs – while the government counts almost 500 people sleeping rough, a figure widely considered to be an underestimate. One doesn't have to believe that property is theft to feel ill at ease when perfectly habitable buildings sit empty for years while families and individuals struggle with homelessness, overcrowding and housing insecurity. Under the circumstances, squatting still seemed to me to make 'robust common sense', as the *Daily Mail* had put it decades ago.

Every squatter I met had a mobile phone – indispensable when constantly on the move – even if they rarely had credit. I used mine to phone the numbers I'd noted down at the ASS. No luck – all the rooms that had been empty were now filled. I spent more time wandering in the streets, looking for possible squats to join or empty-looking buildings that I might be able to open with a group of other would-be squatters, if I met some. But before I had to do that, I got an unexpected text message. I'd told my friends what I had decided to do when I lost my job. Some had been surprised, some worried and some had obviously been gossiping about me. I had never been more glad to be talked about than when a friend of a friend got in touch to say that she heard that I might be looking for a place to stay. She had a mate, Chris, who was looking for people to fill his squat, if I was interested. I phoned the number she gave me, and Chris and I arranged to meet to see whether I could stay at his place, at least for a while.

Chris's easy, straightforward manner was instantly reassuring. Bearded and curly-haired with a slow but sincere smile, he'd graduated from university not long before and had been at a loss to know what to do with himself. He wanted it to be something meaningful, and until he worked out what that might be he didn't want to compete for a sensible graduate job that he didn't really care about. He'd been working as a carpenter until a bike accident left him with a broken wrist and no income. We drank mint tea as we chatted in the kitchen of the Victorian end-of-terrace house where he'd been living for a few months. There were three bedrooms, with one spare because a housemate had just moved home to his native France. He warned me that they might not get to stay for very much longer – the building's owners, the Ministry of Justice, had already started court proceedings to get them out. But I could stay for as long as the squat lasted, which might be another month or two. 'Do you want the room?' Chris asked. I did want it, very much.

I wanted it even though the nursing home residents would be staying put for much longer. Tom had phoned the property developers and they had managed to strike a deal. The squatters would leave without a costly court case when planning permission to level the building went through – and could stay there until that happened if they each paid £15 a week in rent.

Yet another house meeting had been called to discuss the proposal, yet again dragging on into the early hours and descending into shouting and animosity. Tom had made the phone calls, handled the deal and suggested the £15 sum. Some of the others said he should have negotiated a lower rent. Perhaps, some said, they shouldn't accept the deal at all, and should move on as planned.

'We're squatters not tenants,' said Pete, 'that's the point.'

'Yeah,' said Monica, 'don't we want to stay on the outside? Not have a landlord?'

But the chance of cheap stability won over most of the group, and Pete was persuaded that he could satisfy his desire to create a counter-culture by hosting parties, workshops and exhibitions in the space they now had – which might also fetch a bit of money to pay the rent.

With the deal signed, the atmosphere at the squat improved. Knowing that they could stay indefinitely, everyone got to work doing up their rooms and sorting out the communal spaces. Walls were painted, floors were mopped, broken windows were boarded up. But I didn't join in. Tom had turned his attention to trying to get rid of an even newer guy, Jack, who someone else had invited to stay at the squat. I couldn't wait to get out.

I found myself smiling at strangers as I headed across town to fetch my stuff from the nursing home. Knowing I wouldn't have to sleep there again, I noticed the doggy smell in the hall and the bleakness of my room all over again. After living there for almost three weeks I'd made myself ignore it but now that I was leaving for Chris's place, with its back garden, its electric water heater for hot showers, its more convenient location and its cheerful atmosphere, I didn't need to look on the bright side. A note in the kitchen announced yet another house meeting to be held that night. I said a civil goodbye to Tom, a more sincere one to Pete and Monica and couldn't leave the building fast enough.

My room at Chris's place was the smallest in the house, the double mattress that was already in it only just fitting in beside a built-in wardrobe. The walls had been decorated by the guy who had lived there before me, who had clearly spent long hours painstakingly snipping out women's naked torsos from lads' mags, cutting them off at the neck and collaging them on the wall, around a speech bubble which said 'love me'. Perhaps it was art. Given that I had almost no possessions, the room was the ideal size. I unpacked my few clothes into the wardrobe and unrolled my sleeping bag. I hung a piece of floral fabric I'd picked up in the street at the window as a curtain and immediately felt more at home than I ever had at the nursing home.

I hadn't had time to find any food that day so I was expecting to have to satisfy myself with a bit of the increasingly elderly loaf of bread I'd found a couple of days before. But, downstairs, the two Italian boys who shared the biggest room in the squat had come in. They'd brought bags of salad, sandwiches and muffins rescued from bins on their way home from working as gardeners in a nearby park. Massimo and Roberto had been out when I'd come round to meet Chris earlier on but were completely relaxed about me moving in, and told me to take whatever I fancied from their stack of food. Polish Eric, the final member of the household who chose to sleep on a sofa in the living room rather than claiming a bedroom, had also arrived home while I was fetching my bags from the nursing home. 'Can I stay here for a while?' I asked. 'Who can say? What will be will be!' he said with a huge, theatrical shrug before going back to staring at his laptop.

'Best to ignore him when he's in this kind of mood,' muttered Chris. 'He's odd but harmless.'

The house had been a mess when they moved in, Chris said, but they'd repainted the walls in bright colours and the place was cleaner and tidier than many student houses I'd been in. The living room had a motley collection of sofas and armchairs and the kitchen was almost over-equipped, with two ovens, two microwaves and a set each of gas and electric hobs, all rescued from the nearby streets. I needn't have worried about what I was going to eat that evening – the two fridges and two freezers were loaded with scavenged food.

That night, feeling safe and comfortable, I slept properly. When I woke up, I helped myself, as invited, to fruit, a cake and a cup of tea brewed from fresh mint, then sat out in the garden on a swing-seat that Chris had built from an old cane basket chair, its legs removed, secured with long ropes to the tall horse chestnut that towered over the house. The sun shone down through the leaves and I started to read a novel I'd borrowed from Chris. This was the life. Here I was relaxing in a garden on a Wednesday morning as if it was the weekend. I had good food to eat, no need to go to work to pay for it and no pressure to move on. And if we weren't here, the house would be sitting empty and the food would already be in a dump.

chapter three

It only took a few days to fall into a gentle routine. I'd wake up gradually around mid-morning without an alarm clock, doze for a while, then get up, have a hot shower, mooch down to the kitchen and sort out something for breakfast. Maybe a banana sandwich, made with toast if the bread was on the stale side. But there were usually other kinds of fruit and if someone had been to raid the bins of a bakery just down the road there might be Eccles cakes, Chelsea buns or scones. Massimo had bought a big box of tea bags to share, so I'd make a brew for myself and anyone else who was up, then sit in the garden with a novel. When I got slightly bored I'd go out scavenging to get myself better organised and equipped, and to make life feel less like camping.

Things usually seemed to trickle along easily and quietly in the squat, and my arrival didn't make too many ripples. Most of the time we all got on with our own business, companionably if companionship was available and independently if not. The Italians were the busiest, with jobs during the day and occasional punk gigs and parties to go to at night. If they were at home of an evening, we'd play poker for pennies. Chris was calm, quiet company and seemed to want to spend the time just drifting along, waiting for his arm to heal and the right long-term path to present itself. He, like me, passed the days reading and wandering. Conversations with him were usually serious – about politics, economics or the environment. He taught me to play Go, but seemed as happy to be quiet as to chatter. The need for Tom's kind of house meetings never arose.

While staying at the nursing home, I'd been avoiding my friends and family. I knew that I wouldn't be able to make myself sound breezy and cheerful if I spoke to my mum, and that she'd worry if she heard me sounding upset. I hadn't wanted my friends to see me struggling, so I'd sent only brief replies to their emails when I'd gone online on the free computers at the library, and turned down any invitations. Whenever I'd met up with Colin, I'd wept like a hospitalised child at the end of visiting time when I had to leave and go back to the nursing home. I needed to spend time hanging around there to avoid being kicked out like Ernesto for not contributing to the household, and there was no way Tom would have let me get away with inviting Colin round. It had become almost easier not to see him – it was too long a walk, into central London then out the other side, to visit him at his place, and too embarrassing to be tearful in a park or over a glass of tap water in a pub.

Now, though, at Chris's squat, I didn't have to worry. I was welcome in my home and my friends were too. Colin could come round to watch films with the boys in the living room or while away weekend mornings in my room, much as we used to before. If I wanted to see people, they could come and eat dinner in the garden.

'Ha. So you haven't lost much weight, then,' teased my friend Will when I invited him and his girlfriend Bryony round for a dinner of roast chicken and salad rescued from an upmarket supermarket's bin.

'I think this is the best dinner you've ever cooked for us,' Bryony said, and although she was also teasing, she wasn't far wrong either – several friends had worried that I'd end up skinny and ill-fed, but the food I was able to share with them was more luxurious than I'd been able to afford when I was buying it.

Going for a walk turned into going 'skipping' as every scavenger I met called it – looking through skips and bins to find the things you need. Americans call it 'freeganism', 'dumpster diving' or 'dumpstering'. It barely seemed to matter which direction I went. In a stroll down any residential street, I'd pass houses that had been having a clear-out, dumping a pile of junk in the front garden or on the pavement.

Some of it didn't seem worth rescuing – broken-legged chairs that had been cheap and shoddy in the first place or pieces of grubby carpet that smelled damp. But most of the furniture and household gear was still serviceable. I skipped a set of IKEA shelves for my wardrobe and another set of ivory and gold wicker ones to use as a bedside table. On the third day of living at Chris's house, I spotted a feather duvet bundled up next to a municipal bin, half inside a black bin bag. It wasn't smelly, wet or dirty, apart from a couple of small stains – drips of coffee, I told myself. The next day, sticking out of an untied bag on the pavement was a corner of fabric. I pulled it out. A sheet and a duvet cover. Woo hoo! Not colours I would have chosen and the pastel shades didn't go with the egg yolk yellow woollen blanket I'd pulled out of a bin while at the nursing home, but they were inoffensive enough and they smelled as if they'd come from the washing machine, not straight off someone else's bed. And, also in the bag, a towel! Not the fluffiest, and slightly ripped, but far better than the tiny one I'd brought with me. I bundled it all up and took it home, rinsed it in the bath and, when it was dry, upgraded from my sleeping bag to a properly made bed.

All the things I rescued could have been donated to charity shops where they might have been turned into funds for worthwhile causes as well as providing affordable necessities for those who shop there. Much goes into charity shop bins as well, though. I'd always loved poking through their shelves but now I started looking through their rubbish instead. Some of what there was to find among their cast-offs was genuine junk – amusing to pick up since it was going spare but not worth a penny; I gathered several different workout videos from the eighties with impressively leotarded models on the covers. But almost every time I went looking, particularly in well-heeled areas, I found useful things, things I wanted, things you wouldn't have to be in a desperate situation to find useful: a cafetière, a set of cake tins and baking utensils, Tupperware boxes, a dictionary, a Scrabble set, complete with all its letters, a game of Risk, Walt Disney branded soft toys, seemingly never played with.

I left behind far more than I took. I was often aware of other scavengers at the best bins. I'd see figures packing up their findings to leave as I walked up the street, or could see that bags had already been opened and picked through. But there were usually nice things left. In one street where several charity shops had reliably abundant bins, I met an elderly lady with a wheelie trolley. She needed kitchenware and household equipment, she said, and she liked the romantic paperbacks. I also got familiar with a couple of Eastern European men who came skipping with big back-packs to collect things they could sell at car boot sales. But usually I was looking through bags of useful, unbroken things on my own.

Couldn't the shops have a bargain bin inside? Surely the cafetière I found was worth, say, 20p, even though the plunger was a bit wobbly? That would have been 20p more for the charity, cups of coffee for someone who lacked a coffeemaker, and a couple of hundred grams less rubbish in landfill. That isn't the way it works, Rory, the former manager of an Oxfam shop told me. 'You've got to keep the shop looking nice,' he explained. 'Our job is to make as much money as possible for the charity we're a shop for, not to search around for someone who wants to reuse every last thing. The proportion of donations that charity shops dump is tiny, and they definitely reduce waste significantly. But charity shops do struggle to sell clothes and equipment that were cheap in the first place and weren't made to last. If half of your stuff is tatty junk, it's going to make everything look like that – and then you'll make less money overall because you won't be able to charge as much for the things that are good quality, and in good nick.'

But if charity shops don't see it as their mission to find a home for every last unwanted item, 'Freecycle' email lists were set up to do exactly that. As soon as I got online at a local library, I signed up to a couple. The concept is that anyone with anything to get rid of sends a message to every-one in the group announcing what they've got. Anyone who wants it can reply. The giver can choose who to give it to – the fastest respondent, the person who sends the politest request, or the person who can pick it up at the most conve-nient time. No money must change hands.

The first Freecycle email was sent on 1 May 2003 when Deron Beal, working for an Arizona-based recycling organ-isation, sent a message to about 40 friends offering things he'd picked up on his recycling rounds which looked like they needed to be reused rather than scrapped and re-cycled. It was the right idea at the right time – six years later, almost seven million people are members of Freecycle email groups in 85 countries, exchanging an esti-mated 500 tonnes of goods every day. The giver, who has already decided the value of the item is not worth the hassle of selling it or that the pleasure of doing a stranger a favour is worth more, gets someone to come and take away their household junk and has the satisfaction of knowing that their old possessions are going to a good home rather than filling up the landfill sites. The taker gets the item for nothing but the effort of collecting it.

Hundreds of Freecycle emails began to arrive in my inbox every day, offering everything from broken washing machines, broken iPods and broken-up rubble, to baby clothes, knickers with built-in stomach-flattening corsets and even a car. I gained several boxes of fruit tea being given away by someone who had decided to give up caffeine and then relented and was now clearing out her cupboard. I picked up a bag of novels and a couple of pillows so that I wouldn't have to prop my head up on my jumper at night any more. And I managed to give away some of the things I had rescued from charity shop bins, which were of no use to me but too nice to leave behind. A young mum picked up a bag of soft toys. I waited in to give a man a big Spanish–English dictionary but he failed to turn up – an irritatingly frequent Freecycling occurrence and one of the drawbacks of the system, which works purely on trust rather than relying on money changing hands or negative feedback like eBay. If people say they want something on a whim but then can't be bothered to travel to get it, the only punishment comes from their own conscience. But the next person who asked for my dictionary, a girl from Madrid, was glad to have it.

The tiny details of day-to-day life – whether I could drink fruit tea, whether I had a decent towel – took up far more of my thoughts than they ever had before. Acquiring the things I wanted and needed was more difficult than it had been when I could have walked into a shop and bought them, but it was also more interesting and challenging, and more of an achievement when I managed it. Anyway, there was little else to preoccupy me – no immediate worries about food and shelter, and none of the concerns of work either.

Skipping punctuated my days with moments of minor triumph. A little radio! A raincoat! A mock crocodile-skin fifties-style suitcase! I found myself becoming very acquisitive. When I saw something I didn't yet need but which might prove useful to me or a friend in future, I wanted to grab it just in case. When I saw things that could easily be reused I'd feel guilty if I left them to rot. My housemates were the same. Massimo would come home with a packed rucksack several times a week to show us what he'd managed to find in the nearby charity shop bin that day, sometimes holding up pieces of equipment he had gathered without knowing what they could be used for. A hard-boiled egg slicer and a melon baller were added to our kitchen drawer, and a squeaky dog toy was strapped onto Roberto's bike in place of a bell. Our toilet was stacked from floor to ceiling with speakers from stereos – perhaps 50 of them – so it felt like sitting in the middle of a sound-system. Our kitchen had several of almost everything until we gave away a microwave and some hobs to a friend of Chris's who had just moved into a new squat with no kitchen gear at all. If I'd had money to spend, I would only have bought a hot-water bottle when I needed one but when I saw one in a charity shop bin on a warm June evening I wasn't confident that I'd find another one in time for the winter, so I nabbed it and stashed it away.

Now, when I woke up in the morning, I could doze under my duvet with my head on my pillow while listening to my radio. But I was becoming a skipaholic. My tiny room quickly became crammed with stuff. When I arranged to meet friends I'd often be late, having been unable to resist stopping along the way to poke through bins I passed. I'd get back to the squat with an aching back from carrying another armchair for the already over-furnished living room. I asked for a bag of socks on Freecycle, then walked for almost two hours to collect them and came back with more old socks than anyone could possibly need.

By the time Colin's birthday came, I had managed to gather him a large, if ill-assorted, stash of presents. He got two good-quality woollen scarves, found in the street, washed in the bath and wrapped up in newspaper, as well as a yellow high-vis jacket to wear while cycling that had been abandoned in a skip, an eighties football annual I found dumped outside a charity shop, and a dozen of the nicest pairs of socks I had Freecycled. I cooked him a skipped feast, which we shared with a few friends who bought him the birthday drinks I inevitably couldn't afford.

The one possession I still missed badly was a bicycle. Although I was adapting to walking everywhere it felt far too slow and the range of walkable distances was too small. I scanned Freecycle for anyone giving away any sort of bike every time I could get online but I clearly wasn't the only

one after free transport. One or two were given away but
they seemed to be snapped up almost immediately,
presumably by people who were online all day and able to
reply immediately. Far more frequent were people appealing for old bikes. I checked the online classified ads but
even the cheapest bike on sale cost more than I could
imagine scraping together without going back on my resolution not to get a job.

Then I remembered the overgrown back garden at a
friend's rented house. When they moved in it was already
full of junk, and they'd never got round to sorting it out
beyond a clearing a patch of ground big enough for a
barbecue. Hadn't I seen a bike out there last time I went
round? I walked over to their place. There it was. But it
had clearly been sitting outdoors for a while and was in a
sorry state – the frame patchy with rust, the rear tyre split
so that you could see the inner tube, and foam bulging out
of the saddle. The saddle post was too short to raise to my
size, the chain was completely free of oil and it stuck in top
gear. But the wheels went round when you turned the
pedals and it slowed down a bit if you squeezed the brakes.
It was just about rideable and after weeks of tediously long
walks to go skipping, that was enough for me – although,
not really able to stop, I almost crashed into the back of a
bus on the way home.

Once back at the squat, I covered the holes in the saddle
with gaffer tape. Chris gave me some oil and showed me
how to tighten the brakes – a job I would have paid a
mechanic to do before. I struggled along on the bike for a

few days until Chris suggested taking it down to a work-shop he knew of at a former squat south of the river that lent out tools for free so you could fix your bike up.

I squeaked south on the bike and found my way to 56A Crampton Street. At the end of a terrace on the edge of a housing estate, a sign saying 'FREE FIXIN' stood on the pavement, the words marked out in electrical tape with an arrow pointing round the corner. There in a concrete yard were half a dozen people working on bikes. One of the volunteers was teaching a pair of kids from the council estate next door how to fix a puncture on their BMX. The other, Stuart, middle-aged with a relaxed smile, came over to see what help I needed. 'Pretty much everything, I'm afraid.'

'Ha. Yeah, it looks like you do.'

He wasn't going to fix it for me, he said, but he'd show me how to do it myself. I apologised for being such a beginner that it would probably take longer for him to explain to me than just to do it himself. 'You'd better make up for it by not coming back for help with the same problems in future,' he replied. He showed me how to adjust the spokes so that the wheels ran true and how to lubricate the brake cables without making the brakes slippery. He showed me how to get the gears working and gave me oil for the chain and a wire brush to get the rust off.

Once the chain was properly lubricated, though, it constantly slipped off. We realised the pedal cogs were bent and the chain had only been held on by rust before. Even when oiled and adjusted, it looked like I was going to have to get some money together to get the bike back into action.

But inside the workshop they kept boxes and boxes of spare bike bits, salvaged from donated and scavenged bikes that even to them were unrepairable but which had components worth saving. Stuart found me a longer saddle post, dug out a choice of two sets of pedal cogs that might work for my bike, then showed me how to fit the set I chose. It didn't quite fit. 'Needs a shim,' he said, and fished an old beer can out of the recycling bin, cut out a strip of metal and wrapped it round the axle to pad it out. 'Ideal,' he said. 'Can't buy better.' He sorted out a tyre – old, but nevertheless newer than the split one on my back wheel. My old saddle post went back in the box of spares. I held up my old tyre with threads hanging off it and a hole the light shone through and asked Stuart, 'I suppose this is done with too?' Wrong. I'd underestimated their conservationism. The central strip of the tyre could be used to reinforce another one, Stuart said, making it almost unpuncturable. And if it was even beyond use for that, a guy came round occasionally to collect up old tyres to be plaited into belts.

I hopped on to the bike and rode it round the block. It felt great. It ran smoothly, with no clicking or rubbing. The saddle was the right height, the gears changed smoothly and the brakes worked. The frame must have been a decent one originally – though slightly rusty, it was light and robust. The bike still looked like a heap of junk but that made it less likely that anyone would bother to steal it. And quite apart from the miracle of having a fully functioning bike where previously I'd had a rusty bit of rubbish, I now knew what a shim was.

I was taken aback by how much time and attention Stuart had given me for free. The workshop faced few overheads – the building that houses it, an old grocery shop, was squatted in 1988 and used as a base for a non-profit, volunteer-run food co-op and a bookshop-cum-library for political books and home-made zines as well as the bike workshop. In 2003, the squatters negotiated a tenancy with the council to avoid eviction. They now pay reduced rent, which is subsidised by the organic food still sold at the co-op. But the cheapness of the space that housed the workshop and the fact that almost all the bike-mending materials were scavenged or donated didn't explain the generosity of the volunteers helping all-comers with their bikes. Friends had taught me things and helped me to fix my belongings before now, of course, but I'd never been on the receiving end of so much free help from complete strangers. I was as touched and encouraged as when I walked into the ASS on that first day, when Pete and Marie had invited me to stay at theirs, or when I had first turned up on people's doorsteps to pick something up from Freecycle and they gave it to me with friendly but businesslike generosity.

The people who were helping me didn't want my effusive thanks, to hear my story or to be my friend. It wasn't that I was a charity case – they simply had resources to spare and could see a way to make the world a better place. Stuart was clearly a bike enthusiast – his own one was bedecked with stickers reading 'one less car' and he had a bike chain bracelet around his wrist. I could see how hanging out in the yard, with a constant flow of bikes to tinker with and cups of tea and biscuits from the food co-op, could be a nice way to spend an afternoon. Perhaps being paid might have spoiled it, might have turned the visitors into customers, giving them the right to haggle, to make demands, to specify when they wanted the work done by or to complain if he fixed their bike with a bit of beer can. I'd have felt no need to be grateful – I would have paid, he would have done the work, fair deal. When I'd got free-bies in the past, they had usually been a marketing ploy – free samples of biscuits to tempt me to buy that brand in future, a free razor handle so I'd buy expensive blades, or a free newspaper packed with adverts and product place-ment. I'd rarely before had to depend on the kindness of strangers. Receiving it felt great.

The calm of Chris's squat was a relief after the heavy-duty politics of the nursing home, where the people were explicitly anti-society, and sometimes antisocial. Their haircuts, piercings and big dogs looked like fairly deliberate attempts to proclaim themselves outsiders and to upset anyone who didn't like it. And although some of them, particularly Pete and Monica, couldn't have been kinder, others had mistrusted me for not wanting to shun normal life altogether. My new housemates shared my feeling there was something wrong with consumerism and waste. They were squatting partly to avoid being part of a system they were unsure about and to show that it wasn't the only choice. But they also wanted to get on with their lives and squatting seemed a sensible way to do it. They didn't automatically hate, as some of Tom's tribe did, every politician, journalist or person with a university education or any kind of career. There was no demand that you had to be an anarchist to live in the house. You'd never have picked us out as squatters in the street and passing our house you wouldn't have noticed that it was a squat. We chatted with the neighbours across the garden fence, kept a compost heap and put our recycling out. The closest we got to a squat party was when Massimo invited a dozen or so friends round for a barbecue, to take advantage of having a garden.

The biggest disruption to the usual calm was if Eric, short but broad-shouldered and solid with a face much younger than his 27 years, became chatty. Unemployed after being made redundant from a job in a clothes shop and thinking about returning to Poland, he tended to spend most of his days sitting at the table we ate at with a roll-up hanging from his lip, covering sheet after sheet of scrap paper with cartoons or writing in Polish. Sometimes he was silent but at other times he grappled incoherently with metaphysical problems, and then the only escape was to leave the house. We couldn't tell whether his ramblings were incomprehensible because of his poor grasp of English, whether he was philosophically confused, or whether he was sinking into mental illness. The rest of us discussed more than once whether we should do something to help him, but he didn't seem to want help and as he hadn't been working in the UK for long enough to qualify for NHS care, he couldn't have it anyway except in an emergency. We were relieved when he announced that he'd booked his plane ticket home.

In the safe, friendly atmosphere of the house, I began to feel normal again. Now that I was clean and well fed with a room that felt like mine, I had stopped trying to avoid strangers' eyes in the street. I had got used to the way I looked, not made-up and plainly dressed, with my hair tied back. In fact, I gradually began to feel better than normal. After a month or so of idling through the days I began to feel a quietness in myself that I'd rarely felt when I was working. I had time to concentrate on one thing at a time rather than trying to do everything in a hurry and I paid more attention to the minutiae of daily life – what I was eating and what the weather was like. I had less noise around me – I wasn't sitting on rush-hour public transport or in a hectic office and I was rarely out on the streets when the shops were open and the pavements were full, going afterwards instead when everyone else had gone home and the rubbish had been put out. Because I rarely used the Internet, read magazines or newspapers, went to the cinema, watched TV, went into shops or travelled on the tube, I hardly saw any advertising. If I didn't feel like doing anything all day, I didn't need to. I could sit in the garden on the swing in the sun, reading and drinking the fruit tea I'd been given through Freecycle. If I didn't go out scavenging, we might eat less well the next day but someone else might bring some food home, there would probably still be banana sandwiches, and I was easily surviving with the few possessions I had. It was as if I had ripped up and thrown away my mental to-do list.

I'd always slept badly – if I didn't wake around 4 a.m. and spend an hour or so trying to get back to sleep it had been a precious and rare night. I had needed total darkness and silence to sleep at all and had more than once spent whole nights awake in unfamiliar beds. I'd worn earplugs every night since I found myself in a noisy hall of residence at university, thinking of them as the only thing between me and insomnia. But, scared of what I might not hear at night if I wore them in a squat, I'd forced myself not to bring any with me. It was a sudden realisation in the third week of staying at Chris's house that I was sleeping as if I'd been anaesthetised almost every night: no more wakefulness in the early hours knowing that I'd feel tired the next day, no trouble sleeping through the voices in the house or the noise of the road outside. It felt great.

While I'd been at the nursing home, I'd had to keep myself going by reminding myself why I wanted to live for free but that had never erased a visceral desire to return to normality. Whenever I had been on the Internet I'd found myself combing through house and job ads, fantasising about following up those that might help me reconstruct a safe, comfortable life. But now the rational and the emotional portions of my mind were falling into line, and I had stopped wanting to quit, if quitting would mean a return to my old, wound-up, sleepless self.

chapter four

Six o'clock on a clear summer morning and Chris and I were cycling south on the still-quiet roads. Chris had decided we were due for a skipping mission to New Covent Garden and we needed to make an early start. We were heading for the huge wholesale market selling fruit, vegetables and flowers that moved to Vauxhall in 1974 from its former home in central London. The market's new site is very different from the 1630s piazza it used to occupy, now converted into shops and tourist attractions. Hemmed in by industrial estates and a huge supermarket, rows of metal and breeze-block warehouses are divided between traders who sell in bulk to restaurants, caterers and market stall-holders, rather than the public, so there's little effort to prettify the buildings' fronts. The Norman Foster-designed glass and steel flats on the riverfront a couple of hundred metres away seem to avoid looking back at it.

We pushed our bikes up the yellow concrete roads into the main market area past forklift trucks shunting crates and sacks, and pantechnicons and smaller vans rumbling in and out. There isn't any passing trade and few pedestrians. The only people walking were teams of market staff with brooms, shovels and high-visibility jackets who try to keep the place tidy, and us.

The cleaners fight a tide of rubbish. Stallholders prefer to dump box after box of waste produce next to the big skips that line the rows of warehouses rather than lifting them and throwing them in. By the time the cleaners complete one circuit of the market, shovelling the piles of thrown-away fruit and vegetables into the bins, new piles have appeared where they started.

Chris and I found an aisle the cleaners hadn't worked on recently. Heaps of fruit and vegetables were mixed with cardboard, plastic and sacking around the bins. Some was wilted, overripe or bruised but most was perfect to be eaten that day or the next – no good for retailers but perfect for us. I started to fill my bag. Several melons and mangoes. Boxes of blueberries and raspberries. Dozens of peaches as well as bananas, apples, pears and oranges. Inside a skip were a couple of hundred boxes of slightly over-ripe strawberries so Chris gave me a leg-up to pass him out a stack. It was hard to know what to make of a landslide of cherries that covered several square metres. We knew we wouldn't be able to eat many of them before they went bad but I was so used to being unable to afford them in my former life that I filled a carrier bag. Chris, used to the luxury of so much out-of-season fruit, concentrated on gathering the basics – potatoes, onions, carrots, peppers. We found hundreds of avocados. Some were past it, but it was easy to pick out a dozen that were undamaged and perfectly ripe. We could afford to be picky – without bothering with anything bruised we filled both of our big hiking backpacks in half an hour.

We saw a handful of other skippers – conspicuous in the largely deserted concrete forecourts: a couple of middle-aged Chinese people and a few scruffy younger people like ourselves. The cleaners turned a blind eye or even beckoned us over if they were sweeping up stuff they could see was perfectly edible. It would be the security guards in vans that we would have to look out for, Chris said. If they caught us they'd tell us to get out of the market and drive behind us to make sure we did leave, he warned, although if you walked slowly enough they often got bored following so you could double back and hope not to be caught a second time. The market was open from 3 a.m. until 11 a.m., but Chris had found that the earlier you arrived the less assiduously the guards did their job.

The heaps of surplus fruit and vegetables are nothing new – the market has long been a skipper's paradise. Edwardian photos show women picking through the waste at the old Covent Garden market buildings and squatters from the seventies remember going to the market's new site to find their greengroceries. Fruit and veg are perishable and easily damaged and the wholesalers create waste in proportion to the industrial quantities of food they deal in, so where an ordinary market stallholder might throw out a couple of dozen bananas, they throw out five boxes. And because they are selling to shops, restaurants and other market traders the produce needs to be fresh enough to keep for a couple of days before it is used or sold and the traders have to throw out anything which is ripe that day.

Chris and I cycled home far more slowly than we'd come, weighed down by our backpacks. Back at the squat, Massimo and Roberto made us tea – black, because no one had found any milk for days – and we all washed and chopped fruit for an incredibly lavish fruit salad then sat in the garden to eat before the Italians headed off to work. Later, I cooked carrot soup while Chris roasted vegetables. We stewed some of the peaches and apples and packed them in the freezer. The luxury of unlimited fruit and vegetables lasted for days but we didn't manage to get through everything we'd gathered. Our compost heap was growing.

One or two of us usually went to New Covent Garden every week or so, but we also scavenged fruit and vegetables from smaller street markets as they were closing up for the evening. Several stallholders recognised us and pointed us towards the boxes of produce they had decided wouldn't be saleable the next day. They didn't want to see it go in the bin any more than we did.

It was nice to go to fetch a few bananas and oranges and not be treated as filthy scroungers by the stallholders, but the pickings were usually fairly slim. The traders, piling it high and selling it cheap, on tiny profit margins, needed to sell almost everything by the end of the day if they wanted to take money home. They bought efficiently and knew that many of their customers, not well off themselves, would buy slightly inferior produce if the price was right. Most of what there was to be found afterwards needed to have bruises cut out, be eaten that evening, or cooked up and frozen. But we weren't complaining.

I could just about make sense of the waste I found at the markets but the quantity of still-fresh food being dumped every single day by cafés, restaurants, bakeries and supermarkets blew my mind. When I first left home, I had foraged haphazardly. If I saw piles of bin bags on the pavement outside a sandwich shop, I would go over to have a look inside one or two. And I had usually done all right, eventually finding decent sandwiches, cakes and salads to take back to the nursing home.

But the way I had done it then had been time-consuming and unpleasant. I'd have to open several bags of real rubbish – coffee grounds, used dish-clothes or mashed together food – before finding anything worth having. I had never needed to pick out the half-eaten sandwiches and muffins thrown away by customers along with their used paper cups and napkins – I always found a bag of unsold goods sooner or later. It felt like a victory when I found loaves of bread that usually sold for £3 each or untouched boxes of salad packed with smoked salmon, Parma ham and other luxurious ingredients. But I avoided looking up in case I caught the eye of passers-by and saw disgust or contempt there. I didn't want to feel that I was eating rubbish. I could tell myself that it was safely encased in cardboard and plastic and that nothing had happened to the food since it was displayed in the sandwich shop except that it was now in a bag rather than on a shelf. But I needed to carry the food a good distance away, take it out of its packaging and put it on a plate to end its association with black bags and wheelie bins, and to avoid feeling unclean.

Over time, though, and with tips from Chris and the others, I got the process of finding food down to a fine art. I learned when various cafés and shops threw out food so I could adjust my foraging route according to the time of day and what I fancied eating. Friday evenings were particularly good in areas with lots of cafés catering to office workers. Most would be closed all weekend so I'd find sacks filled with fruit and pots of Greek yoghurt as well as the normal heaps of sandwiches. Bags containing food tend to weigh more than those full of empty cups and boxes. Before unknotting any sacks I located the heaviest ones then felt through the plastic to work out whether it was weighed down by boxes of sandwiches or damp paper towels and mop heads. I opened bags of bona fide rubbish far less often, beginning to find bread, fresh juice, salad, cakes and sushi on the first try almost every time.

On a Friday, I'd try to gather enough food for the weekend so I could have a break from going skipping every evening. At the end of the week, I got into the habit of meeting Colin and his colleagues in a pub round the corner from the architecture practice where they worked, and would usually arrive laden down with the treats binned by the nearby cafés. I'd offer round coffee shop muffins and patisserie from upmarket bakeries, and although some of Colin's colleagues found the idea of eating something that came out of the bin too disgusting to take a bite, several started to consider it a distinct let-down if I turned up without any goodies.

Passers-by barely seemed to notice what I was up to when I was going through the bins. Like most skippers, I tended not to do it too ostentatiously. And the public – whether because they didn't want to see, or because they were caught up with their own business, distracted by iPods or mobile phones – didn't look. But I began to want other people to see what I was seeing. Every time I went scavenging, I would find enough food for scores of people, far more than my little household could possibly get through. The bags of food were sometimes so heavy that lifting them out of the bins was difficult. There were often other people at the bins, or I would see that others had visited before me because the bags would only be loosely tied. But even at the most popular bins we couldn't take everything away. If I went late, hours after the bins had been put out and the most efficient skippers had been through them, I'd still find enough to keep my whole household going for days if we were content to eat only the most boring kinds of sandwiches.

I discovered where and when to find the bins of several local supermarkets. Inside there would always be a sack filled with bread, croissants and muffins from the in-store bakeries. Such treats go stale quickly, but look and smell appetising when displayed piled high in the stores, and the high profit margins they command seems to outweigh the cost of throwing the surplus away every day for most stores. Cuisine de France, which supplies fresh croissants and bread to small convenience stores, promises shopkeepers 40 per cent profit on their items compared to the 10 per cent profit on most grocery items they sell. But a girl can't live on patisserie alone. The real draw of the supermarket bins was the opportunity to find ready-meals and the ingredients to cook from scratch as a change from sandwiches and salads.

The food we ate was almost always great quality – better than I'd been able to afford when I was buying it. The more upmarket the supermarket, the more they seemed to throw away. The shops at the bottom of the market, such as Co-Op and Iceland, stocked the lowest quantities and narrowest ranges of perishable food and cut their prices to the bone at the end of the day. I rarely found more than a couple of packets of reconstituted ham or perhaps a ready-made pizza in their bins as well as the inevitable bread, cakes and pains aux chocolat.

At more expensive stores – Marks and Spencer and Waitrose, for instance – we would be able to pull anything you'd normally find in their fridges out of the bins, and often less perishable products too. I'd come home weighed down with vegetable lasagne, butternut squash soup, salmon fishcakes or ready-to-roast chickens in their own baking tins, and sometimes dried apricots, breakfast cereal, bread sticks or boiled sweets.

The stores stock a wide choice of fresh, preservative-free food, and a lot of it seemed to go out of date before they could shift it. Cutting prices too heavily at the end of the day isn't their style. Marks and Spencer only began reducing their food with the onset of the recession. Before that, an M&S spokeswoman said that reducing food 'is not right for us. It just wouldn't fit with the M&S brand.' Even in the depths of the recession, most of the food in the bins hadn't been marked down.

The shock of seeing so much food thrown away cut through the pleasure of the free lunches it made possible and sometimes left me feeling sad. I'd find the treats my mum used to splash out on for birthdays and celebrations – expensive luxuries like tuna steak, smoked salmon or goose eggs. They had seemed special at the time. But if the products were so valueless to the shops that they could be dumped in quantities like this, perhaps we'd been conned.

Many shop workers seemed to have it in their job descriptions to chase us away if they saw us looking through their bins and some did it with determination. A Co-Op assistant came out and grabbed a loaf of bread from my hands one evening, shouting with real anger: 'It may be rubbish, but it's still our rubbish!' before jamming it back in the bin and shooing me away. In the yard at the back of a branch of Marks and Spencer, the security guard blocked the exit while a shop assistant pulled my backpack out of my hand, grabbing my wrist to make me let go of it when I held on since it also contained my house keys and mobile phone. The pair watched as I placed everything I had picked up back in the bins. The assistant looked into every corner of my bag as if I might have hidden a sandwich somewhere before letting me out. A greater deterrent was the security guard who caught me raiding bins at another branch of M&S and, rather than telling me off, tried to get my phone number so we could meet for a date, reaching out to touch my arm while we stood there in the supermarket's dark backyard, surrounded by skips. I started to avoid those bins so as not to meet him again, but the tellings-off sometimes made me even more determined to return to get my own back.

Many shop assistants – presumably aware of how ridiculous they would sound telling us off for taking things they'd already thrown out – turned a blind eye. Some told us when they'd go off duty so we could come back when it would no longer be their responsibility. One man who worked at a branch of Pret A Manger would point out which bag had the food inside if he came out to dump them while we were by the bins, but he was a kindly exception. Dustmen tended to be friendlier than shop workers. Some were stony-faced if they came while we were still looking but many gave us a chance to finish before loading the bags into their vans. One crew told me about another good set of bins when they caught me in the act outside a branch of EAT. Another crew loaded sacks that were clearly full of food into the cab of their dustcart. When they came across skippers, they'd pass us down the bag to take our pick from what they had saved while they continued loading their dustcart with other rubbish.

The most common way to discourage skippers was to ruin the food or make it inaccessible. I once bit into a skipped croissant and found my mouth instantly growing numb. I spat and spat, then rinsed with water until I wasn't sure whether the remaining tingling was only in my mind. The food must have been splashed with bleach. I hadn't swallowed and no harm was done but I reverted to far higher levels of caution afterwards and never went back to those bins.

Some shops emptied floor-sweepings or coffee grounds on top of the food they chucked out – an accident, possibly. But it is no accident that many branches of Marks and Spencer sprayed their waste food with blue detergent which stays wet and stains hands and clothes. Marks and Spencer refused to comment on the policy. It might have made sense if there was a risk of anyone raiding the bins to sell the food on, but it was all out of date anyway so the purpose of the dye was almost certainly to put off those who wanted to take it and eat it themselves. It wasn't a major problem – the food was so heavily packaged that most of the dye sat harmlessly on the plastic or cardboard.

Staff at some sandwich shops, including many branches of the EAT chain, open all the packaging and then empty out the food at the end of the day, turning it into a soggy mess at the bottom of the bag. You'd have to be very desperate to try to eat such an unpalatable mush. But I still saw people trying to salvage something from the ruined bags – and was glad when I could give them a few sandwiches from stashes I'd found elsewhere.

We had to shunt each other over walls or squeeze under gates and through gaps to get to supermarket skips. Basic locks on bins could sometimes be opened with a pair of pliers or a home-made key. The business of skipping was tolerable if you were young and determined. In fact, it was almost fun if you liked cat and mouse games. Chris, Massimo and Roberto clearly enjoyed the adrenalin kick they got from it. The risks were fairly minor and the prizes were good – roast duck, strawberry tarts, chocolate cakes. If you were angry about the waste these stores were producing, as most of the skippers I met were, it was a very small way of doing something about it. But it seemed insane that we had to go to so much effort to 'liberate' food that no one was going to eat otherwise. And the whole business was much less fun and much more serious for the people who needed food more than my housemates and I did.

Twice police cars slowed down when they saw me opening up bags late at night. I steeled myself for trouble. Chris had told me about a man called Ben Nunn who was arrested while carrying away seven bags of food from the Co-Op's bins to share with his fellow road protestors at a camp near Bristol. He was charged with theft but the charges were dropped within days. I was luckier. The cops just shouted that I should make sure I left the area tidy when I'd finished. Sure thing, officer.

Though I felt morally comfortable with raiding the bins, it is legally a grey area. The rubbish still belongs either to the shop that owns it or the company that's due to collect it, so you are, in fact, stealing it by helping yourself. Even if it's out on the pavement so you don't have to trespass on private property to take it, it is 'theft by finding' – just like pocketing someone's dropped wallet rather than handing it in to the police station. In New York, bin raiders can be fined up to $2,000 (a measure primarily intended to make sure valuable recyclables such as metal and cardboard aren't siphoned away from civic recycling programmes on a large scale, so it only applies to those who use a car or van to carry away their findings). Fortunately, the British police rarely feel the need to interfere.

The waste I was finding was produced in such consistent quantities – from day to day at individual stores, and from store to store within a chain – that it must have been built into the shops' and cafés' business models. Throwing it away must have made economic sense for them. If customers are paying upwards of £3 for a sandwich, it seems reasonable for them to expect very fresh food and not to have to settle for a chicken and mayo wrap when the BLT sandwiches have run out, for instance. Much of the price customers pay goes on running the stores, paying the staff and publishing adverts. The mark-up on the cost of the ingredients is high enough that it is better to send spare sandwiches to the dump than miss out on one or two possible extra sales or, worse, annoy customers and make them switch permanently to a competing chain.

I was usually unable to carry all the food I'd find in half an hour or so of searching but what I was seeing was a tiny fraction of the 18 to 20 million tonnes of food being wasted every year in the UK, according to estimates from government-funded agency WRAP (Waste and Resources Action Programme). The idea of poking through domestic rubbish for food never crossed my mind and I never needed to – I was already drowning in unsold food. But household waste is a huge and well-publicised problem – we're throwing away 6.7 million tonnes of food a year, a third of what we buy. That's 70 kilograms each. Only 1.3 million tonnes of that total is unavoidable waste such as vegetable peelings, tea bags and meat carcasses, according to a study WRAP carried out, in which they picked apart the contents of 2,000 households' bins. Another 1.3 million tonnes could have been eaten if the food had been prepared differently, or if people didn't choose to avoid it – such as bread crusts and potato skins. The rest – 4.1 million tonnes – is leftovers, or has simply been allowed to go bad. It could be avoided by buying less and cooking more thriftily, paying less attention to best-before dates and using up any surplus in stocks, soups and old-fashioned dishes like bubble and squeak.

Families and individuals are often nagged to waste less. If I'd gone through household bins I don't doubt that I would have found food but it would have been truly disgusting – old, half eaten, and mixed up with other kinds of garbage. And I never needed to – food was being disposed of all the way back up the chain, by shops, manufacturers and farmers. Although these groups receive less public hectoring, put together they throw away far more than households, and the food they throw out is, mostly, still good enough to eat.

Farmers are often forced to plough large amounts of perfectly good fruit and vegetables back into the land because of fixed contracts with processors or retailers that specify the size and shape of fruits and vegetables and the exact number needed. It isn't unusual for 30 to 40 per cent by weight of all food grown to be unsold, according to the National Farmers' Union (NFU), but these quantities are not included in the WRAP figures because most is returned to the land or fed to animals rather than being dumped. Being unable to provide as much food as was ordered could result in the farmer being dropped by the supermarket they supply which could ruin their business, so they typically plant more than necessary to allow a margin for error. The excess might previously have gone to wholesalers, but this market has shrunk and now cannot absorb the huge volumes of surplus produce. Consumers share responsibility for this wastage with retailers, said Phil Hudson, chief horticultural adviser of the NFU. 'We now always look for a specific size and shape of food in supermarkets. Anything outside that is left on the shelf. But is this human nature or are we being conditioned by retailers to look for this? We have certainly created a level of expectation which encourages large-scale waste.'

Meanwhile, shops chuck 1.6 million tonnes of food, hotels, restaurants and bars 3.3 million tonnes, and food manufacturers 4.1 million tonnes according to WRAP – almost half as much again as households when put together. The rest of the waste comes from institutions such as hospitals and schools.

Although the numbers are huge, they may be underestimates because they were calculated by extrapolating from the waste statistics provided voluntarily by businesses on condition of secrecy. They have never been independently verified and, because neither WRAP nor anyone else has gained access to commercial or industrial bins to examine them in the detail that household waste has been subjected to, it is impossible to know how much of this waste is unavoidable, how much could be avoided if manufacturing techniques were thriftier and how much is still edible when it is binned.

Most manufacturers were based on remote industrial estates out of rage of most skippers but we had slightly more luck with restaurants. Usually the unpackaged food was mixed up inside the bins at the backs of pizzerias, gastro-pubs or takeaways, and we were never hungry enough to need to bother with it. But Massimo knew of an east London curry house that handed out unsold food at closing time. We cycled down one evening, getting there early having been too hungry to risk missing out. By the time the restaurant staff had finished cleaning up and were ready to serve out their leftovers, about 20 people had lined up outside – a few local Bangladeshi men, a couple of rough sleepers and a few squatters – twenty-somethings like Massimo and me. The queue was slightly tense, with a bit of scuffling for position and a faint mood of anxiety about whether there'd be enough to go round tonight. The staff scooped out curry and rice for us – free if you'd bought your own box or plate, 20p if you needed one of their takeaway containers. Massimo and I ate, perched on a wall around the corner, with a couple of other squatters we'd got chatting to while waiting. 'Why are you giving it to us?'

I'd asked the man who had served me. He'd shrugged: 'We'd only throw it away otherwise.'

But I never heard of another restaurant that thought about things the same way. And a few months later even that restaurant stopped doling it out: it had got too popular and fights had begun breaking out in the queue, the manager said.

Perhaps if you own something you can do what you like with it, including putting it in the bin. But wasting food has a wider impact. That classic way of nagging children to finish their meals – 'think of the poor starving children abroad and eat up your broccoli' – is too simplistic. But the market for food is, today, a global one. The use of crops as biofuels rather than food has been blamed for causing food shortages, particularly in the developing world. By taking a greater proportion of the supply than we actually eat, we are arguably pushing up prices for everyone in a similar way, hitting the world's poorest hardest.

The food I was looking at was scheduled to be collected along with all the other rubbish and, still wrapped in its plastic, cardboard and foil packaging, incinerated or land-filled. In a landfill site it would add to the stink of the tip and attract flies and vermin. Most of it would also rot without air, contributing to emissions of methane, a green-house gas 23 times more damaging than carbon dioxide. If the stinking, yellow-orange liquid that seeps out of rotting waste, leachate, is allowed to escape, it deoxygenates and pollutes nearby water, killing fish, plants and animals.

Even if it were disposed of better, every scrap of food

waste represents the waste of the resources and energy used in producing it. We all have the message drummed into our heads that we should be trying to eat seasonal, local produce. Each meal going to waste represents the waste of every mile it has travelled, every hour in an industrial fridge, and every drop of fertiliser used in producing it.

Seeing perfectly edible, good-quality food destined for landfill is upsetting however you look at it. Most obviously, it could have provided a tasty, nutritious meal to a person who is going hungry or is eating unhealthily. An estimated four million Britons suffer nutritional deficiencies because they can't afford healthy food, and one in seven pensioners is seriously malnourished. Meanwhile, enough square meals to feed several armies are going into the bins every night. At first glance, it shouldn't be too difficult to put the two together.

Schemes to redistribute the food only manage to hand out a tiny proportion of the total being wasted, though. Pret A Manger, to its credit, runs a food redistribution scheme, heavily touted on its packaging, using a fleet of branded and ostentatiously right-on electric vans. But the chain is constantly searching for more charities to take the surplus food they generate, which must, they stipulate, be eaten by 2 p.m. the following day. It would be impossible to doubt the earnestness of their charity coordinator Edward Metcalfe, who claims that 96 per cent of Pret's surplus food goes to charity and that only 12 of their branches have not yet found a nearby charity to accept their leftover food, but that wasn't how it looked from their bins. When I phoned

Metcalfe, he said that if we squatters wanted to collect food, regularly or as a one-off, they'd consider supplying us. It was a kind offer, but to my squatmates and I it seemed easier just to pick the food out of the bins. That way we didn't have to make regular appointments to collect it and we didn't have to present ourselves as grateful charity cases. As it was we'd found piles of unopened sandwiches in Pret's and other cafés' bins so often that I and everyone else in my house had got sick of them and stopped bothering to go and fetch them when alternatives were available. Perhaps the same thing had happened to some of the charities that had agreed to pick up Pret's leftovers.

Many other companies also try to redirect their waste food to hungry mouths by cooperating with national charity FareShare, which collects unwanted food from shops and manufacturers to be redistributed to charities. The project was started by homelessness charity Crisis in 1994 and became an independent organisation in 2004. Today, it operates in 12 locations across the country, distributing 2,000 tonnes of food a year – 7.4 million meals – to a range of charities, saving the food from being simply dumped, and saving the charities an estimated £5 million in food-shopping bills. The charity accepts everything from Kellogg's cereals to Ben and Jerry's ice cream.

I began to volunteer at the FareShare centre in London that summer. The metal warehouse on an industrial estate south of the river where the charity is based was packed to the roof with food whenever I went. Groceries, such as breakfast cereals, tins of beans and jars of instant coffee, lined big shelves in the main hall and two cold rooms at the back were packed with perishable foods. The charity never sends out any food past its 'use by' dates or even its 'best before' dates, so doesn't collect the food that has been displayed in store and has come to the end of its shelf life – the food we skippers got our hands on. They work higher up the chain, distributing food which would otherwise have been chucked out by warehouses and manufacturers and which they can collect in large quantities, making the logistics of sorting and delivering it worthwhile.

Jeredine, the enthusiastic manager of the London depot, showed me round and explained how the food came their way. If a package of several hundred cartons of fruit juice gets knocked while being loaded onto a lorry and one or two cartons are squashed or spilt, the company will jettison the entire crate rather than unpack and repack the salvageable juice or risk irritating their clients by including a few damaged boxes of juice in their order. A packaging misprint might make a thousand boxes of cereal unsaleable. And almost every manufacturer produces more food than the store they're working for has ordered – just in case some is spoiled or damaged or the store wants more after all. If it weren't for FareShare such food would have gone straight in the bin and most of it continues to do so.

We volunteers sorted the donations then made a round of phone calls to ask what the charities could most easily use that day. Refugee drop-in centres would request tea and biscuits while residential homeless shelters would get legs of lamb and jacket potatoes. A team of volunteers – a mix of professionals, students and pensioners who helped more vulnerable or disabled people to learn the tasks – then packed the orders into crates for other volunteers to deliver by van.

Since FareShare does not charge any charities for the food they deliver, their system relies on donations and the efforts of volunteers to function. Continuing increases in the cost of sending waste to landfill will help FareShare and similar organisations by giving businesses a greater motivation to reuse their waste rather than paying to dump it. Such taxes have already risen from £11 a tonne when they were introduced in 1996 to £40 a tonne in 2009 and will rise by £8 a year until at least 2013. These charges may not be high enough to force businesses to significantly reduce the amount of food waste they produce – they are still tiny compared with the cost of producing a tonne of unsold food, an expense the companies are already willing to absorb. But they are allowing FareShare to consider charging businesses for waste disposal to increase their revenue and expand their operation. The charity would also be helped by laws to protect those who donate food from litigation in the unlikely event that someone becomes ill after eating it, which could be modelled on the USA's Good Samaritan Food Donation Act, which was passed in 1996 to encourage food redistribution. At the moment, to guarantee food safety, FareShare only supply food to charities that serve meals on the premises rather than sending clients home with parcels of edibles. The charity aimed to throw out no food itself – and the only snacks available to the volunteers were a few fun-size chocolate bars from a sack that had split before it could go to a homeless shelter.

FareShare are without doubt doing a worthwhile job but the bins at the back of shops are also helping some very vulnerable people. Some of the most desperate people I met going through the bins had fallen through the charities' safety nets, didn't want to depend on others for handouts or didn't want to eat their meals in a charity's dining room. They were elderly people stretching their state pensions, rough sleepers or out-of-work migrants, ineligible for state benefits. They were taking food that was too close to going out of date for FareShare and other similar charities to distribute, or which was available in quantities too small for it to be worth their while to fetch and sort. Unless business models change radically, despite FareShare's efforts there will still be food in the bins.

Maybe gut instincts tell us that it isn't fair for one person to get something for free when others have to pay for it. But it would not be unreasonable for businesses to see it as part of their corporate social responsibility to let skippers get on with it. Even if stores chose not to make it easy by giving handouts, they could at least ignore those who made the effort to be in the right place at the right time, between the rubbish being put out and the bin men picking it up. Those who eat waste food already have to put up with heckling from taxi drivers, the composting stink of some of the supermarkets' skips, and the risk of putting their hands in puddles of yoghurt, soup or worse. They have to take what is there and eat it within a day or two. Those disincentives would probably put off most of those with enough money to have the choice to walk through the front door of the shop whenever they felt like it to buy what they fancied, even if shops did not pour bleach on the food or surround the bins with razor wire.

Pret seemed to tolerate skippers – they may have been less successful than they would have liked at donating the food, but they never ruined what ended up in the bins and I was never told off by a member of their staff. Feeding yourself from the bins is better than going hungry or eating badly because you can't afford decent ingredients or fruit and vegetables. But the idea that there are thousands of middle-class 'freegans' going through bins by choice was, as far as I could see, almost entirely a myth, perhaps propagated by the fact that it is voices like mine which get heard, rather than those of the people I was usually going through the bins alongside.

Some shop assistants cited 'health and safety' when stopping people from skipping, telling us that we would get ill then sue the company. It seems unlikely that such litigation could be successful, even in the absence of a law along the lines of the Good Samaritan Act in the States. If you bought the food, ate it after its 'use by' date had expired and became ill, you would not be able to blame the store. The same is doubly true if you took it out of a bin. Other assistants told us we had to be stopped from taking the food because we'd make a mess. It is possible that skippers sometimes left food strewn across pavements or shops' yards but I rarely saw it happen. The fact that we skippers received so little hostility from bin men, who would be the ones responsible for clearing up after us if we were making a mess, perhaps shows that it was a rare occurrence. If one person ripped the bags or dropped sandwiches on the floor, someone else would usually tidy up. The sensible majority knew that leaving the bins in a bad state would be a quick way to irritate the shops and cut off everyone's food supply, so didn't let it happen.

We didn't worry about 'best before' and 'display until' dates in our household. They refer more to quality than safety, and appear on products that will not be dangerous if eaten when a bit past their prime. It is legal to sell food after its 'best before' or 'display until' date, and online shops exist to sell out-of-date cans and bottles at rock-bottom prices. Bread or cakes might go stale, apples might lose a bit of crispness, and cereals could possibly lose a bit of freshness, but even if the food tasted less good, it wouldn't make you ill. Before dates of minimum durability for pre-packaged food became compulsory in 1996, everyone would have done what we did, giving our food a look, a poke, a sniff then taking a bite to work out if it was still worth eating, an idea one of Colin's housemates found utterly disgusting, preferring to put unopened packages in their house bin the day it went out of date. More than once I sipped from a bottle of skipped orange juice to find that it had fermented, going fizzy and alcoholic. But generally things stayed good days after the packaging warned that they might be past it.

We didn't let 'use by' dates, which appear on food that goes off more quickly and is more dangerous if rotten, such as meat and fish, worry us too much either. Many manufacturers take into account the risks of buyers failing to store their food carefully – driving it home in a hot car or forgetting to put it back in the fridge. Walkers Midshire, one of Britain's largest food manufacturers, has a lab dedicated to abusing its products in the various ways customers might, testing the outcome, and then factoring the results into the 'use by' dates to be on the very safest side. Some skippers stuck with vegetarian food to avoid the risk of food poisoning, but as long as we found meat, fish and ready-meals the day that they'd gone out of date so we could be reasonably sure they hadn't been sitting out in the sun for 24 hours or more, we didn't worry about eating them the following day or putting them in one of our freezers to defrost when needed.

I tried to avoid eating very perishable things like prawns or sashimi beyond the evening I found them – as delicious as they might have been for lunch the next day, they didn't seem worth the risk of illness. But I was probably being over-cautious. Milk, where you can instantly tell whether it's gone sour or is still good to drink, carries a 'use by' date but always seemed to last a good three or four days beyond it. And neither I nor any of my skipping friends ever got food poisoning.

Even if some of the food waste really wasn't safe to eat and the companies couldn't avoid creating it, it didn't need to go into landfill. It might once have been fed to animals.

But collecting food from restaurants and other caterers, which used to be turned into pig swill by boiling it for an hour, became illegal after the 2001 foot and mouth epidemic which is thought to have stemmed from a single farm where imported meat infected with the disease was fed to pigs without being properly treated.

The food could still be composted or, with higher-tech methods, fed to an anaerobic digestion plant, which can provide energy by burning the gases it emits as it decomposes and which also yields good-quality compost. Some supermarkets are making use of the technology – Sainsbury's, for instance, has promised to invest £9 million to build five anaerobic digestion plants by the end of 2010. Tesco promises that it will be diverting 95 per cent of its waste from landfill by the end of 2009, and Marks and Spencer hopes to send zero waste to landfill by 2012, both chains intending to rely on anaerobic digestion to dispose of food.

But anaerobic digestion is an imperfect solution. The energy it releases is a small proportion of that which is used in producing the food, and the electricity produced by the digesters is not currently worth enough to cover what it costs to build and run them so the companies that operate them depend on government subsidies and the fees the waste-producing companies pay for their rubbish to be dealt with. As with any kind of recycling, anaerobic digestion is better than doing nothing and simply sending the food to landfill but it does not compensate for creating the waste in the first place. It would be better not to produce more food than can be sold. If the waste had to be produced, it would be better for the environment if it was being eaten. If that couldn't be done it would be better to feed it to an anaerobic digester. But the food I was quite literally up to my elbows in almost every day was simply going into landfill, along with all the cardboard and plastic in the bins alongside it.

As long as I didn't think about it all too much, though, things were great – which friends and family found hard to believe. Whenever my dad came to London – once a month or so – he would insist on taking me out for a meal and would try to give me packets of biscuits or bags of crisps to take away. It was nice to have them, of course, but I was eating healthy, delicious, luxurious food almost every day.

I could see no point in boycotting battery eggs once they had been thrown out – it would have been an empty gesture, making not the slightest difference to the number of eggs the store ordered in future. The planes flying prawns in from Honduras and raspberries from South Africa had already made their trip – it was irrelevant to their carbon emissions whether I ate the food or simply left it to rot. Many of the vegans I met were happy to eat animal products rescued from bins – they wouldn't have to feel personal guilt for the animal's suffering. Unlike shoplifting, which would still leave a gap on the shelf that the store would need to replenish, therefore increasing demand, my eating habits had absolutely no effect on what was produced or stocked.

Everyone in our house except Eric went skipping at least

every couple of days. It was hard not to bring home more than you could eat. We liked to have enough food to last a little while – even though we'd probably find more the next day, it might be raining, making foraging a damp and tedious job. And the skips weren't completely reliable. A couple of times I went out searching and came home with nothing but doughnuts.

Eric had a phenomenal appetite and quite similar tastes in food to me, so it wasn't so unusual to go to the fridge to get the thing you fancied for dinner only to find it had already been eaten. Cheese, since it isn't particularly perishable, was a relative rarity in the bins, but once when I found a wedge of brie one evening, Eric had managed to eat the whole thing before lunch the following day, leaving only a bit of rind wrapped up in the cellophane in the fridge. I would have felt too stingy if I'd started writing 'mine' on things I found – I hadn't paid for them, except by putting in the effort to cycle around at night, so claims to ownership seemed less clear. The best solution, I found, was to bring home enough stuff to act as a decoy, to keep Eric away from the things I really wanted to eat.

I rarely met with anything other than cooperation and help from the people I met at the bins. One set of bin bags was often visited by a grubby-looking middle-aged man, paunch pushing through his T-shirt, who would barge anyone else who was there out of the way then sometimes step back without taking anything, muttering about how we were no better than pigs to be eating rubbish. He was an exception, though, and I was on nodding terms with the other regulars at my favourite spots. If you opened up a bag you got first pick of the stuff inside it, although completely cleaning it out would attract irritated mumbles from others. But there was usually so much food that it was difficult to look greedy.

I liked the element of chance skipping brought to my diet. I'd always tried to do my shopping as quickly as possible, buying the same things as usual by rote. I'd been exactly the customer who'd be irritated if a supermarket had run out of the particular kind of pitta bread I liked, so they probably had to overstock to be sure of being able to satisfy me. But I grew better at enjoying what was in front of me and at having to be a bit more creative about organising a meal. If I wasn't sure whether I'd like something I found, I could just try it. If it wasn't nice and no one else in the house fancied it either, it hardly mattered if I binned it – it had been on its way there anyway.

I became a skipping evangelist, taking interested friends on tours of my favourite spots. 'We're inspecting your bins,' one friend, Lucy, told an assistant in a branch of Starbucks when we were caught helping ourselves to their muffins and – perhaps because Lucy, dressed in smart clothes having just finished work, was a more plausible inspector than a raider – the assistant turned tail and left us to carry on with our 'inspection'.

I enjoyed my friends' company, but also their astonishment at what we found, since my own surprise had more or less worn off. They'd be wowed when I opened a bag of sandwiches even if the haul was less good than usual. I wanted them to see what was going on, partly so that they wouldn't worry about my diet but mostly so that they would understand why I was so angry. If the government wasn't going to compel businesses to release accurate waste figures so that their customers could see what was going on and apply some pressure to get things changed, I was going to tell as many people as I could myself. None of them started skipping regularly, since none of them were so poor that it was worth the effort and lack of choice that getting your food from the bins rather than the shelves entailed. I would have been glad if I had converted them, though. Of course there were people who needed it more than them, but there was more than enough spare food to feed every-one who was willing and able to turn up at the bins, and every sandwich, cake or ready-meal salvaged meant that slightly less food needed to be produced from scratch and a few grams less would go into landfill.

chapter five

In my first two months as a squatter and a scavenger I'd spent 54p. Less than a penny a day. Ten pence had gone on a sheet of photocopying for the nursing home residents' deal with the owners and the other 44p had bought me a KitKat Chunky, comfort food at my lowest ebb in the first week. Since then, getting through the days without cash had become routine.

Before I set off, I'd told my mum not to worry, that I'd be fine. Privately, though, I'd steeled myself for discomfort and dirtiness at the very least, and I knew I was putting myself in danger. As it turned out, though, I'd slept on a mattress every night and hadn't had to go more than two days without a wash. I'd been worried I'd have to live with chaotic, unpredictable housemates, hardened by exclusion from ordinary life. Tom and Eric had been difficult to deal with, but I'd been able to at least rub along with everyone else I'd met and positively liked most of them. I'd asked Colin to expect a text from me every evening to tell him where I was and that I was still OK, so that someone would know fairly soon if something had gone badly wrong. But, after the first couple of nights, I felt silly writing a message.

Even if I was low and lonely, that I was safe seemed to go without saying. And now I was sitting in a sunny garden eating berries and Greek yoghurt, feeling good.

A few worries still lurked. I would need some money soon. I'd been using up my squatmates' cooking oil and loo rolls without contributing any in return and I was getting to the bottom of my bottle of shower gel. Although my mobile phone contract cost only ten pounds a month, I hadn't paid last month's bill. At the back of my diary, I'd started a list of what I wanted the moment I could afford anything, which was running at about a dozen items including lights for my bike, a tube of sun cream and a set of panniers so that I could carry all the things I found without dangling heavy carrier bags from my handlebars.

I couldn't shake off the fear that I had got this far largely through luck, stumbling on a safe path through a minefield and due for a misstep soon. When I was away from the house I'd find myself fretting about what I'd do if I got home to discover that the owners had come round while we were all out and boarded the place back up, locking us out of our home, and our stuff inside it. There'd be nothing to stop them – squatters' rights not to have the door kicked in only apply when someone is inside.

It rarely happened, Chris assured me. The house had been squatted for more than five months with no visits from the owners, the Ministry of Justice, since the first fortnight. Chris and the others had assiduously made sure that at least one person was at home all the time for the first month but there had been no attempt to evict them except through court, so they had stopped worrying too much. As it was, Eric was usually in the house. But not without fail. If my phone rang I'd feel faint dread as I fished in my bag for it, afraid it would be one of my house-mates warning me that some sort of emergency was under way. What if I lost even the few possessions I'd brought with me, the bare essentials?

I didn't want even to think about where I might go when we got evicted, which was bound to happen sooner rather than later. Chris had already announced that he was going to move out of our house and out of London, going back to his parents' house in Dorset rather than putting up with the hassle of finding a new squat when he wasn't particularly enjoying city life anyway. As the pound plummeted against the euro that spring, Massimo and Roberto had decided to go back to Italy. Why bother to slog it out in England when they could go back to their friends and family in Tuscany and earn as much there in better weather? Since Eric was leaving too, I was losing my entire, easy-going household. I was safe right now, but I had no idea where I'd be living or who with in a month or so. I was walking a tightrope and the cash I had in my bag was a flimsy safety net.

Some reassurance came from the local network of squatters Chris introduced me to just before he left. Walking into my first meeting through the ranks of bicycles left in the hallway of the squat that was hosting it, I found a circle of about 20 people, some dreadlocked and pierced, others fairly conventional-looking, sitting on the mismatched armchairs and sofas of the big living room of a long-standing squat. I was 45 minutes late but the meeting still hadn't started. A couple had brought their baby with them. An American girl, wearing an extra-extra-extra-large T-shirt decorated with pictures of cats, was cutting New Covent Garden potatoes into chips while a huge pot of tea did the rounds.

Two men on a sofa budged up to make space for me. Jamie, on my left, was tall and striking, his haircut somewhere between a scruffy short back and sides and a Mohican. Wearing a brown and cream cardigan of the sort you can only knit yourself or find in charity shops or bins, he still managed to make it look desirable. Luke, on my right, with short, suedehead hair and a nondescript lumberjack shirt, looked easy-going and friendly.

The squatters, from about a dozen houses within a mile or two, got together once a month to chat and eat, to share information, tools and skills, and to try to protect each other from the difficulties that come from living on very little in buildings that don't belong to you. When the meeting finally got going, information about new squats and recent evictions were swapped and a communal film night and meal cooked with skipped food was planned for a fortnight's time. The network had a shared mobile phone and everyone chipped in what they could for credit at the end of the meeting. If trouble arrived on anyone's doorstep, the threatened squatters could text the phone and the message would be forwarded to everyone else. Fellow squatters would cycle over if they were nearby to provide safety in numbers or at least to be witnesses or negotiators if the owners decided to break the law and try to evict the squatters by force.

The meeting was good-natured and as we all sat eating chips afterwards it became clear that although I'd been lucky to meet Chris, he wasn't the only calm, thoughtful and likeable squatter in my district, let alone the city or the country as a whole. The people in the room did not seem to be squatting because they were feckless thieves or because their lives were chaotic and desperate. Few were signing on for benefits – most did a bit of casual work now and then to pay for non-skippable essentials such as tools, mobile phones, beer and fags. If they had not been squatting, it seemed unlikely that they would have been sleeping rough. Like the people at the nursing home, most were in touch with their families, had non-squatting friends they could go and stay with in a crisis and seemed to have the skills and resources to get a job and rent a flat if necessary. Their faces were relaxed and I felt overwhelmingly glad to be surrounded by them all.

Jamie was squatting because he simply didn't enjoy going to work, he said. He was the kind of boy who had joined and very shortly afterwards quit the Scouts; he didn't get on with authority figures and didn't like having a boss. He'd had a couple of full-time jobs since finishing a history degree but had left each one after a few months. While unemployed he'd decided to give squatting a try. None of his friends were squatting so, like me, he'd had to go to the ASS office to find out how to do it and get in touch with others to open a house. That was more than three years ago. Now he worked about one week in five as a freelance sound engineer building recording studios and spent the rest of the time doing his own thing – reading, making films, writing songs or getting stoned.

Meanwhile Luke, who lived in the house that was hosting that evening's meeting, was on sabbatical from a PhD in biochemistry. He struggled with depression and had almost dropped out of university altogether but had negotiated a year-long break to get his head together. He'd started squatting a few years before when he was offered a room in a squat by friends he'd met through protests against the arms trade. He carried on because he liked being surrounded by people – living more communally in a large group, as is hard to avoid when squatting, suited him. The absence of pressure to earn much money allowed him to spend a lot of time watching maths lectures on the websites of American universities, usually at one and a half times the usual speed. I went home from the meeting with the network's emergency phone number in my phone as well as Jamie and Luke's numbers, and the promise that I could call if I needed any practical help with finding a new place to go when we were evicted.

I drew on examples of others who lived without money. Between 1974 and '75 Alex Smith managed for year without a penny. Smith's home at the time, one of several dozen early Victorian houses in Tolmers Square, Camden, north London, was squatted for 17 years. The buildings were scheduled for demolition in favour of an office block and were occupied in 1962 by a group who bitterly opposed its redevelopment. 'It seemed like opting out completely was the only way to stand against the whole destructive, wasteful, corrupt system – exemplified by Camden Council's decision to destroy Tolmers Square,' Smith says now. 'I just didn't want any part in it.' He had also come to the end of his money and didn't want to go and earn any more. So, with the advantage of not having to move squats, he found ways of surviving entirely without money or utilities from the grid. He collected water from the roof, filtering it through sand for washing and sand followed by charcoal for drinking. He gathered wood from builders' skips to heat the house and power the Swedish-style sauna-bath he built. He grew his own food as well as visiting a circuit of three reliable skips – New Covent Garden market, a dairy distribution centre near Regent's Park where he found milk, yoghurt and cream, and a natural food whole-saler's, where he used to sweep the floor in exchange for taking away the grains and cereals in the floor-sweepings.

Talking about it today, Smith barely seems to remember any dangers, discomforts or inconveniences that came from doing without money. 'I treated living for free as a job, really,' he says. 'I went to work looking in the bins, and I got my income – food, wood to burn, all the other things I needed. It took about 25 hours a week. The rest of the time, I could do as I liked – which was mostly lying around soaking up the sun, like a cat.' He spent a lot of the year dressed in a white fluffy rabbit costume he had found in a bin, the rabbit's head dangling down his back or pulled up like a hood. 'It was convenient,' he says, 'and warm.' When he was given a £5 note for Christmas in 1974 he used it to light the fire.

The main downside was his family's disapproval. 'The shame of it almost destroyed my mother – when I quit university, where I'd been studying architecture, and became this dropout in a squat, it went completely against what she'd hoped for me. Sadly, the last time I saw her, when she was dying of ovarian cancer, I was still this disaster of a son. But it was the only thing that made sense for me at the time.'

In November 2008, Bristol-based Mark Boyle also embarked on a year without spending any money whatsoever. After Freecycling a caravan, building a wood-burning stove out of old olive-oil tins and spending £350 to kit himself out with a solar panel and a second-hand laptop, he used a hole in the ground as a toilet and ate a combination of skipped, home-grown and wild food harvested from the forests near him. The solar panel powered the laptop, from which he wrote a blog at www.justfortheloveofit.org/blog.

Boyle brushed his teeth with dried cuttlefish bones on a twig, and if his pen ran out, he planned to go into the forest near his caravan and harvest inkcap mushrooms, which have spores that can be dried to make ink. 'Does the guy who works on the assembly line of the pen factory have as much fun as the guy who makes his own?' Boyle mused in his blog. 'Does it make him a more satisfied, fulfilled and creative human being? Does the industrialised pen mean anything to the person who makes it? Does it have a story, will its user respect it, or will it get lost behind the sofa or behind the printer because the user has no appreciation for the energy going into it? Will the user enjoy every word he writes with the 25p pen, or will he curse it when it runs out?'

I was glad Boyle was doing his project, glad I could read about it but glad I didn't have to do it too. I liked having possessions that were ready to hand when I needed them and I felt no inclination to drop out of society to the extent that Boyle chose to. I also didn't have an ideological problem with using money or technology per se, whereas Boyle wrote in his blog that he saw pharmaceutical companies as being on a moral par with paedophiles and hoped his project would lead everyone towards a moneyless, agrarian life. But market-driven technological advances and the division of labour facilitated by the exchange of money have made life much easier, safer and more efficient for most of us. Medical and technological innovations continue to improve life. Although there is something going wrong in a society that, facing environmental crisis, continues to throw out enough still useful stuff to feed, shelter and clothe tens of thousands of people as a by-product of our appetites for convenience, choice, delegation and luxury. Arguably, even if we managed to eliminate all the waste created by our lifestyles, there'd still be fundamental problems with our obsession with consumerism. But that isn't reason enough to abandon the whole edifice – money, technology, medicine, mass production and all.

Of course it would be logically impossible for everyone to live, like me, off society's waste. It would also be very difficult for everyone to go back to small-scale agriculture. We can't undo the seventeenth-century agricultural revolution, which increased the land's output and freed the workforce for the industrial revolution, even if we wanted to. Britain is now more densely populated than China, Pakistan, or any African country other than Rwanda, and we currently import 40 per cent of our food. Environmentalists disagree over whether we have enough farmland to feed everyone who lives here, and it seems unlikely that we could do so with the small-scale allotment gardening that Boyle is practising. But even if it were possible, I didn't want to go back to the land. I love city life. For me, if not for Boyle, it was time to get a bit of money together, to buy a new toothbrush if nothing else.

If I could feed, clothe and house myself from other people's rubbish, perhaps I could also earn a few quid from it. Smith managed to do so and used it as the foundation for a business which now has a turnover of £4 million a year. After a year without money, his then-girlfriend was bored with it. The very day they decided to give it up, he found £2 on the pavement. The pair of them borrowed a friend's Morris Minor van and used the money to pay for vehicle entry to New Covent Garden market one morning so they could rescue and bring home a serious quantity of fruit and vegetables. They sorted it, washed it, displayed it appealingly on a stall at their squat and managed to sell it all, to fellow squatters and other locals. They earned back their £2 so the next day they did it again. By the end of the first week, they were making up to £5 a day, so in the second week they used the profits to buy flour and yeast and added freshly made bread to their wares. With the next chunk of profit they went to the wholesalers to buy rice, dried beans and pulses to shift. Turnover went up to £40 a day. They started selling home-made muesli, mixed in the kitchen of their squat, to scores of regular customers and, eventually, to health food wholesalers. When the squatters were evicted, after a legal battle with the council and the developers followed by protests in the street, Smith had made enough money to buy a lease on a non-squatted building. Today Smith's company, Alara Muesli, sells almost 200 varieties, making products for supermarket and other brands as well as a range under his own brand name

'I didn't see it as selling out,' says Smith. 'I prefer to call it buying in. By living for free, apart from making some kind of ideological point, I was essentially having no impact on the world. I wanted to do something positive and to do that I needed to be back inside the system. Now, as well as producing muesli, I can use my knowledge, money and influence to have an effect.' Smith's company is waste-free, sending nothing to landfill, and his was the first cereal company in the world to be certified organic and fair trade. Smith was named a 'London leader in sustainability' by Mayor Boris Johnson, who gave him the task of helping other businesses to cut down on waste.

Today, Smith is a tidy-looking middle-aged man in shirt and tie. He's clearly keen on muesli but is far more animated when talking about his business's side projects.

He has converted one patch of wasteland around his ware-houses into gardens, growing strawberries, apples, aloe vera and walnuts, and has paid for raised beds to be built on another large patch to provide allotments to three local community groups. 'I spent about six years living in Tolmers Square – they were very formative years,' he says. 'And very exciting.' He still looks in skips when he passes them, he says, cycles everywhere, and stops to pick up coins he sees in the street.

Now when skipping I started to think about things I could turn into money. I don't know what made me give a cardboard box from a paper shredder a kick as I walked past it in the street but when I did I realised it wasn't empty. Inside was the original shredder, just as pictured on the packaging. Must be broken, I thought. But I jettisoned some of the food I was already carrying in order to take it home; I didn't need more sandwiches but I definitely needed something I could sell.

When plugged in it worked perfectly. The next day I went straight to the library and posted an advert for it on a classified ads website. A couple of days later, after meeting a man at a nearby tube station to hand it over, I had an extra £15 in my purse. In the meantime I'd found a television on the pavement within carrying distance of my house. It was smallish and had its remote control sitting on top of it. This time I wasn't so surprised to find that it worked when I got it home – it was the boxy, analogue kind and had been sitting next to a cardboard box from a flat-screen version which it had, I assumed, been replaced with. TVs were the new video players, Luke had told me. His squat had a VHS machine and a huge stack of films the group had gathered, but you didn't find them so often any more, he said, now that almost everyone had converted to DVD players. You occasionally found functioning DVD players – Chris's house had two of them. But you could find old-fashioned tellies and non-flat-screen computer monitors every day if you were looking for them.

I came to expect every gadget I brought home to work perfectly as soon as I plugged it in or to spring into action if I changed the fuse in the plug. If it didn't, though, it was unrepairable. 'Cheaper appliances are almost being sold as disposable items now,' Shaun Claridge, a repairman at Electrical Aids, an Oxford electrical appliance shop and repair company, told me. 'Demand for cheaper prices means they're almost being sold at a loss – particularly in supermarkets. It's almost inevitable that the cost of repair is going to be more than the original price. And because they're being made a lot cheaper, you're probably only going to get a year or two of use out of a cheap toaster, for instance, before something breaks and can't be fixed.'

The policy of making electrical goods semi-disposable makes a kind of sense. If gadgets are constantly being outmoded or going out of fashion, there can be little point in giving them a longer life expectancy. Industry insiders acknowledge that plasma TV screens will not last as long as cathode-ray screens – but the chances are that they'll have been pushed aside by a newer innovation before they've had a chance to fail. The kettle and toaster I rescued from a skip in a municipal dump had simply outlived their owner's desire for them. They still heated water and cooked bread, but perhaps they had begun to look a bit passé.

Most charity shops won't accept electrical items because they can't take the risk of selling dangerously faulty goods and being responsible if a customer gets an electric shock. But several charities exist to collect functioning white goods from homes, check them, then sell them at very low cost to the needy. Other charities collect outmoded mobile phone handsets to send to the developing world. Homelessness charity Emmaus aims to fund itself entirely on proceeds from donated goods, which they collect then sell in their own shops and on eBay. Homeless people are given places to live within communities run by the charity, funded by jobs sorting, testing, reconditioning and reselling unwanted white goods and furniture as an alternative to living on benefits.

Even if electrical items are irreparably damaged they shouldn't be sitting on the pavement waiting for the dustmen. Manufacturers are obliged, under EU legislation known as the WEEE directive (Waste Electrical and Electronic Equipment), to pay the costs of recovering and safely disposing of the goods they make via shops which sell electronic goods. The rules became law in the UK in 2007, and also impose a duty of care on householders who should ensure they only pass their waste batteries and electronic equipment to an approved WEEE collection point.

We are still creating more than 1.8 million tonnes of electronic waste every year in the UK, and over 75 per cent of this waste ends up in landfill, where lead, mercury and other toxins can cause soil and water contamination. Even if the waste is rescued for recycling it often ends up in poor countries. It is illegal to export electronic waste from Europe, but Greenpeace has revealed that companies are sending waste to the developing world by saying, falsely, that they are second-hand goods for reuse. While many charities genuinely do put old computers and phones to great use in poorer countries, other traders employ workers – often children – to break apart old mobile phones, computers and televisions to extract valuable metals, releasing harmful substances in the process. In one area in Ghana where electronic waste is stripped down, Greenpeace recently found high levels of lead, dioxins and phthalates, which can damage the liver and testes. Similar degrees of contamination have been found at electronic waste dumps in India and China.

The TV I'd found didn't need to be in the bin at all. Giving unwanted items away on Freecycle or to charity shops may be good for one's karma and faith in human nature, but recycling and reusing make no less environmental sense when motivated by money. Ebay does a great job of linking sellers of niche goods with the few buyers who consider their wares treasure rather than trash. When I stuck an advert for my telly on the Internet, a couple were delighted to come and pick it up. They already had a flat-screen TV in their living room, but they wanted a little extra one to go in the bedroom, and left me with their thanks and another £30 in my pocket.

So in a week I had converted rubbish into £45 and was itching to go out and buy the things I needed and couldn't get for free. Since what I needed wasn't going to use up all my cash, maybe I could treat myself to one or two of the things I merely wanted – a bag of ground coffee, for instance, or a bar of chocolate. I decided to wait a day or two before my spending spree. I didn't want to blow the money all at once then realise I'd bought the wrong things, and I was enjoying planning what treats to buy.

Saturday night came and Jamie, from the squat network, was having a 29th birthday party at his place, a former library a mile or two away. The building, which closed as a library several years ago, had been guarded by Camelot, a company which places 'property guardians' in empty buildings to protect them from squatters and vandals. When the roof began to leak, Camelot refused to put guardians there any more, leaving it empty until Jamie and his five housemates moved in, repaired the roof and made themselves at home. I cycled over, taking some skipped birthday cakes. It was a low-key event – a couple of dozen friends and friends of friends, many of them familiar from the network, sitting around and chatting in what had previously been a meeting room, now the house's sitting room, furnished in typical squatter style with mismatched sofas, curtains and tables, all brought home from skips.

Someone strummed a guitar, whisky was drunk, joints were passed. We climbed up a ladder onto the library's flat roof to watch dawn break. Then I decided to call it a night. I'd dropped my bag and coat in a corner so I went to fetch

them. I felt in the front pocket of my bag out of habit. Odd
– my purse wasn't there. Checked all my other pockets.
Nothing. Perhaps I'd left it in the pocket of my only other
pair of trousers or by my bed. I used it so rarely these days
that it was perfectly possible that I'd simply left it at home.

On the way home, drunker than I thought after the first
alcohol I'd had in two and a half months, I hit a kerb and
came off my bike. No major damage done – just a couple of
grazes but I was shaken. When I eventually limped into the
house the sun was well risen. I checked everywhere and my
purse was nowhere. I texted Jamie, who replied that at least
two other wallets had been taken too. Whoever had taken it
had been someone I more or less knew and would probably
consider a friend or at least an ally. Almost everyone at the
party had been a squatter so whoever had stolen the purses
had known they were stealing from other squatters. Now
I'd lost not only my newly earned £45 but what remained
of my original £20 too.

All my plans for what I might buy evaporated and, with
even less money than I had started with, I felt far more
vulnerable. Worse, the confidence I had that I was
surrounded by basically decent people following some
sort of ethical code had fallen apart. Although they were
disobeying some of the rules and conventions of normal
society by squatting, scavenging and working as little as
possible, I'd assumed that they had worked out which
rules were worth breaking and which ones deserved
respect. A lot of conversations I'd had with squatters had
turned to discussions of the rights and wrongs of the

present political and economic situation and what might be done about them. If a building is empty and set to stay that way then I didn't see a problem with turning it into a home, if it could be done without affecting the neighbours' lives. But I did see a major problem with stealing someone's belongings, especially if you'd looked them in the eye and chatted and smiled with them moments before. At least one of the people around me seemed to have decided that it was OK to take whatever they wanted, regardless of the consequences for the person they were ripping off. I didn't want to live like that or with people who lived like that. I didn't think that was what we were all doing by moving into other people's empty buildings. But maybe I was kidding myself.

Losing my purse, in the normal way of things, would have been a hassle but I could have just withdrawn some more money from the bank. Now I couldn't even buy antiseptic and sticking plasters for my grazed arm. I didn't want to cycle any more but I didn't have the money for public transport. And I still couldn't pay my overdue phone bill. I didn't want to get out of bed.

So I didn't, sleeping and listening to the radio while I got over my hangover, aches, exhaustion and sense of betrayal. I had no idea how to get cash at short notice. Even if I got a job it would take weeks to get paid and I'd probably need some smarter clothes if I wanted to get through an interview. I lacked the musical skill to busk. Although I'd gathered a collection of potentially saleable junk from charity shop bins, none of it was worth more than a couple

of quid and would take days to sell through the online classifieds if it sold at all.

I went back to walking the streets. Before, I'd felt like I
was tripping over useful things. Now I wandered for hours
finding nothing. Eventually I found another TV. But it was
in a worse state than the last one and was missing its
remote. I put an advert up for it. No one replied. On the
online classifieds website, a club manager in Soho was
advertising for girls to tout his club on the street. It wasn't
a strip joint, he insisted. He didn't care about visa status
and he'd pay cash in hand – he just wanted people to go up
to passers-by and entice them in. I considered it but I
couldn't face it and I wasn't even sure if I'd be capable of
doing it. But what other choices did I have? Pinch someone
else's wallet? The thought made me feel marginally more
sympathetic towards whoever had nicked mine.

Going out to skip some food cheered me up, as it often
did. Along with the ordinary sandwiches and ready-meals I
found several dozen organic lemons. We had a bag of sugar
at the squat, I remembered. And I vaguely recalled the
recipe for home-made lemonade from when a friend had
shown me how to make it a couple of summers before. I
took the lemons home and got to work, juicing, zesting and
leaving it to infuse. The next day was sunny so I decanted
my lemonade into some glass bottles with caps which, in
my acquisitiveness, I'd picked out of a recycling box a
couple of weeks before simply because I'd liked the look of
them. I put some ice in a bucket and took it to the park,
along with some disposable plastic glasses we had in the

house, which was cluttered precisely because all the junk just sometimes came in surprisingly handy. I felt self-conscious touting lemonade at 50p a glass to office workers taking a break in the sun, but after a couple of hours I seemed to have some satisfied customers and I had magicked up almost a tenner.

The following Sunday I took my bags of junk down to Brick Lane where an unofficial scrap market cropped up every weekend. I'd seen people laying out motley assort-ments of jumble in previous weeks, some selling probably stolen bikes, some touting painted T-shirts and home-made accessories but most selling the kinds of cast-offs I'd managed to accumulate from the backs of charity shops. Because the stalls were unofficial there was no charge for selling there, so people laid out rugs or blankets with scrappy selections of items – a few bangles, a knot of computer cables, some crockery and a set of rechargeable batteries, for instance – displayed as appealingly as possible. I had a few books, some clothes, and a couple of soft toys. I hadn't expected them to go like hot cakes and they didn't. But by the time the council staff came round to bully the sellers into packing up their stuff and going home, kicking one couple's collection of wares across the street, I'd made another £8.50. I paid off my phone bill and replaced the sugar I'd used in the lemonade. Everything else would have to wait.

chapter six

Whenever I heard the letterbox snap, I had to drop whatever I was doing and rush to see what was waiting on the mat. Breakfast would stick in my throat and I wouldn't be able to focus on whatever I was reading until I was sure whether or not the new papers from court had arrived, telling us when our eviction hearing would be. Chris had told me that they were on the way before I'd moved in but for weeks the post had just been junk and our home had been safe.

Eventually, inevitably, the thick wad of officially stamped papers arrived, with one bundle posted through the letterbox and another set taped to the door. The others were still asleep. I crumpled onto the sofa. The owners of our house, the Ministry of Justice, wanted us out. They had already taken Chris and the others to court about a month before but had made mistakes in their claim. The judge had adjourned the case to give them time to sort it out. Chris knew, from the court papers and from talking to the neighbours, that the row of 30 or so terraced Victorian houses had been used to house prison wardens working at a nearby jail. The government wanted to sell all the buildings off and they wanted to do it in one go. So when the prison warden who had been living in our house left his job two years before they hadn't moved anyone in. The neighbours, who were all Ministry of Justice employees, knew they would have to move out sooner or later, but since the property market had crumbled they assumed it would be later. Our home would be disused until then.

Chris had written to the ministry's property manager, suggesting a deal similar to the agreement the nursing home residents had managed to strike: he would carry on living in the building then leave without a fight when it was needed. In the meantime he'd take care of the building and stop it from being re-squatted, vandalised or stripped of scrap metal. No luck, though. We had to get out. And now they'd reworked the court papers to make them watertight.

Our little house hadn't been a bad squat. It had provided a relatively long-term home because it had genuinely been disused and was set to stay that way. Most squatters are painfully aware that they can be evicted very quickly if they try to move into any building which is actually inhabited or about to be brought back into use and do their best to avoid it – a fact rarely publicised by media keen to whip up public anxieties about the idea of filthy squatters moving into the homes of hard-working families while they are away on holiday or even popping out to the shops. As the *Squatters Handbook* had already taught me, if squatters took over someone else's home it would be an offence punishable by up to six months in prison if they refused to leave when asked. The should-be occupier could call the police who would arrest the squatters if they tried to stay and, very likely, charge them with criminal damage or theft too. The same applies to tenants or owners just about to move in. If they have a tenancy agreement or a sale deed and the only thing preventing them from moving in is a group of squatters, the squatters must walk away or be carried away in the back of a police van. A sense of self-preservation, even in the absence of a sense of morality, drives any sane squatter to look for a long-term empty like ours, avoiding a house with any visible signs of occupation – furniture, belongings or food in the cupboard.

Even if a building is empty and the owners want squatters out at short notice, whether because they need to work on the building or because they simply don't want the squatters to be inside it, they can apply to the courts for an Interim Possession Order which, like an Antisocial Behaviour Order, turns something which is not a crime – trespassing in an empty building – into a criminal offence. The orders, which were introduced with the Criminal Justice Act of 1994, make life difficult for squatters. The time between owners applying for an IPO and squatters having to leave or be arrested can be as little as five days, making it a desperate scramble for the squatters to seek out a new home and move their possessions before the deadline. The orders are also slightly more awkward for landlords, however. Owners who want to get an IPO have to apply for it within the first 28 days of knowing that the squatters had moved in and have to make their case to a criminal standard of proof, showing 'beyond reasonable doubt' that they have the right to evict squatters rather than, as in a civil case, showing it 'on the balance of probability'.

Chris had picked his home well. The Ministry of Justice was in no urgent hurry to have the house empty so had only applied for a common-or-garden possession order, a method that takes longer to get squatters out. It involves only civil law, so would be enforced by court bailiffs not the police. All landlords have to do to gain the order is to prove that they have the right to immediate possession of the property. The question of who would put the building to the best use is irrelevant. The Ministry of Justice wanted us booted out so that the building could sit empty, wasting taxpayers' money and its potential as a home because they would not rent it out. Even if we had been far needier and more deserving than we were, the judge would still have had no choice but to grant the owners the possession order.

I took the new batch of papers to the ASS in the hope that the volunteers, who are not legally trained but who know the small corner of property law that concerns squatters inside out, might find new flaws in the Ministry of Justice's case. Greg, the volunteer again on duty that day, could see only one minor mistake in the solicitor's arguments. His advice was to start looking for a new home.

Squatters always lose their homes sooner or later, I'd been warned by Greg in the ASS office on that first day. Cases of adverse possession – where squatters live in a building for so long that they gain ownership of it – have always been rare, and have become more so since a change in the law in 2002. Before 2002, squatters could attempt to claim ownership if they had lived in a place for 12 years or more without permission from the owner, whether or not they had ever contacted the owner to ask for permission. Now, if a property is registered with the Land Registry as almost all buildings are, squatters who hope to gain adverse possession must ask the Land Registry to contact the owner after they have been living in the building for ten years and will only gain adverse possession if the owner does nothing for a further two years. Only if the owner neither attempts to evict them nor gives them a licence to stay during that time will they gain ownership, and even owners who have left a building squatted for ten years are rarely negligent enough to just let the property go. In fact, squatters who have been living safely in buildings for ten years or more now think twice before attempting to gain adverse possession – they are far more likely to prod the owner into evicting them than to end up owning their home.

Armed with Greg's flimsy legal argument, Chris, Eric and I cycled to court. There was nothing funny about the drab waiting room, lined with people looking at their feet while waiting to hear whether they were going to have their houses repossessed or the bailiffs sent round to seize their possessions. Chris and Eric sat quietly but I couldn't stifle an urge to chatter and giggle nervously.

We were in the waiting room for half an hour but in and out of the courtroom in ten minutes, feeling stupid, scruffy and powerless. When the judge asked me a question, I could hear the wavering in my voice. She was uninterested in the technicalities Greg had highlighted. Even if the government solicitors hadn't made their case very well, it was now clear that it was their building, that we were trespassers, so we should leave. A possession order would be issued and handed to the court bailiffs who would schedule a date to come and make sure we left. We'd get a letter warning us when the bailiffs would arrive and if we hadn't already gone the bailiffs would use 'reasonable force' to break in and eject us, by the scruffs of the neck if necessary.

From then on, with everyone except me planning to quit the city, the household fragmented. Knowing the door was due to be kicked in, the house was less homely. Now we were on borrowed time there was no point doing any more decorating, gardening or DIY, and hardly a motive to do any significant cleaning – the windows wouldn't have time to get really filthy before we left. Chris knew, from talking to other squatters in the network, that it would probably be at least a month before the bailiffs came. I'd fretted when eviction was just a vague threat. Now it was real and I felt paralysed with worry.

I had almost no money and few bright ideas for getting any. I was too preoccupied by the looming eviction to focus on earning. But my normal routine of skipping and scavenging continued and several of the things I would have bought before my money was stolen and which I'd assumed would be unskippable landed in my lap for free. I found a rear bike light lying in the road and picked up some sun cream offered by a Freecycler. A website listing freebies offered by companies trying to drum-up custom led me to some free sanitary supplies. And one evening while out foraging for sandwiches I spotted a bin bag behind an upmarket chocolate shop. I couldn't imagine they would be throwing much away since I'd never known a chocolate bar go bad but I had a quick look anyway. Inside, I found half a dozen bars of chocolate in exciting flavours – dark chocolate with spices, and milk chocolate swirled with raspberry-flavoured white chocolate. The bars were cracked – not the right image for a shop where 100g of chocolate costs upwards of £2.50, perhaps. They weren't even close to their best before dates.

Days later, I found a bin bag outside a café full of un-ground coffee beans. They looked glossy and smelled rich so I filled a carrier bag. I'd stashed away the wobbly cafetière I'd found behind a charity shop, though I'd held out little hope of finding coffee to use in it. And I'd noted a coffee grinder at the squat that had most recently hosted the network meeting. Luke was more than happy to let me use the grinder – particularly because I left half the beans with him and his squatmates when I ground the other half for my own household. We even had milk to drink it with – Massimo had found about a dozen bottles in a bin a few weeks before, so we'd frozen them to use gradually. I had long ago got over my physical need for a caffeine kick every morning but almost three months later I was still missing the luxury of a good cup of coffee and a chunk of chocolate

– far more, I surprised myself to find, than I missed a gin and tonic or a glass of wine.

While popping into the ASS office I'd got chatting to two boys who were there, like me on my first day, to look at the noticeboard. They seemed sane and likeable; Martin was an art student from Berlin and Italian Fabio was a waiter at the famous restaurant the Ivy. Both wanted to squat because they were low on cash but also because they were looking for adventure. I liked them and I also remembered what a favour Pete had done me in inviting me to his place when I was at my wits' end. Chris was leaving in a few days so we'd have a spare room, and the emptying house was making me feel increasingly hopeless. I invited them to come and stay.

It was the right decision. New people brought new energy to the house. Fabio cleaned the kitchen from top to bottom and cooked huge dishes of pasta to share, while Martin was cheerful and gentle in a slightly puppyish way that contradicted his clean German features, square jaw and broad shoulders. But both were even less experienced as squatters than me so homelessness still loomed.

Viktor, a tall, skinny Hungarian with thick dreadlocks and a calm manner, had visited the house several times when Chris was still there. He smiled rarely, raising his eyebrows as if surprised to find that you had provoked him into cracking a grin when he did, and gave considered answers to any question you asked him, including, 'How are you?' It was he who had opened the building for us all to live in, Chris had told me. Another group of squatters had been living in it before Christmas when the Ministry of Justice had won a possession order against them and sent the bailiffs round. On the day they were due to come everyone had left the house, trying to make it look as abandoned as possible. Only Viktor had stayed behind, crawling into a tiny, hidden cupboard with a torch, a bottle of water, a book and some food. He'd waited and listened while the bailiffs came in, checked the house, changed the locks and left. Then he'd waited another couple of hours. That night he'd crawled out, changed the locks once more and kept a low profile for a week before letting his housemates come home.

When Viktor heard that Roberto and Massimo were leaving he came round, bringing 30 bags of skipped crisps, to ask whether he and a pair of friends could move back in for a couple of weeks. He'd left the little house to join friends living in a squatted pub, but the pub was now due for eviction before our little house. Crisps or not, he was welcome. He seemed sensible and since he'd been squatting for three years, maybe he'd help all of us to find a new home.

But when he came back a couple of nights later I was less sure. The two friends he brought barely spoke. With partly shaven heads and with hands and forearms covered in tattoos, they didn't make eye contact and they returned smiles with creepy grins. It was too late to change my mind and turn them away – they'd been evicted that morning so had nowhere else to go, and had walked several miles to our house with guitars on their backs and their few possessions packed into granny-style shopping bags on wheels. Jozsef and Istvan carried their things to the Italians' old room and didn't come out for the rest of the evening. In the room next to them, with my non-locking door, I slept badly.

They barely left their room for days, sleeping in their jeans or sitting on the beds sketching or playing computer games on portable consoles. But I gradually began to suspect that they didn't smile, meet my eye or come down to the living room because they were nervous, not evil, and they didn't start conversations because their English was bad, pronouncing the 'k' in know and knit, and relying on Viktor to explain anything complicated in his better English. They were slight and physically unthreatening, addicted to computer games but not, as far as I could tell, anything else. I looked again at their tattoos. Jozsef had the little bones of his hand tattooed onto the skin, but cartoon-ishly, like a Disney skeleton, and a game of Pac-Man stretching up his arm. When they began to leave their room, to bring home piles of food or to play computer games downstairs instead, I felt feeble for having let such harmless people scare me and guilty for letting my preju-dices and my insecurity cloud my view of them. They would deep-fry huge portions of chips and cook up pans of salty, spicy but otherwise tasteless stews, then look down at the floor while quietly telling us that there was dinner ready if we wanted it.

Every conversation in the house began to revolve around where we should go next. Time was ticking away. We'd received a warning letter from the bailiffs, telling us they'd be coming in just over two weeks. Empty buildings were at the front of my mind and I began to see them everywhere. Just as I'd never noticed the bags of food sitting outside cafés and restaurants before I began to rely on them for food, I now started to notice the empty buildings and consider their potential as homes.

I went out for a recce with Jamie, methodically cycling down every street in a patch of the city we'd picked out, him looking to the left and me looking to the right. We stopped to walk up paths and peer through windows of any buildings that looked like they might possibly be empty. We'd chosen an area not too far from where I currently lived – not so smart that neighbours would find the entire idea of our squatting there odious but not so poor that we'd feel vulnerable walking in the streets – but posher and more central to London than the areas I'd been able to afford when paying rent.

After an hour or so of looking in the single square mile we'd chosen we had a list of eight buildings that were definitely disused. We had ignored anything with a sign saying it was for rent or for sale. But we'd spotted a maisonette above a shop where open windows and smashed panes of glass let pigeons fly in and grimy curtains billow out. We saw a disused shop, every surface thick with dust. A three-storey house, part of what had been a mansion that was now subdivided into flats, had steel shutters over windows and doors. And, most promisingly, a row of three massive houses, part of a terrace now knocked together into a single building, not boarded up but entirely stripped of furniture, carpets, curtains or other signs of life. Junk mail spilled out of the letterbox where the postman had been unable to fit any more into the slot. A basement window wasn't locked.

If I'd found it hard to understand how so much food could be thrown away, it was even more difficult to make sense of the empty houses. One look was enough to see that the buildings we had noted down had been empty for months if not years. Although property prices had begun to decline that summer, these buildings had been sitting empty through much of the steep and sustained property boom, during which the massive price rises had been blamed partly on an undersupply of housing. But while the government had been cajoling developers, housing associations and councils to build new homes to ease demand, these and several hundred thousand other perfectly habitable houses had been sitting empty. It wouldn't have been hard to write the estate agent's spiel for these 'elegant, well-appointed period homes in a highly desirable area'. But for whoever owned them, it seemed to make sense to keep them empty, even though the Empty Homes Agency estimates that empty properties drag down the values of neighbouring properties by as much as 10 per cent.

EHA chief executive David Ireland had some explanations for the swathes of property lying disused. We talked for some time and he essentially said that if homes are allowed to fall into poor condition they often stay empty. The owner may be unable or unwilling to spend the money to put things right and make the house habitable again. Then, when houses are disused, their condition usually deteriorates further. A small leak in the roof turns into a bigger one then becomes a collapsed ceiling. The cost of making the home habitable escalates, making it ever more likely to stay empty.

He also suggested that property speculation also leads to empty buildings. What he calls 'buy-to-leave' purchasers might acquire a property for its investment potential then leave it uninhabited before selling it on or redeveloping it, as had happened at the nursing home. Huge house price rises in the first half of this decade made things worse, as generous capital appreciation reduced the motivation of many buyers to gain rental income. The problem continued even when house prices dropped. Finished properties stayed unsold, untenanted and empty as investors were reluctant to sell at a loss. Construction projects stalled, leaving buildings that had been bought by property developers with plans to demolish and replace them standing disused.

The third large group of empty houses are publicly owned, said Ireland. Local authorities and government departments might have compulsorily purchased homes with a view to regeneration, or emptied out flats or houses ahead of plans to renovate the buildings or sell them off, as was the case at Chris's house.

The government is making some effort to get the empty homes brought back into use, but not, Ireland thinks, anything like enough. Owners pay zero council tax on empty properties for the first year they are disused and only half the normal council tax rate afterwards – a policy the

EHA calls 'a public subsidy for keeping properties empty'. Since 2003, local authorities have been able to cut the level of tax discount in their area but only half have done so. The EHA is calling for the discounts to be removed altogether and for higher, punitive levels of council tax to apply to long-term empty houses.

The VAT system also demotivates owners considering bringing empty homes back into use. While building new homes is zero-rated for VAT, anyone who wants to refurbish an existing building has to pay the full rate of VAT if the building has been empty for less than two years and 5 per cent if it has been empty for longer. Only after the building has been empty for ten years does the rate fall to zero – and a building allowed to stand neglected for a decade is more likely to be ready for the wrecker's ball than renovation in any case. So, for many developers, it makes more economic sense to demolish and rebuild, or grub up previously unused land for new developments, than work to fill empty buildings.

Local authorities received new powers to bring buildings left empty by private landlords back into use in 2006, with the introduction of Empty Dwelling Management Orders. EDMOs allow councils to take control of buildings left empty for more than six months, do any renovation works needed to make them habitable, then rent them out. The council keeps the portion of the rent that will pay for any work done on the building, plus a management fee, and the excess is paid to the owner. EDMOs can be imposed temporarily or permanently. The threat of such orders has probably prompted many owners to bring their buildings back into use and may inadvertently help squatters since a squatted building does not count as disused for the purposes of an EDMO. But, despite the hundreds of thousands of homes that lie empty for far longer than six months, less than twenty EDMOs had been imposed in the entire country in the first three years after the legislation was introduced.

Back on the streets, it was well worth putting in some effort to find out exactly why a property was empty and just how much the owners were ignoring it, Jamie told me. Doing proper research was the best way to avoid the risk of an IPO or a speedy possession order. Long-term empties, left neglected for any of the reasons listed by the EHA, were what we were scouting for. I went back several times over the next week to check the houses I'd spotted, making sure that the little bit of sticky tape I'd left stuck between door and door frame of each of them hadn't been disturbed, a sign that someone was using the building. If people came out of nearby houses, I'd try to strike up a conversation. Neighbours were often irritated by the empties and glad to complain about the negligent council or property developer who left them vacant, blighting the street.

I checked the most promising buildings on the Internet, looking them up on the Land Registry to confirm who owned them – big companies and councils were better bets than private individuals, since councils and companies tended to take the problem of squatters less personally and were less likely to come and threaten us on the doorstep. I checked the local council's website to see whether planning applications had been made on the buildings I was looking at – if planning permission had been granted, the owners were more likely to want the building vacant quickly so they could start work.

Looking at the buildings from the outside and imagining the task of getting inside, I began to feel qualms. I'd felt all right about moving into established squats but, just as it's easier to eat a hamburger than to butcher a cow, the business of finding a way into someone else's empty building was morally dubious. But I reminded myself that moving in wouldn't be illegal and, even if I was breaking the socially accepted conventions towards property, I could feel little sympathy for the large-scale landlords or property developers who had chosen to leave these buildings empty year after year.

The six of us in the little house – Martin, Fabio, the Hungarians and me – pooled the lists of empties each of us had spotted. With just over a week until our eviction date, we had a shortlist of half a dozen promising-looking new homes. The three huge houses converted into one looked like our best bet. They had been empty since the local council had sold them to a housing association in 2007, they hadn't been touched in the days I'd been watching them and we could get in easily and legally. The main drawback was the fact that planning permission had been granted. We had no way to find out for sure whether the owners intended to carry out the permitted building work in the near future but, unlike in a building without planning permission, we couldn't be sure that they wouldn't. Planning permission is often gained a long time before building work starts though, and does not necessarily imply that the permitted work will ever actually happen. We decided to take our chances and to move in a couple of nights later.

The next day, Jamie phoned. He'd been round at another squat from the local network that was set to get evicted before long, and had asked where they were going to go next. 'Oh, we've seen this great place – three massive houses knocked together into one. And there's an open window.' Jamie had told them that my group had been eyeing up the same place. They'd been planning to move in a couple of nights after us. The solution was obvious. We should all squat it together – more people would be an advantage in such a huge building.

A dozen people crowded into the living room of our little house to reformulate the plan – me and my five housemates and six from the other household – four women and two men, all of them earnest, skinny vegans, as familiar with the task of finding a new home as Viktor. We'd stop in and drink tea until around 11 p.m., it was decided, when the police would be at their busiest dealing with pub kicking-out time. The streets would be quiet but there'd be nothing suspicious about our being out and about then. A team would go ahead to climb in through the unlocked window and open the front door to the others. We'd rush in, close the door behind us and get to work securing the doors and windows as quickly as possible.

Eleven came. A couple of the girls from the other house and I went on ahead, reckoning that passers-by might find females less suspicious. On trembling legs I followed the others down the stairs to the unlocked basement window, opened it, climbed in and closed it behind us. So far so good. We stood and looked at each other for a moment, smiling with relief. Then Anita pushed open the door from the room we were in and the shrill howl of an alarm began to sound. Quick! Quick! Get out! Get out! Our nerves already strung out, we panicked, shoving the window back open and bundling out, falling over each other and almost breaking the window in our desperation to get away. Back in the street, we forced ourselves to walk rather than run, in case neighbours were twitching curtains at the racket.

Round the corner, sitting at a bus stop to make ourselves look less suspicious, we met up with the boys again. No point going back in now, we decided when our heart rates had returned to normal. Leaving had been the right thing to do, even if the decision to escape had been based on instinct not thought. Now we could wait and see what the reaction to setting off the alarm might be and then, armed with that knowledge, go back the next night. The alarm had already stopped sounding when we walked back up the street. I was happy to sit and watch and wait for police or security guards, I said. Two hours passed and I calmed down enough to notice what a lovely summer evening it was. An urban fox, out on a skipping mission of his own, came and sniffed at me. No one came to check the alarm.

The next night we were ready when the alarm went off,

its screeching setting our teeth on edge. Two of us were tasked with trying to make it shut up while the others methodically went round doors and windows putting on new bolts and locking closed existing ones. I couldn't think of a time I'd felt more adrenalin in my bloodstream. I was terrified but felt strangely good – my mind was clear, my tasks were simple and manageable and I could rely on the others to do their parts of the job efficiently too. When we put down our screwdrivers and drew breath, I was astonished to realise we had been working solidly for more than an hour. It had felt like minutes.

We were just about to start exploring the house when there was a hammering on the door. 'What's going on in there? How did you get in? This is private property. Who are you?' The security guard had arrived, a bit late.

'The window was open,' Anita, one of the vegans, said. 'We live here now.'

'I'm phoning the police,' he replied.

We heard him walk away from the door and speak into his phone. Ears pressed to the door, we grinned with relief when we heard him tell them that we'd got in through an open window. We hadn't done anything illegal so the police wouldn't come now. All the security guard could do was go back to his car and watch us from the outside. We inside watched him. The sky was getting light when we decided it was time to get some sleep. Curling up on the floor, we pulled on the sleeping bags we'd brought, taking it in turns to stay awake and make sure all stayed quiet.

The next morning, as we sat on the bare floor, our sense

of triumph was tempered by the contents of one of the back rooms. Filled with tools, with plans of new floor lay-outs stuck up on the walls, it was hard not to read it as a sign that building work was about to start. A bottle of milk left on the side had gone lumpy with age and no one had disturbed the sticky tape that I'd left stuck to the door for ten days, but the building clearly wasn't as empty as we'd hoped. We faced a dilemma: should we pour in the effort needed to move our possessions over and fix the building up as a home, knowing we were unlikely to be able to stay for very long, or should we abandon it and focus on something else? The contractors' phone number was on one of the plans. Trying her best to make it sound like an innocent enquiry, Anita called them and asked when work was due to start. In a fortnight's time, came the answer. Not only were we bound to get IPOed, we decided, we would also be making life miserable for the building's owners. There was no point in staying.

It felt rotten walking away from the house. I was tired and achy from a night on its floorboards and glad to go back to spend the day in my soft bed at the little house, but I'd already begun to imagine the new place as a home and had worked out which of the rooms I'd like to have as my own. Now we were going to have to go through the entire terrifying business of opening a new building all over again.

Our next best bet for a new home were a dozen tiny houses formed out of an old converted warehouse that Martin had spotted. The entire row was empty, with wooden boards over the ground-floor windows and weeds pushing up between the paving slabs in the front gardens. The owners, another housing association, had made a planning application to add an extra storey to the houses but had been turned down. Climbing up at the back to look in through the first-floor windows, Martin had realised that the windowpanes could be slid out without damage by unscrewing part of the frame. Although each house was miniature, our household and the vegans could squat several and have room for everyone. Even if the owners made another planning application it would be months or even years before work could start – making the owners less likely to evict us with an IPO.

We made a new plan, which this time involved going back several nights in a row to climb in through the back windows and change the locks on the houses from the inside. Then we'd take off the boards on the front all at once – if we did them one at a time, the owner might well make sure the remaining few houses were better secured, stopping us from moving into them. We started the next night but the job took longer than we thought. Three nights later, we were still going back to work on the locks, with a few people going inside while others sat outside as look-outs. Mercifully, the dry, warm weather continued. But all of us were exhausted, ground down by nightly anxiety and increasingly fed up and tetchy.

Our eviction day came before we'd finished getting the houses ready to move into. We dismissed the idea of trying Viktor's trick of hiding in our old house for a second time – surely we wouldn't be able to fool them twice. But still,

Viktor told us not to worry. 'The first time the bailiffs come, they don't really mean business,' he said. 'They're expecting you to have walked away. If you just say you're not leaving and make it look like it would be a bit difficult for them to get in and kick you out, they'll just come back with reinforcements in a week or two – and that'll be long enough to get the new places ready.'

The front windows of the house were already boarded up so we piled the fridges and furniture up against the glass patio doors at the back. We sent a text to the squat network phone promising skipped croissants and coffee for anyone who came to support us when the bailiffs were due early the next morning. And, to be on the safe side, we trekked the mile to Jamie's library with the possessions we couldn't afford to lose if we were evicted after all.

Right on time, six bailiffs showed up, two of them looking like human battering rams, leather-jacketed, with heads that met shoulders without narrowing at the neck. A representative of the Ministry of Justice, a self-conscious woman with a clipboard, had come to supervise the eviction. One of the bailiffs, a skinny, rat-faced man with broken capillaries in his sunken cheeks and a Russian accent, came to our window. 'Are you leaving?'

'No.'

He shrugged and went back to his gang for a discussion out of earshot.

A handful of people from the squat network turned up; we winched them down some hot croissants from the first-floor window, as promised. The bailiffs called the police and a pair of officers arrived – to prevent a breach of the peace, they told us, not because we were doing anything illegal yet. Our little front lawn was crowded. The stand-off continued for more than an hour. If the bailiffs looked up at us and caught our eyes as we looked out of the first-floor windows, they didn't smile.

Suddenly, something was happening. The bailiffs were coming round the side passage of the house, into the back garden, pushing aside the old mattresses we'd used to block the gate. Jozsef and Istvan sat on top of the pile of furniture and fridges, tapping on everything within reach with spoons. 'We're coming in,' one of the battering rams said. 'You'd better get out of the way!'

They gave us a chance to move. We didn't. 'They'll give up soon,' said Viktor, though he had finally begun to look slightly anxious.

The bailiffs didn't give up. They went back to their car parked in the road and came back with a hammer. 'Step away from the glass,' they said. 'We're going to break it.'

One of the squatters standing outside phoned me. 'The police say they'll give you a chance to get your stuff if you leave now,' she said. 'But not otherwise.' The bailiff raised his hammer.

'OK! OK! You win! We'll leave!' We moved the fridges and opened the door. The police made the bailiffs stand back. We rushed around picking up everything we could carry. I grabbed blankets, coffee beans, a hacksaw, a scavenged DVD player. My brain had stopped working. It didn't occur to me to collect crockery or cutlery, or, most useful and valuable of all, the electric shower Chris had plumbed into the bathroom. We stood, dazed, while the bailiffs waded in and started throwing the possessions we hadn't managed to rescue out of the house and into the back garden.

The ratty little man sidled up to us. 'Why didn't you put up more of a fight?'

'I thought we did,' I replied. 'What else were we supposed to do? He was going to break the glass, and then he'd have been inside.'

'Back when I was a squatter, me and my gang, we'd have been standing inside waving an axe around. Then they wouldn't have come in.'

'Back when you were a squatter? If you used to squat, what are you doing as a bailiff?'

'Ah, well, what I like is a good fight. I grew out of squatting. This seemed the best way to use my skills. Now they pay me to do it – and the Ministry of Justice is going to be paying me to live in your home from now on. You got a place to go? I might be able to give you a few tips. I still look out for empties – it's not a habit you get out of.'

We couldn't work out whether he was trying to cosy up to us or to drum up business for the security company he worked for. Either way, he clearly felt no obligation either to squatters or to his new employers. Rat-man offered his hand to Viktor, who refused to shake it. We picked up our motley collections of belongings and walked away, hiding the few things we couldn't carry under a nearby hedge to return for later. At the vegans' squat, we decided that the only thing we could do was carry on working on the row of houses – that night and for as many more nights as it took.

Finally, after five nights of working on the locks, we were ready to lever the nailed boards from the fronts of the houses. We borrowed as many crowbars as we could so that we could do them all at once. It would be noisy but no one had noticed us in almost a week of climbing in every night. I was posted as lookout on one of the streets leading to the houses. I heard the crack as the boards came off and saw Anita, the other lookout, coming over to tell me it was time to go inside. Then we heard the sirens. Someone must finally have heard us and called the police. There was nothing we could do but watch as a squad car drew up outside the houses. We prayed that they'd see that the problem was squatters, not burglars, and leave. But they didn't. One police car was joined by another and officers started inspecting the damage to the boards from the fronts of the houses, shining torches inside and shouting at whoever was inside to come out and be arrested for criminal damage. Anita and I sat at a bus stop, watching and feeling sick. Suddenly, Fabio walked past us, jaw clenched, clearly forcing himself not to sprint. He didn't look at us. Then we saw Viktor running in the opposite direction.

Around the corner, Fabio explained what had happened. Jozsef, who had also been waiting outside, had heard the police coming. But rather than running while he knew he had the chance, he'd climbed up the back of the houses and slid out the panes of glass we had been using to get in and out on each of the houses we were opening, risking being spotted by the police. The window hinges only opened a crack and the panes could only be removed from the outside, so everyone had been trapped until he'd released them. The police hadn't yet climbed over the wall protecting the backs of the houses so everyone had got out before they noticed.

Anita and I went back to the vegans' place and waited for everyone to reassemble there, pale but relieved. The last to arrive, well after sunrise, was Martin. He'd decided to climb a tree rather than run away and had sat up there for three hours until the police gave up and left. We were all safe but we were exhausted. We'd wasted a week on the stupid little houses and we were still homeless.

chapter seven

The solution, when it came, was almost too easy. All of us were numb with tiredness and anxiety and desperate for a way out. Bickering was breaking out over trivialities. Anita's well-meaning but brusque manner was irritating the boys from my house, and they were winding up the vegans with their tendency to fill the fridge with skipped food then leave it there well after it had become inedible. All of us were dragging ourselves along but we couldn't afford to rest since it was only days until the vegans' house would be evicted as well.

It was time for our groups to split back into two. None of the houses left on our lists were big enough for all of us, particularly not if we wanted a vegan and a non-vegan kitchen. And trying to achieve anything as a team of more than a dozen, where several members were barely on speaking terms with each other, was becoming increasingly painful.

Those of us without jobs had it easier than those who were working or studying. If I was exhausted I slept in but Viktor, who made sandwiches in a café, had to get up for an early start every morning even if he had been up until daybreak. Three of the vegans, so fed up with the turmoil of squat-hunting, scraped together the money for deposits on rented flats. Viktor's minimum wage, combined with his need to send money back home to Hungary to pay debts he'd accumulated while studying history in Budapest, didn't offer that escape route.

I went to Jamie's library, looking for a break from the tension in our group and some sympathy. Jamie did better than that. He had heard about a knack for opening the metal doors security companies put on buildings due to stay empty in the long term and he wouldn't mind testing it on the house that was part of a former mansion broken up into smaller homes that I'd been keeping an eye on. It was owned by the local council, who hadn't yet applied for planning permission on it. A passer-by had told Viktor it had been empty for years, but hadn't been able to tell him why.

Jamie and I cycled over to it that night, waiting until gone midnight when the neighbours would be safely tucked up in bed. He went on ahead to work on the door while I stayed on the pavement, watching out. Minutes later he reappeared to take his turn waiting while I went inside.

I knew the house was empty. Since we had done no damage while getting in, I was doing nothing criminal simply by being inside. But as I swung a torch into each room, my breathing was shallow. I was braced for a phone call from Jamie warning me of trouble outside and I couldn't escape the sensation that I was about to walk in on someone asleep or waiting for me around a corner. Whoever had lived there had left in a hurry. The house's four bedrooms had curtains, furniture and institutional-looking single beds with plastic-covered mattresses, some of them still with sheets and duvets. Notices on the walls asked residents to please not throw litter out of the windows or play loud music after 10 p.m. Rubbish and belongings were scattered on the floor – a weight-lifting bench and weights, a bottle of antidepressants, family photos, pornography. I ran my finger through the dust on a porn magazine, reassured by the visible trail it left.

I turned on a tap in the bathroom. Yes, there was water. I flicked a light switch, less optimistically. Nothing. Oh well. It's rare for buildings to be entirely disconnected from the electricity or water mains unless they are completely derelict so we'd probably be able to sort it out with a bit of fiddling, as we would have had to at the row of little houses. And electricity is less essential than running water, in most squatters' views, so if this place didn't have power we could always use it as a staging post while continuing the hunt for a more suitable place.

Walking down the stairs, I flicked another switch. Wait a minute – the neon tube was flickering slowly into life. Down in the kitchen, three fridge-freezers lined one wall. Without thinking about it I opened the door of one of them. It was still switched on, chilling a box of choc ices that had gone out of date two years previously. I'd seen enough. Jamie closed the door and I went to tell the boys that we might have a new home.

*

The next night Jamie went on ahead, with me, Martin, Fabio and the Hungarians following ten minutes behind. By the time we arrived, Jamie had gone and the door was open. We walked in, bolted the door and sat down at the kitchen table, looking at each other with a slight sense of anticlimax. After all those nights of wasted effort at the other places we didn't feel as if we'd worked hard enough here to have earned the right to celebrate. But Martin pulled out a bottle of wine, which he'd bought in the hopes of toasting success at the row of tiny houses and had carried with him while hiding up the tree all night. Without cups or glasses, we drank from the bottle, talking quietly so as not to alert the neighbours. Barely able to keep our eyes open, we pushed the fusty bedding off the beds in the boarded-up rooms, unrolled our sleeping bags and collapsed.

'I'm going to have to break some stuff so we can have something to fix,' Viktor joked the next day. The house could have done with a lick of paint but was perfectly habitable. We found more signs that it had been empty for two years – an old newspaper, opened post. The first task was to take down the boards from the windows, to let the light in and the musty, shoebox smell shared by all abandoned houses out. I hadn't thought of trying the hot taps to see whether they ran warm when checking the house. Martin turned one on to wash his hands. 'It's hot!' he whooped. The gas, widely considered an out-and-out luxury by most squatters, had been left on for the two years the building had been empty, despite the risk of fire. We phoned the utilities companies to tell them that we had just moved in and ask them to set up accounts in our own names. We didn't mention that we were squatting, and they didn't ask – unless the quarterly bills went unpaid, it wasn't their problem. We would work out how to find the money when the bills arrived, Viktor said. I ran myself a hot bath.

The room I chose had an armchair where I could sit looking out of my window at a leafy square behind the mansion and was painted the shade of pale green which hospital, school and prison managers seem to consider calming. I unpacked my few possessions into a chest of drawers, ripped the nagging notices down from the wall, dusted with a damp rag and put my blanket over the bed, but I couldn't get rid of the waiting-room atmosphere.

There was no need for discussion about who was going to stay at home to keep the place safe. We were all exhausted and glad to stay in as much as possible. After a couple of days, I found the energy to go and hunt down a double mattress to replace my nasty single one. There is something unpalatable about sleeping on a stranger's discarded mattress left out as rubbish in the street, so I had to remind myself that I'd always slept on hotel beds or beds of furnished rented flats without a second thought. And there were so many mattresses abandoned in front gardens and skips – I spotted four within a half-hour cycle – that I could avoid those that were stained or torn. I also rescued a glass vase from a recycling box so I could have flowers saved from a florist's bins I discovered nearby. I found a lampshade at the back of a charity shop for the bare bulb in my room. We had been paying for our stupidity in forgetting to pick up our crockery during the eviction, eating from plastic wrappers and drinking out of jam jars, so we were grateful for a dusty box of mismatched plates, cups and glasses offered by a Freecycler having a garage clear-out.

On the first afternoon, I'd looked out of a window to see a smartly dressed blond woman frowning up at me. Viktor and I went down straight away – whether she was the owner or a neighbour, we needed to be on the right side of her. 'I see,' she said when we explained that we were squatting. She seemed to weigh us up and decide to give us the benefit of the doubt. 'I live next door. When I heard you inside the house, I thought the people who used to live there had come back,' she said. 'So in a funny way, I suppose the fact that you're just squatters is a bit of a relief.'

Our house, she said, had been used to house recently paroled prisoners. She had spent years complaining about fights, noise and swearing in front of her kids and had been relieved when it closed down two years ago.

An elderly Irish man who lived in a council house directly opposite our front door spent most of his time sitting on a chair in his front garden watching the people who came down the path. Wearing a battered 'Mighty Ducks' baseball cap if it was sunny, a woolly beanie on chillier days, he said a gruff hello to those he knew. If he was sitting inside, he'd leave his front door open so that he could see who was passing while watching the telly. We couldn't enter or leave our house without him noticing during the day. All of us tried to give him a smile when we passed but his face didn't soften.

I was lugging home some bags of skipped food one evening when I smiled at him as usual. 'D'ya need some chairs in there?' he asked, curtly.

'Have you got some spare ones?' I asked.

'Yes. There's three out back. Yours if you want them.'

The truth was that we were doing quite well for chairs, with armchairs in every room and enough upright chairs for us all to be able to sit round the kitchen table together. But even if I didn't want the chairs, I wanted to encourage the thaw his offer seemed to represent. 'Thanks! That'd be great!' He dragged out three decent wooden chairs, the varnish slightly bubbled from lying out in his back garden. 'And here's a pot of varnish so you can smarten them up,' he added.

The next day, I laid down some newspaper in our front yard to do the unnecessary work on the unwanted chairs where he could see I was doing a proper job of it and took him a skipped Mr Kipling cake.

Paddy, the conduit of local gossip, became our best ally in the neighbourhood. When rumours that we were stealing electricity came his way, he challenged us, blunt and abrupt, which gave us a chance to rebut them – and, via him, reassure everyone else living nearby. When a woman from the council was sent to our doorstep to tell us to leave, he stomped over to see what was going on and reiterated what we'd already pointed out to her – that we were doing no harm and that it was silly to simply leave the house empty.

Life settled back into a calm, easy routine: waking gently with the radio on, a luxurious breakfast of skipped croissants or yoghurt and fruit while sitting in my armchair by the window, then a day out in the late summer sun, or reading at home if it was my turn to stay in. My friends came to visit me, and I could go out to see them. With the pressure off, we were back on speaking terms with the vegans, who had also found a safe new home. We found some good new local skips and lived close enough to the ones we'd relied on in the previous house to take advantage of those too. Because the house was owned by the council, we weren't worried about a violent, illegal eviction and the risk of a quick legal eviction with an IPO disappeared as the time limit for the council to request one slipped past.

My money worries were also over for the foreseeable future. Just before we had been evicted from our previous home, I'd spotted an advert on the online classifieds from a woman prepared to pay £150 for a brown, buttoned leather sofa – just like the one we had in our living room, which Chris and I had pulled out of a skip before he'd left town. I'd replied to the advert straight away. We'd almost given ourselves hernias carrying the sofa home, so although it was comfortable we wouldn't have been able to carry it to a new house even if we had known where we were going. The woman replied to say our sofa sounded perfect and sent a van round, leaving me with a bundle of ten-pound notes. Since I was in the money, I'd paid for our household's moving expenses, which had amounted to a new lock for the door and a few drinks for Jamie. So I still had more than £100, even after paying all my outstanding phone bills.

My 27th birthday approached and friends and family asked what I wanted. There must be essential things I was struggling without, or luxuries I was missing. But although I'd spent the first month cheering myself up by cataloguing what I'd get if I had the money, I now struggled to think of things I wanted. I didn't need food and I no longer needed cash. I'd got used to not wearing make-up and there was no point in asking for anything nice to wear if I would have to cycle and climb in it, kneel on the floor, or get it dirty while skipping. Anything expensive or delicate would only be more of a pest to wash than my current vests, shorts and trousers, plus a shirt for going to court, which I bunged in the bath, covered with hot soapy water and stomped on as if I was pressing grapes whenever they got too grimy.

There were certainly things I missed – an electric toothbrush, for instance, or some nicer bed linen. But leaving the last house so quickly, taking only what we could carry, had highlighted the pointlessness of accumulating possessions I didn't need or passionately want. I was bound to find myself carrying or abandoning everything I owned again before too long.

Presents I'd hate to lose or leave behind would only have rekindled my fear of being deprived of all my belongings in a surprise eviction or some other catastrophe, a worry that was fading. After four months I was increasingly confident that I could find, borrow or improvise the things I really needed and could do without most of what I'd previously considered indispensable. My acquisitiveness dropped away as I realised that it wasn't sheer luck that I was finding useful things, so I didn't necessarily have to grab everything available. I'd had opportunities to replace almost every-thing I'd originally brought with me – sleeping bag, clothes and wash-kit. I'd even found a spare *A–Z*, one of my most useful possessions, dropped in the street. I was basically unscathed despite the turmoil of the last house move and the loss of all my money. I thought of my mum, for whom a house fire or a burglary in her carefully looked-after home would be a cataclysm. For now at least, it seemed worth doing without a perfect home for the liberation of travelling light, with nothing I would really mind losing. I didn't want to clog myself up with the gifts people wanted to give me.

But although I had the basics covered, I was beginning to feel faint boredom. It crept into the time I spent reading, wandering the streets or waking up slowly, time I'd previ-ously revelled in as a rare indulgence. I'd got better at entertaining myself but I longed for the stimulation I used to get from culture and sport. I asked my mum for cinema tickets and tea bags. My dad paid the inexpensive training dues for my Sunday League football team. One sister gave me a tiny MP3 player, while the other gave me some albums to listen to on it. Colin took me to the theatre, then out for unskippable treats – chips, ice cream and Belgian beer. The boys in my house found me a cake.

But over the increasingly comfortable weeks in the mansion, the tedium worsened. Life had got too easy. If I didn't get up until lunchtime then spent the rest of the day doing sudoku puzzles, I'd survive just as well. But it wasn't enough. I certainly didn't want to go back to the job from which I'd been made redundant. But work had filled up my time and given me a sense of usefulness, which I now lacked. Even if, in my former job, days passed without my feeling proud of specific achievements, at least I could tell myself that I'd done what I had to do. I'd got up, gone to the office, done what I was told and hadn't told the boss where he could shove his BlackBerry. I could tick off each day as a task completed and the wages turned up in my bank account every month as proof. If people asked me what I did, I could answer succinctly, and I could explain it to myself, too. I couldn't have predicted how much I'd miss the sense of purpose and identity work had brought.

Now, I couldn't blame having to go to work if I failed to achieve the things I imagined doing. I had time and mental space in abundance so if I didn't get anything worthwhile done it was no one's fault but my own. I used to feel that I'd earned the right to time off on holiday or at the week-ends. Not now. After a day of drifting around, I'd feel as if my brain was going mushy from lack of exercise. Without distractions, I'd too often find my attention turning self-critically inwards, dissecting my own character flaws, my appearance, and my past and future failures, a process which only made me miserable about being so silly as to be wasting time making myself miserable.

Everyone around me had ways to fill their days. Viktor and Fabio worked long hours to save money and to send some home. But Jozsef and Istvan, although they worked at the weekends collecting glasses in a nightclub, had time on their hands. Jozsef drew and painted, copying Old Masters but reworking the characters as Terminator-style mutants, while Istvan coaxed computers found in skips back into life then used them to play games. Jozsef used some of his earnings to buy a tattoo gun and started practising – first on a piece of leather, then on his own thigh, the mechanism making a wince-inducing whirring from inside his room.

I started borrowing philosophy books from the library to struggle through for the first time since I finished my degree. I Freecycled some wool, borrowed a book of knitting patterns from the library and started working out how to make things to give in return for my birthday presents. I persuaded a friend to give me basic chess lessons. I borrowed a book of jam recipes, collected jam jars from recycling boxes in the street and splashed out some of my sofa money on sugar so I could preserve a glut of berries harvested from New Covent Garden market.

It was easy to get involved in projects within the squatting scene. I wasn't alone in finding acres of unfilled time a drag, and most squatters who weren't working seemed to have projects that gave them a sense of purpose as well as passing the days. Martin and I started helping out at a squat in Stoke Newington, north-east London. The couple living there hadn't chosen it for the building, an ugly house owned by the council that had been allowed to fall into total disrepair. No one except local kids messing around or drug addicts looking for a place to shoot up had used it for several years, it seemed. Suzy and Stefan had repaired the broken windows with whatever they could find – glass cupboard doors, old car windscreens and colourful Perspex – and had patched up the plumbing, using a scavenged baby's bath with an added plughole as a kitchen sink.

Although they could easily have found a better house, they'd have struggled to find a better garden. The building had a huge plot by London standards and backed on to Clissold Park. It had once been the park-keeper's cottage, but Hackney Council had earmarked the site for a new block of flats, then taken no action for years. Suzy had set herself the task of turning the plot into a community garden, inspired by those set up in vacant lots in New York starting in the 1970s, many of which have now been officially recognised as miniature parks. She wanted vegetable patches, a pond, benches and a barbecue space to be shared with the neighbours who had much smaller gardens, if any at all. The weeds had to be cut down and composted and broken glass had to be sieved out of the soil. The pond had to be dug and benches had to be built. It felt good to be outside, digging up soil and stomping down nettles. Neighbours were suspicious at first but some gradually began visiting and several donated plants. A few mothers began bringing their children. A team of gardeners contracted to the council surreptitiously donated some surplus turf.

It felt like a real achievement. We had turned nothing into something, a patch of wasteland into a sunny, leafy space, with paths built out of cracked paving slabs rescued from a skip and beans trained over a rusty supermarket trolley that had been lurking in the undergrowth. The *Hackney Gazette* ran photos and the tomatoes were ripening. Perhaps Suzy had managed to do what she set out to do – to show that squatters aren't inherently evil, and that it was possible to turn unwanted buildings and land into something worthwhile.

Then the court papers arrived. The council wanted Suzy and Stefan out straight away. They weren't prepared to enter into any discussions. Suzy and Stefan had no permission to be in the house, therefore they had to leave – no chance of the council simply tolerating their presence. A petition from the neighbours cut no ice. We knew the building would stay empty, since it was uninhabitable by any normal standards and no planning permission had been granted to replace it. We carried on gardening, but only half-heartedly. We might harvest the beans but bailiffs would arrive before the pumpkins were ready.

Looking around for other worthwhile ways to fill my time, I spent a few Saturday mornings cooking with the East London Food Not Bombs group, who scavenge or scrounge the ingredients for vegan meals then serve them up free of charge to all-comers in the street. I was welcomed to the squat where the group did its cooking by Jonny, a slightly chubby man with a big ginger beard, who was unloading New Covent Garden fruit and vegetables from his bike trailer with a couple of other volunteers. 'What do you want to make, then?' Jonny asked me.

I was thrown, having expected to knuckle under and do what I was told as one might when volunteering for a more conventional charity. The group is part of a movement which started in Cambridge, Massachusetts, in 1980 by anti-nuclear activists who hoped to sow the seeds of non-violent social change – as well as feeding people who fancied a meal – by cooking and dishing out food that would otherwise go to waste. Non-hierarchical organisation is a fundamental precept of the movement and each group is independent but subscribes to shared values. The groups, of which there are more than 500 across the world and around 20 in the UK, sometimes volunteer to feed protestors, setting up kitchens at Climate Camps as well as bringing meals to marches. They sometimes serve their food outside big supermarkets or branches of Starbucks while trying to persuade people not to shop there. They fed rescue workers after the 9/11 attacks, and survivors of Hurricane Katrina. Usually, though, the groups just set up on street corners, feeding all those who turned up. No one has to show that they are in need of charity before being fed but anyone who turns up for a serving has to be prepared for a seasoning of radical politics.

I surveyed Jonny's bruised and tired-looking selection of veg and suggested that maybe I could turn aubergines, courgettes, peppers, tomatoes and onions into ratatouille. 'Perfect,' said Jonny, who got working on peeling potatoes and cutting out the eyes that they had begun to sprout while another man got on with stewing apples. A couple more volunteers drifted in and helped with the chopping, peeling and boiling.

By lunchtime, we had filled huge pans with stew and

mashed potatoes. We sat down to eat before heading out to feed everyone else. The food was edible, though slightly tasteless and mushy. My ratatouille proved that I needed practice at cooking for 50 but the others' efforts weren't bad. Jonny's bike trailer, which he had made himself and adapted specially for Food Not Bombs events, included a pair of gas burners in the base to keep the food warm, so we fired them up and headed to a nearby park.

Giving away the free food wasn't particularly easy, even though it was hot and the day was cold. Many of the more conventional-looking people, perhaps too used to being hassled in the streets by free newspaper distributors, charity muggers and nutcases, blanked us. I'd got used to anti-capitalist aesthetics – the dreadlocks, holey jumpers and hand-painted banners explaining what we were up to, but the respectable public hadn't and didn't want to. Most of our clientele were local rough sleepers and street drinkers. Giving them a hot, healthy meal was probably a worthwhile job, but when the pans were empty the group was slightly downcast. The battle to draw the attention of ordinary passers-by to the wastefulness that made the meal possible and the benefits of veganism and anarchism would have to be fought again the next weekend.

I got to know a group of art-school graduates who, calling themselves the DA! collective, squatted a series of multi-million pound buildings in Mayfair, where they hosted exhibitions and events. Well spoken and elegantly dressed in vintage dishevelment rather than muddy-coloured charity shop bin-findings, the group were mistrusted by many long-term squatters, particularly because they courted press attention and because many of them admitted to having homes to go to when their buildings got evicted. A brief visit to one of their squats was enough to see that they weren't really trying to find a place to live. They slept in shared rooms, in sleeping bags on camping mats, rather than scavenging mattresses and furniture. And their choice of building was attention-seeking rather than practical and not what any squatter looking for a long-term home would have gone for. The chances of owners turning a blind eye to their well-publicised occupation of such huge, valuable properties were far slimmer than for a less ostentatious home in a shabbier part of town.

But while they didn't keep their buildings for very long, they made great use of them while inside. The atmosphere was easy-going and far more welcoming for those unused to squat life than many more-anarchist-than-thou squats, where even I, in my shabby clothes, would sometimes feel not quite punk enough. I turned up at one of DA!'s spaces on a day of workshops to look at the schedule. Two p.m.: skipping. Boring – I already knew everything I wanted to know about skipping, but I went along just in case I still had things to learn. I was slightly late and walked into a room full of people running around, playing tag. 'We're just warming up,' called one of the girls running the workshop. 'Join in!' It was a bit cold inside the draughty mansion, I thought, so I did. When we stopped, I expected everyone to sit down for a discussion of favourite supermarket bins and the best wall-climbing techniques. But no

– I was handed a rope and taught some real skipping-rope tricks by the trio of girls leading the workshop who, calling themselves Skip Theatre, incorporated skipping into dance and had performed in music videos, at club nights and to publicise Diesel jeans. The whole thing was quite silly, as everyone in the workshop, including the leaders, acknowledged. But I spent the afternoon laughing and left the squat light-hearted.

Squatting has long given would-be artists and musicians a bit of breathing space to work out what they wanted to do without having to worry about whether it was going to pay the rent. The Clash's Joe Strummer formed his first band from his west London squat – and called it The 101'ers after his squat's door number on Walterton Road in Maida Vale. Fashion designer Gareth Pugh, who designed costumes for Kylie Minogue's Showgirl tour and now shows his collections during Paris Fashion Week, lived in a squatted south London warehouse from 2004 to 2005. As part of a collective known as !WOWOW!, he hosted notorious parties in the space, one of which was attended by Lauren Bush, daughter of George W. Bush, along with two CIA bodyguards. In the meantime he used the luxury of living rent free to experiment with hopelessly uncommercial clothes, such as a jacket with shoulder-pads a metre wide and a poodle costume with condoms for ears.

One squatted shop in Shoreditch, a fashionable part of east London, stayed open as the NO:ID gallery for more than a year, housing shows by new artists and a screen-printing workshop upstairs until the group was evicted in

2009. A couple squatted another empty shop on Redchurch Street not far away to host installation art in place of a window display, on which the shutters were down during the day but opened at night on brightly lit displays. It worked well for almost a year, tolerated by the shop's owners, until yobs put a brick though the window one night in 2008 and the shutters were permanently closed, putting an end to the exhibitions.

I had got into the habit of popping into the ASS office for the company and the coffee, even when I didn't need advice. So when Lesley, one of the volunteers, mentioned that the collective was looking for more members and maybe I should join them, I said an immediate yes. I liked everyone who worked there, all of them squatters and ex-squatters. The little office, with its bare wooden floorboards and draughty windows, the bodged lock on the door and the worn chairs, was a friendly, interesting place to spend time, a hub for news of what was going on in squats up and down the country, with a constant flow of people passing through and phoning up.

The volunteers avoided the patronising tone of charity workers, giving people the information they asked for and preparing civil court defences when requested, but not intervening in people's lives or prying into their back-stories. If people might be eligible for housing from the council they told them so, but for those who had already decided that squatting was the best option for them – because they couldn't afford or didn't want to rent – the

volunteers set out the law and practicalities straightfor-
wardly, making sure that they knew they needed to find a
genuinely empty building if they wanted to stand any
chance of staying there for long. The ethos was to encourage self-sufficiency. Plenty of people came in hoping to
treat it as a squatter's estate agency where they might pick
up a list of disused buildings ready to move into, or be allo-
cated a place in an existing squat. They were given leaflets
and advice instead.

Even if I didn't like all the squatters who came through
the office, the public stereotype of drug-addled scroungers
stealing other people's houses was clearly not accurate. The
ASS is the only group that helps squatters to squat legally,
avoiding as much disruption to their own and others' lives
as possible. Most charities and organisations funded by the
government or large donors disown squatting, or at least
don't endorse it. Instead, the Citizens Advice Bureau as
well as various charities refer people to the ASS when they
are squatting or want to start and need to know their rights.

Several newspapers created a stink in 2008 when Tory
MP Eric Pickles noticed that many local authority websites
offered links to the ASS's website on pages intended for
homeless people or those at risk of homelessness. Their ire
was directed at the fact that councils seemed to be endors-
ing squatting, with headlines such as the *Daily Telegraph*'s
'Squatters taught to pick locks by council leaflet'. This
referred to the ASS's *Squatters Handbook*, even though
every council's website explicitly disowns the content of
outside links and the handbook has never been funded by

councils or anything other than its £1.50 cover price. It doesn't even include any lock-picking tips or any advice on housebreaking, except to tell squatters very clearly that they must avoid causing criminal damage. If the *Daily Telegraph* wished to stir up anger, a better target might have been the combination of urgent housing need and the swathes of long-term empty properties that makes squatting make sense, and many councils' failure to use the powers they have to put the buildings into use legitimately. By including a link to the ASS, councils were tacitly admitting that their homelessness services exclude people, leaving them to resort to squatting. But after the news stories, the councils removed the links from their websites.

Personally, I was glad to put some of my surplus time and energy into helping others to access resources that were otherwise going to waste, to share the liberation I had found in living for free and perhaps to repay some of the freely given generosity I'd received along the way.

chapter eight

I, like all my housemates and almost everyone who passed through the ASS office, was homeless according to government definitions, and all of us were skint. Socialising with some of my conventional friends – particularly those I usually met for gigs or parties rather than for quiet nights in – had become more difficult, since most of their pastimes involved spending money and I'd have to explain again and again why I was, for instance, drinking tap water, or couldn't come out for the restaurant part of a birthday party. But the default assumption among squatters was that no one could afford anything, not even to reply to a text message. My extreme thrift, which had so far seen me through almost six months on an average of about 50p a day, mostly spent in a few large chunks on locks and phone bills, with most days passing entirely without cash, was unexceptional.

But the squatters I was surrounded by didn't consider themselves homeless. Our squats were homes while they lasted. And, although many of us were thoroughly sick of coffee shops' surplus muffins, none of us was hungry. But if food and shelter were there for the taking, why did anyone need to sit in the street with a sign saying 'homeless and hungry – please help'?

Squats that felt homely seemed to hugely outnumber the squalid, dangerous crack dens I'd expected to find when I decided to become a squatter. But the real misery and chaos of homelessness, when it meant a choice between sleeping outside or inside somewhere terrifying, filthy or dangerous, was closer than it had been when I was earning, renting and shopping.

I met Bill at a particularly reliable set of Pret A Manger bins, a favourite with skippers because the bins were inside a garage at the back of the shop which was always unlocked, and were collected very late, so if you failed everywhere else you could usually find at least a sandwich or two there. Bill was fairly tidy-looking with a white beard, someone your eye would slip over in the street. An ex-serviceman, he had been homeless for five years. With two other tramps, he slept behind the Pret bins every night. They woke up and cleared out with their bedding and belongings before the Pret staff arrived every morning, spending the day at a drop-in centre for the homeless where they could get a cup of tea and have a shower.

Avoiding attention was a survival tactic. Hidden in their faintly garbage-smelling nook, they ducked 'Operation Poncho', a scheme operated by the City of London Corporation, in partnership with the police and homelessness charity Broadway. Council street cleaners, accompanied by police, rouse rough sleepers in the early hours, move them on, then hose down the doorway or alley they had been sleeping in, leaving it so wet that the tramps have to find another place to rest. Howard Sinclair, chief executive of Broadway, said: 'The whole point is to make it uncomfortable for people to sleep on the streets, to make them confront the fact that it is not doing them any good, and to engage with services.'

But Bill and many others like him simply found out-of-sight places in which to elude the jet-washers, which also meant that they did not appear in counts of the rough sleepers in the area. In 2009, these official surveys counted 464 people sleeping in the streets across the UK, but many homelessness charities consider this to be a drastic underestimate, with charities such as Housing Justice accusing counters of including only people who are sleeping in open view and massaging figures downwards by stepping up council and police interventions in the run-up to the count to meet the government's target of zero rough sleepers by 2012.

Hiding also kept homeless people safer from crime. Those who sleep on the street or in temporary accommodation are 13 times more likely to have experienced violence than the general public, and 47 times more likely to have been victims of theft, according to a survey by homelessness charity Crisis, which found that they were harassed and attacked by ordinary members of the public as well as fellow homeless people. Out for a walk and a skip late one night, I saw a pair of boys running down the street laughing. That's nice, I thought to myself. They're having fun. It wasn't until I walked another hundred metres or so that I realised what they'd found so funny. They'd just pissed on a tramp asleep in a doorway, something that has happened to one in ten rough sleepers according to the Crisis survey. I called the police and gave the guy some of my cash from the sofa proceeds, but could think of little else to do but walk on.

While I was working in the ASS office, an elderly man came in. He had been sleeping on one of the bendy buses, which travel long routes 24 hours a day and which are popular places to rest at night for the roofless, since they are dry and warm and it's easy to dodge the fare. His pocket had been picked while he napped. Without anywhere to leave anything safely he had been carrying all his possessions, including his birth certificate, with him. He lost all his cash and, worse, every scrap of ID. He couldn't claim benefits until his documents were reissued, so he hadn't had a penny, except what he could beg, for weeks. He didn't have a mobile, so he needed to use our office phone to find out whether it was going to be much longer before he got his papers replaced.

The choice between squatting in a mansion like mine or huddling in a doorway all night, vulnerable to thugs and council staff, might seem obvious. But things aren't so simple. For some of those who sleep rough, sleeping indoors seemed even more dangerous. When I dropped into Bill's garage one night to get some sandwiches, he asked me where I lived. I said I was a squatter, and he sucked his teeth. 'You want to be careful,' he warned me. 'I've been in a few squats, but I wouldn't piss in the same pot as most of the squatters I've met. Better in the street.'

A couple of weeks later, I saw what he meant first hand. At another set of bins, I got chatting with a couple in their late twenties with dreadlocks and piercings, but friendly faces. After we'd shared out that night's rations of bread, salad and cake, we hadn't finished our conversation, so Cristina and Tony invited me back to theirs, just round the corner. 'By the way,' they added as we walked. 'It's probably only right to mention that someone got knifed at our place a few weeks back.'

We walked round the corner to their home and I realised we were going to the warehouse I'd seen squatters being let into on the first day but had shrunk away from approaching. Having already said I could do with a cup of tea, it seemed too awkward to change my mind and go home. A scrawny, hunched man with patchy ginger stubble, pale, unhealthy skin and a black eye opened the door and let us in. The light inside was dim, but not dim enough to conceal how grimy and bare the huge warehouse space was. Crude, uncreative graffiti spread across the walls and the floor was empty apart from a cluster of furniture in one corner. There, a man with another black eye slept on a mangy sofa and a fat Asian bloke played a fighting game on an Xbox. He barely looked up when Cristina said a brief hello. Smaller rooms opened off the main one, all of them empty, some of them with puddles on the floor from a leaky roof.

A scrawny, small woman in her late twenties jigged up to us. 'Oh man!' she ranted, unprompted. 'I went raving last night. It was A-MAZE-ING! The talent on display was just awesome! It was BRI-LI-ANT!' She dropped the exclamation marks for a moment. 'Mate, I really need some Valium. No? None of you? Got a fag? Anyone? How about you?' she asked, standing far too close as she jabbed a finger at me. 'No? None at all? You're sure?'

'Sorry, Steph,' Cristina said as Steph rattled away to the furnished corner of the room.

I was biting my cheek, trying to maintain a calm façade despite being inside the nightmare I'd imagined before moving into a squat. Tony and Cristina's room, once an office for the bakery company that used the warehouse, was upstairs, removed from the main hall. I left my bike in the corridor locked to a banister, at Tony's suggestion, an idea that would never have occurred to me when leaving my bike unattended inside any other squat I'd been to. Cristina unlocked a padlock on the door their room, we went inside and she bolted the door behind her.

Suddenly we were back in a world I recognised. A mattress had cheerfully coloured sheets on it, clothes sat on shelves, and photos and newspaper cuttings were stuck to the walls along with a couple of stencilled anarchy symbols. Tony went to the stereo to put on some music and Cristina opened one of the bags of cookies we'd just skipped – pieces of minor comfort and self-care that had been absent downstairs. Tony and Cristina had moved in a few months ago, they said. They'd seen that this building was squatted, so had asked if there was room to spare. They'd run out of money for rent, so had decided to give squatting a try.

The murder, which Cristina called 'the accident', had happened only a few weeks before. Unsurprisingly, it was still the only thing on either of their minds. The household had never been united, they said. There had been about a dozen teenagers living there, some of them on a break between school and university. They'd been toying with communal living, going to raves and parties, taking ketamine, getting stoned and all sharing one of the big warehouse spaces as a bedroom. The teenagers had moved in with the dozen or so people who had opened the squat in the first place. That group, in their late twenties and thirties, had moved between squatting and living in caravans for years and had harder drug habits. Cristina and Tony, who had moved in after the teenagers, hadn't been part of either group.

As Tony told the story, they, the teenagers and the long-term squatters had all been out raving one weekend. When they got home, wasted, in the early hours, a row had been brewing. No one knew how it had started, really. Perhaps a taxi fare, perhaps a bong, borrowed and never returned. Someone's girlfriend was head-butted and a fist-fight broke out. Everyone had thought the fight had settled things. But then the head-butter, who had come off worse in the fight, had gone to his belongings, grabbed a knife, and stabbed the attacked girl's boyfriend, they said. Tony had seen it happen, had called the ambulance, had seen the paramedics decide it was hopeless to try to resuscitate the dead boy, one of the teenagers.

In the wake of that pointless death on the grimy floor,

the man everyone in the house saw kill the boy was on remand, awaiting trial. All the squatters had been taken to the police station for DNA samples and the forensics team had taken over the building for a week. But when the police left, some of the squatters had found a way back into the building, and the owners, property developers who were seeking planning permission to demolish the warehouse and replace it with 50-odd new flats, still seemed to be turning a blind eye. Tony and Cristina had made efforts to patch things up in the household. But during a communal dinner Cristina had cooked, another fight had broken out, resulting in the two men's black eyes.

Tony and Cristina were looking for a new home but were still hoping that things in the warehouse would get better. I felt the shaky sensation of having survived a near miss. What if I had got to the door of this squat more quickly on that first day, before the squatters had closed the door behind themselves? Maybe I was as naive and reckless as I considered Tony and Cristina to be, or had been when I first left home. What, after all, was I doing right now, if not sitting in a place my instincts were screaming at me to avoid because I hadn't wanted to commit the social faux pas of turning down a cup of tea? I felt a deep gratitude to Tom for being only a bully, not violent or drugged into irrationality. And I counted my blessings all the way back to my lovely, clean home, where I could sleep with my door unlocked and leave my possessions on open view without fear of my housemates touching them.

I already knew only too well that squatting is no easy option. Finding and getting inside a disused building that's likely to make a long-term home can't be done opportunistically if you don't want to get arrested or moved out at short notice. It takes patience, organisation and practical skill. And opening a building is only the first step. You then have to fix anything that's broken, find furniture and keep the place constantly inhabited for the first few weeks. You have to convince the owners you're not going to burn the building down, and the neighbours not to complain so much you get moved on straight away. Committing any kind of crime inside, such as drug use, gives the police a ready-made excuse to break the door down. And you have to do it all over again every time you get evicted. In the seventies, squats might have lasted for years, but now staying in a place for six months is considered lucky. As long as you've got the money or the state is paying, renting is a far easier option. And for some, sleeping rough is an easier or safer option as well.

When searching for empties, we'd sometimes come across places which were being used as places to crash by rough sleepers, but couldn't be described as squats any more than Bill's garage. Rather than changing the locks and asserting their legal rights, they defended their homes with threats of violence. An elderly alcoholic was sleeping in the carcass of a pub that had burned down years ago, as Martin discovered when he peered in past one of the sheets of corrugated iron that was hanging loose from the window frame. And when Viktor went to have a look through the perforated metal covering the window of a huge house in central London, he was chased away by a tramp wielding a stick who was living in the basement coalhole, not in the house itself.

Perhaps most difficult of all, squatters have to live in a group. Maybe the warehouse squatters had got it together to find and secure a suitable building. But everyone in your household has to be relied on not to bring trouble to the door if you want to feel safe in your home. The mystery of the money stolen at Jamie's party gained a likely explanation after his household asked one of their squatmates to move out – a girl who had arrived as a guest but had never left. Only once she had gone did they mention that she had been struggling with a heroin habit. She'd been managing to keep up some semblance of normality and her housemates had been trying to help her. But when she was sacked from the pub she'd worked at after being caught stealing from the tills she'd gone into a downwards spiral and her thieving, lack of personal hygiene and tendency to bring fellow addicts home had eventually made her impossible to live with. They didn't know where she had gone. To a squat with other addicts, they suspected. They hoped she'd be OK but had decided that their responsibility for her was over. Jamie thought she had probably stolen my purse and the others at his party. They had decided to give her the benefit of the doubt then, knowing that she'd be in more danger elsewhere, but their patience had eventually run out.

The situation is no longer what George Orwell found

when down and out in Paris and London in the late 1920s. Orwell describes lying in a bug-ridden bed, weak with hunger, desperate for a slice of bread and dripping despite being willing and able to work. Today, thanks to charitable and government help, quite apart from the fact that there are hundreds of thousands of empty homes and sacks of sandwiches in the street every night, long-term rooflessness and starving hunger are often the visible symptoms of deeper problems such as addictions and mental ill-health for those lucky enough to have full rights to live and work in Britain – although there can be few better incubators of such problems than life on the streets. The tragedy of the situation is that those very problems make it difficult for long-term rough sleepers to accept the help offered by the dozens of institutions trying to relieve the most visible cases of homelessness, let alone find and maintain a safe, stable squat, even when their beds are being hosed down nightly. The solution to such profound chaos in people's lives is not as simple as putting a roof over their head or a sandwich in their hand.

The decline in absolute if not relative poverty means that the raw desperation that drove tens of thousands of British people into squats to escape overcrowded slums after the Second World War is largely a thing of the past. Food poverty means stretching the weekly income by doing without fruit and vegetables, not lying in bed because you're too famished to get up, as Orwell describes. Local authorities have a duty to house anyone who is in 'priority need' – those who are entitled to help from the British government, unintentionally homeless and are ill, have just left foster care, or have children. Even if the housing offered is a grim bed and breakfast hostel during the long wait for a secure council flat, it represents reliable shelter – more reliable than that offered by most squats. And government benefits will pay or at least subsidise the rent for people the council does not have a direct duty to house.

It is something to be proud of that, today, it is rare for people with full rights to the support of the British government to be forced by pure financial hardship into a choice between squatting or sleeping rough, and it's rare to meet British children who live in squats. In the ASS office I met British people who had chosen to squat rather than stay in overcrowded, inappropriate accommodation or remain with a partner they'd broken up with when they couldn't afford separate flats. I met people who squatted rather than shuffling their possessions from one friend's sofa to another, or falling out with their family by overstaying their welcome. Many squatted rather than working long hours for bad pay, only to see most of their income swallowed up by expensive rent. And I met scores of people who had chosen squatting rather than abandoning their ambitions to study, write or make art or music because they couldn't make ends meet while devoting time to their projects.

But before we all start patting ourselves on the back for having moved closer to making poverty history, it's worth remembering that the situation is very different for the millions of people who are in the UK, but who have fewer rights to state help. There are an estimated 500,000 failed asylum seekers in the UK, who are banned from working, and cannot receive support from the government – which would consist of supermarket vouchers and no-choice accommodation rather than cash – unless they sign an agreement consenting to be removed from the UK at a later date. Since many fear torture or abuse if they return to their home countries, only 9,000 are receiving the support, according to a report by refugee charity Pafras.

Only a tiny proportion of those people who choose destitution over deportation find a solution in squatting. The vulnerability of their position means they have to keep a low profile, since any kind of trouble with the authorities could result in being sent home. Squatting might bring them to the attention of the police, who might start asking difficult questions, and who have the right to break into a building which they have reason to believe is occupied by people who are in the country illegally. Some charities working with refugees gave out ASS advice leaflets, but had to do so surreptitiously for fear of attracting media controversy or the ire of financial backers if they were seen to be encouraging squatting. Some squats hosted failed asylum seekers, letting them stay in the background while those who had full rights to be in the country dealt with the police and other authority figures. But most failed asylum seekers seemed to consider it better to stay covertly with compatriots who did have the right to remain in the country, or sleep in the streets, even if that laid them open to exploitation and abuse.

Far better off than the asylum seekers were the citizens of Poland, Hungary and the six other countries that joined the EU in 2004 and became known as the A8. Their citizens gained the right to travel to the UK freely and to work here, while citizens of Bulgaria and Romania, the A2 countries, gained restricted rights to work when they joined the EU in 2007. Citizens of the A8 or A2 are only eligible for government support if they had been employed here for a year, registered as a worker and were paying tax. If they are out of work for more than a month within the first 12 months or if they only find casual, temporary or unofficial work, the clock goes back to zero and they are on their own, ineligible for unemployment or housing benefit. Under European law, homelessness services are not obliged to help them if they find themselves sleeping rough, although many charities do.

Even those in work sometimes couldn't make ends meet. Many, like Viktor, earned the minimum wage which, for a 40-hour week, came to just over £200 before tax. When it's a real struggle to find even a room in London for less than £100 a week the sums often didn't work out, especially if you wanted to save or send money home, or, just possibly, enjoy yourself a bit. I met A8 workers who were sleeping in dorms, renting a bunk bed in a room shared with half a dozen others, to save money.

The rules on A8 and A2 workers may be fair and necessary. But for some of that army of immigrant labour, the famous Polish plumbers and the cheerful Slovenian barmaids who kept prices pleasantly low during the boom by working cheaply, squatting made sense, particularly if they had lost their jobs or hadn't yet managed to find one that paid a decent wage. They had the economic motivation and they had already found the guts to move to an unwelcoming, unfamiliar country where they wouldn't have the safety net we Britons had – family and long-standing friends if we were lucky and at least the support of the state if we needed it. Putting up with the hassles and stresses of squatting for many wasn't a problem.

Whenever Eastern European squatters made tabloid headlines, they were painted as a bunch of bums, coming here to take advantage of our state's generosity and, in the meantime, living in filth and disrupting their English neighbours' civilised lives. But it didn't look like that to me. No doubt some were self-centred opportunists, seeing an easy way to get a free ride by taking advantage of Western European prosperity, coming to London where we are so rich the streets are paved with free food, if not gold. But the majority seemed to have come to work. If a lean period or the need to save money meant the hassle and effort of squatting, they did it.

In the ASS office, English accents were rarely the majority. Arty graduates using squatting as a window of opportunity for experimentation were exceptional, as were dangerous, ruthless scroungers. Instead, I met a steady stream of people in difficult situations who were looking for a way to sort themselves out, and who had realised that squatting was a sensible solution. Back at home, my Hungarian, Italian and German housemates made our house a cheerful, safe place to be. I'd been proud of myself for leaving behind my possessions and my flat. They'd done all that, on top of moving away from their country, language, friends and family. I could only admire their grit.

chapter nine

Summer was slipping away and our time in the mansion was coming to an end. I'd found the court papers for the council's claim to evict us stuck to the front door one morning. Now we'd have to go back to hunting for empties then face the fear and risks of getting into the one we chose. We'd have to carry all our stuff around again, jettisoning the luxuries that were too heavy to transport. Even if we found a place we could stay in for a while, it would take weeks to make it feel homely. The quiet routine I'd got into – reading, skipping, hanging out at the squat with the boys, inviting friends round or meeting them out and about – would be shattered. But the papers had been more of an irritation than a source of dread. Like most squatters, we'd tried to make a case for the council simply leaving us alone until the building was needed when the council officer had called round. I'd faxed her, because she had asked to see it in writing. She hadn't responded, and now my fax was included in the bundle of court papers.

Moving couldn't be worse than last time, and that had worked out all right in the end. Martin, Fabio and Istvan were going home, but Viktor, Jozsef and I had agreed to stick together. I now had more of an idea of how to open a squat and a far wider group of squatting friends who would help if needed. Evicting us wasn't a high priority for the council so they'd only gone for an ordinary possession order. The court date wasn't for several weeks, and even if my ASS colleagues couldn't come up with a defence to get the case adjorned for another few weeks, we would probably still have a month or so between losing in court and the bailiffs arriving at our door. There wasn't much point in scurrying around looking for empties straight away. But, as before, the knowledge that we were going to have to move out sooner or later eroded the sense of homeliness that had grown in the mansion.

It was time to take a break from London. Mikey, one of my best friends, had persuaded me to come along on my first hitch-hiking trip while we were at university. Back then I'd been embarrassed as much as scared. Of course standing on the side of the road asking to get into a car with a stranger went against all the safety rules I had been taught as a child. But almost as bad was having to effectively announce my inability to pay for the train or the coach to every passing driver. Mikey, a natural extrovert whose daring sometimes edged into recklessness, was in his element. Afterwards I was forced to admit that we'd got to where we were going, we'd got back and we'd had a good time.

It was time to do it again. Mikey, who was self-employed and at the end of a couple of months' work, was also at a loose end so we decided to go on a little spree up to Scotland before I'd have to focus on finding a new home and he'd have to find another job. We wanted to visit a road protest site I'd been told about by one of Jozsef's friends, Piotr, another Hungarian who had what looked like a piece of pasta stuck through the middle section of his nose where a bull might have a ring. The camp was a scattering of tree-houses in a patch of ancient woodland, Piotr said, intended to save the trees from road builders. It had been there for more than five years and there was no immediate prospect of the bulldozers arriving. He'd loved it.

Mikey came to stay at the mansion and we set our alarms for an early start. We needed to cover more than 400 miles that day – optimistic but not unrealistic, we reckoned. Hitching out of the centre of town was likely to be a chore, since most of the drivers would only be making short hops. For the sake of speed, and to save ourselves from too much emphasis on the hiking part of hitch-hiking, we treated ourselves to a bus out of town to the North Circular.

We'd looked at a map and spotted a promising set of traffic lights which drivers going north would have to pass. We'd checked an online satellite picture of the junction and seen that there would be a pavement for us to stand on and a lay-by for drivers to pull into. Mikey had brought two marker pens, one green and one black, and I'd found a cardboard box to make a sign. The plan was to start with a sign saying Edinburgh, then make a new sign for our specific destination once we were close enough for people to recognise it.

Mikey, who rarely travels except by thumb, took charge of making the sign. The knack, he reckoned, was to write

179

the central letter first, then the first and last letters, then fill in the rest. If you start at the beginning, you almost always end up with too much or too little space for the last letter, whereas if the middle letters are bigger or smaller than the first and last, it just gives the sign a jaunty look. Two colours were a worthwhile luxury, in his opinion, because then you can add shadows to your letters – and who wouldn't be more inclined to pick up a hitcher with nice typography rather than dull black capitals?

We arrived at the junction we'd chosen, dropped our backpacks and stuck out our thumbs. We had a captive audience in the queue of morning rush-hour drivers waiting at the lights so we tried to look smiley but not irritatingly so, as if we'd be good but undemanding company for anyone who decided to let us into their car. We focused on trying to catch the drivers' eyes, deliberately not wearing sunglasses, and holding the sign up high for a lorry driver, down low for a sports car. The easier we made it for drivers to ignore us, we reckoned, the more they would. But if we managed to force them to meet our eyes, it was harder for them to pretend not to see us. If they decided not to give us a lift then, they had to admit to themselves that they'd made the decision to leave us by the side of the road. A psychology study carried out by academics at Stanford University in 1974 bore out Mikey's theory. Hitch-hiking was then so common that researchers used it to test people's reaction to eye contact. They found that if hitch-hikers stared at drivers' eyes it more than doubled the drivers' probability of stopping, compared with looking away from oncoming drivers' faces.

We had waited barely ten minutes when a car pulled over. We sprinted along the verge to it. 'I'm not going far,' said the driver. 'Just a few junctions, but it's on your way.' We jumped in anyway, then jumped out again less than 15 minutes later. Although a steady stream of cars flowed past our new spot, everyone studiously ignored us, not gesturing that they were about to turn off or that their cars were too full, or even shaking their heads for 'no'. We tried to stay cheerful-looking, jumping and stamping our feet to stay warm. After about 40 minutes a building-site manager picked us up on his way to a meeting in Northampton. Over the hour or so of driving, Keith explained the difficulties of working on shop refits, but mostly wanted to talk about the prospects of the youth football team he coached for the coming season. They were on good form.

In the eight years since my first hitching trip, and during scores of lifts from harmless people like Keith, I'd more or less reasoned myself out of my fear of hitch-hiking. Most homicide victims and most people who are raped are attacked by people they know. Or so statistics and logic said. Emotion disagreed. The stories of those who are harmed randomly by strangers simply for being in the wrong place at the wrong time stick in the mind and receive endless press coverage. As with winning the National Lottery, another random and unlikely event that millions of people nevertheless gamble on, it could be you. Several of Fred West's victims were hitch-hikers he picked up. Ivan

Robert Marko Milat killed seven hitchers in Australia in the nineties. Nineteen-year-old Dinah McNicol disappeared in 1991 while hitching home from a music festival, and Peter Tobin is due to be tried for her murder after her remains were found in his back garden.

Even thinking about such tales made me want to rush back to safety. The risk may be tiny but there are easy ways to avoid it – pay up for public transport or stay at home. As life gets less dangerous and life expectancies increase, a tiny danger grows in relative riskiness. But people lay themselves open to statistically far more dangerous things without a second's thought. Smoking, not wearing sunscreen or not fitting a smoke detector in your house are – like a million other incredibly tedious things – far more likely to take years off your life. And even if it is attacks by strangers you want to avoid most of all, anyone who wanted to attract innocent victims would do far better to advertise a job or a lonely heart on the Internet rather than cruise around looking for hitchers.

Still, on that first hitching trip, I'd made a promise to myself not to hitch-hike alone. As a woman, standing by the side of the road waiting for lifts sounded too much like asking for trouble. Ever since, Mikey had done his best to convince me it was unnecessarily cautious. I'd ignored him, but I was pretty sure that as long as we were a twosome we'd be all right, too much for any but the most motivated and deranged psychopath to take on and, since we were hitching, clearly too broke to be worth robbing. I was fairly sure that the most dangerous aspects were standing close to the edges of busy roads and the variable levels of driving competence among the people who picked you up.

The next ride came from a soldier, heading up north to visit his girlfriend for the weekend. He was a PT instructor who told us about his daily fitness regime as well as filling us in on just how tough you have to be for a military yomp, a long-distance, high-speed march in full kit, which can weigh as much as 80 pounds, he said. When we stopped for petrol, he came back from the mini-supermarket on the forecourt with three bottles of water. 'Got to keep hydrated,' he said as he passed them round.

A cheerful couple from Leeds picked us up from the service station where he dropped us and offered to pack us into the back of their white van, where we sat among the boxes of home-made chutneys and chilli sauces that they were delivering for the small business the girl's mum ran. Sitting in the pitch black among the clunking boxes, we had no idea where we were or how far we'd gone, but they let us out, blinking, at some traffic lights on the junction to Leeds, insisting that we take one of the bottles of hot sauce.

A retired Geordie couple gave us the next lift. They'd been out just for the sake of going for a drive and now they were heading back to Newcastle. We chatted about the virtues or otherwise of hard work, which the man, a retired headmaster, was thoroughly in favour of for its own sake. From the junction where they dropped us, we got a ride with a stand-up comic in his Volkswagen camper van. He was driving to Edinburgh for a gig and offered to put us on the guest list if we fancied it.

He took us into the centre of town, where we jumped out and cheered. Hello Scotland! It had been a bitty journey, with shorter lifts than we had hoped for, taking ten hours – slightly longer than the National Express London to Edinburgh coach. Although we'd spent time waiting by the side of the road, the bus went slowly on a less direct route, stopping on the way to give the driver a break. If we had loaded ourselves onto the coach that morning, we would have crawled off it, achy and cranky, after a boring day staring out of the window, rather than being filled with a sense of achievement as we were now. The train would have taken less than five hours but would have set us back around £100 for the cheapest return ticket – unaffordable for me, obviously, but a stretch for most people. Actually, we were now better off to the tune of a bottle of chilli sauce, two bottles of water and a pair of tickets for a comedy show. But far more importantly, we'd had an exciting, stimulating day, chatting to interesting people we had little in common with and who shared few of our views, whose paths we'd never normally have crossed but who had decided to do us a good turn for no reason other than that they were going our way and we needed a lift.

For all the talk about the increasing fearfulness and isolation of society, our 40-minute wait on the edge of London had been the longest that day, with most waits lasting only 15 or 20 minutes. And that was despite the fact that there are just as many stories of hitchers killing drivers as the other way round – in 1950, Billy Cook hitched a ride with a family of five from Illinois and murdered them all.

He also killed a travelling salesman he got a lift with. His story was made into the grisly 1953 film *The Hitch-hiker*. Fictional slasher flick *The Texas Chainsaw Massacre* also features a hitch-hiker who is a murderous cannibal.

Unsurprisingly, most drivers ignored us. But the tales hadn't stopped every driver from deciding, in the moment they had to think about it before passing by, to stop for us. I only once failed to get where I wanted to go by hitching. Colin and I had decided to go to Margate. It should have been easy. It was before lunchtime and Margate was only two or three hours away by car, so we should have been able to get there, check out the disused wooden roller-coaster we wanted to see, dip our feet in the sea and get home before nightfall. We found what should have been a decent hitching spot on a slipway onto the main road towards Kent. Half an hour passed. An hour. Our optimism was fading. Eventually, a young couple going home from the shops pulled over. Did we want a ride as far as south London? All we wanted was to get off that rotten strip of asphalt, which for some reason seemed to be cursed for hitchers. The place they dropped us should have been quite good too. But after another hour of waiting, and after the third carload of boys had responded to our thumbs with two fingers and jeering suggestions that I should provide them with a variety of sexual favours, our chances of having time to get back from Margate even if we eventually got there were looking slim. We picked up our bags and walked home.

But one failure had to be set against dozens of triumphs.

Colin and I were invited to a wedding down in Dorset in the early autumn. By that stage, I'd got over my shame at having to go to the ceremony in a skirt rejected by a charity shop, and I actually thought I looked quite nice with the knitted flower I'd made for my hair and some Freecycled nail varnish. As wedding gifts, I had jars of homemade jam and chutney to offer, and I was also able to give the couple a day of my time to let workmen into their house while they were away on honeymoon. We arrived in plenty of time for the ceremony after a man we had at first thought a bit charmless, driving a very grimy car with footwells full of junk, refused to let us out. It was raining and he insisted on going 30 miles out of his way to take us to the church door.

Ken Welsh, the author of *The Hitch-hiker's Guide to Europe*, first published in 1971 and out of print since 1996, summed up the attitude hitching demands perfectly. In the introduction to the first edition he wrote: 'Hitch-hiking is a game of chance. In this world where we expect things to run on time or to be in a certain place by three o'clock, it is a refreshing experience. Just because the ninth car doesn't stop doesn't mean the tenth will; nor the hundredth, nor the thousandth. But you'll get there.'

The book's two main claims to fame are that it was for a while the book most commonly stolen from public libraries, and that it inspired Douglas Adams's *The Hitchhiker's Guide to the Galaxy*, first aired as a radio play in 1978. Adams appropriated Welsh's advice that a towel is the most useful item a hitcher can bring. You can use it as a scarf, a groundsheet, an extra layer of clothing, a poncho to keep your clothes drier if it's raining, a flannel, if you kept one corner exclusively for washing your face, and you can even use it to dry yourself after a shower.

Welsh's book was almost the opposite of a guidebook, providing little guidance about what to see or do in the cities you might end up in, instead giving readers the information and encouragement they might need to go and work it out for themselves. It laid out tactics for finding a good hitching spot and persuading drivers to pick you up, as well as summarising pitfalls and money-saving tips for cities across Europe – how to get stale bread in France and the regulations regarding sleeping on Portuguese beaches, for instance. Anyone travelling without the attitude Welsh recommended, who expected star ratings and helpful maps rather than just waiting to see what happened, and who perhaps liked to carry a scarf, raincoat, groundsheet, flannel and an extra jumper as well as a towel, would have found his guide almost useless.

Most of the drivers who picked us up commented on how few hitchers you see these days. My parents, who were young in the seventies, describe having to queue up with other hitchers to take it in turns to stick their thumbs out at particularly good spots in the UK and Europe because so many people were using it as a way to get around. Many lifts came from former hitchers, now middle-aged and able to afford cars of their own but also able to remember what it's like to stand by the side of the road. Today, Lonely Planet travel books, aimed at a similar demographic to

Welsh's guide, explicitly discourage hitch-hiking and provide one or two paragraphs of basic tips for travellers who decide to take the 'small but potentially serious risk'.

If hitching was a 'refreshing change' from normal attitudes in the seventies, as Welsh put it, it is even more so today. Real adventures, where you genuinely don't know how things are going to turn out and you need to be on your toes to make sure you end up all right, are increasingly rare in normal life. Going backpacking means stepping onto a well-worn route of banana pancakes and lager unless you make a real effort to avoid it. So-called adventure sports may generate adrenalin but involve little element of chance – what happens when you jump off a bridge attached to a bungee rope is entirely predictable. Shops offer instant gratification. As long as you have money in your pocket or credit on your credit card, you almost never need to just wait for a solution to present itself. So hitching – setting out knowing where you want to go but not how, when or with whom – is a long way from how most people go about their lives today.

But it isn't only the fault of our uptight age. The falling prices in real terms of private cars and public transport combined with rising prosperity make paying your way far more affordable than it was in the sixties and seventies. If it's possible to book a coach, train or plane ticket for less than a fiver, it's understandable that no one heads onto the road equipped only with optimism and a thumb. But of course most tickets cost far more than that, and you have to know where you want to go weeks if not months ahead of leaving to have any hope of getting a bargain. A journey like mine and Mikey's, planned at the last minute when the mood and the opportunity arose, is discouraged by the pricing structures. Hitching eliminates the question of 'can I afford it?' from the question of 'do I want to go?'

Hitching is now so rare that it's little wonder that even people who are broke, brave and easy-going don't bother. Although most of the squatters I met hitched as a matter of course when they needed to travel, Mikey and Colin were the only non-squatters I knew who considered it a sensible option for getting anywhere – and Mikey had proved to me that it worked, and I'd taught Colin. If you have never spoken to anyone who has succeeded in getting to their destination by hitching, it would be easy to assume it could never work. I have more than once had to explain to groups of teenagers what I was doing standing by a road with a sign. 'You mean drivers are just going to stop and take you there? Why would they want to do that?' Even I, despite having proven to myself again and again that drivers do stop, sometimes wondered myself.

The Internet might help to spark a revival. Websites such as digihitch.com and hitchwiki.org have sprung up, built, Wikipedia-style, from the contributions of hitch-hikers across the world. Over the last couple of years they have reached critical mass, and have begun to fill the niche Welsh's book once occupied. Websites to coordinate lift-sharing have also developed, although they are probably of more use to commuters than one-off travellers. I signed up for a few such sites but never succeeded in finding anyone who was making the same journey as me, with most rides offered for short, regular hops by people hoping to find commuting partners to share the petrol costs. Even if I had found a lift for a trip I wanted to make, I'd have to fit in with the time the driver wanted to set off and discuss meeting points and how to share out the petrol costs ahead of time. Doing it the old-fashioned way seemed less of a faff.

Hitch-hiking may have got us to Edinburgh, but Mikey and I now faced another problem. It was getting dark, we weren't at our final destination, and even if we could get a lift to the nearest village to the camp, getting to the site itself was going to involve a walk through the woods. We only had Piotr's directions for how to get there from the road and his assurance that we'd probably be welcome when we did arrive. We didn't fancy getting lost or finding our way to the camp only to irritate the protestors by arriving late and unannounced, imposing ourselves if we weren't welcome.

Mikey had brought a tent just in case we had been marooned by the motorway, so pitching it in an unobtrusive corner of a park or a playing field was a fall-back possibility. But an Edinburgh-based friend picked up the phone on the third try so we took him to the comedian's show, presented him with the chilli sauce and got invited back to his to sleep on the floor.

The weather had turned drizzly and cold the next morning when we headed to the camp. We found the tiny, unmarked gate Piotr had told us about, and followed a rough path into the woods. The huts, with roofs made from loud-coloured tarpaulins, were visible in the trees from a distance. The protestors, most of whom had dread-locks or dyed, hacked-around hair and grungy clothes, were just waking up, making coffee on a campfire. When we introduced ourselves, people said hello and invited us to sit down on the logs under a tarpaulin roof where the campers were gathered, but then paid us little attention. 'Who're these clean people?' a protestor arriving at the circle asked, and we introduced ourselves again, but mostly we couldn't join in with the chat about recent parties, highs and come-downs.

Most of the campers were in their twenties but there was a scattering of older people who looked to be in a bad way, their faces weathered, perhaps by too much drinking and uncomfortable living. Several members of the circle were cracking open cans of Stella and Strongbow while others drank morning coffee. They were clearly used to guests, as Piotr had said, but that didn't seem to explain their almost complete lack of curiosity about who we were, where we'd come from and what we were doing there. Eventually, we got into a conversation with one of the more together-looking campers, who pointed out the various parts of the site so we could go and explore for ourselves.

Most of the houses were built high up in the trees, based on poles tied between two or three branches. Floors were made of planks and walls were a motley selection of chip-board, plastic signs and bits of broken-up furniture, all the materials gathered from skips in the nearby village, as well as towns and villages further away. Few huts were bigger than a double mattress and some would only have space inside to sit or lie, but others looked tall enough to stand in. Most had slanting tarpaulin roofs and glass windows, some made using glazed cupboard doors. I couldn't imagine how you would even start to build something like that, or put up with a long winter in one of them. Back at the campfire, the protestors shrugged off the skill and toughness it involved. First you winched up the poles and built the frame, then added the rest of it, improving it over time by adding windows, a better roof, more headroom as you found the materials and the energy to get on with it. And winter wasn't so bad – you just made your hut as draught-free as possible, and used a hot-water bottle and lots of blankets. You get used to it, they shrugged.

The camp had a basic kitchen with drinking water collected in huge containers carried in a wheelbarrow from a standpipe in the village Mikey and I had walked from, and Scotland's abundant rainfall collected in a butt for washing. A few villagers were involved in the camp but although villagers and protestors seemed to get on fairly well they were very separate communities. One supportive villager let them charge up a couple of car batteries at his house most days so they could power mobile phones and a stereo but otherwise they were completely off the grid, using gas lanterns and candles for light and spending as little money as the London squatters. Food was skipped from nearby supermarket bins and cooked on the fire or eaten cold. A huge shed was the larder, where the food was stored in switched-off fridges to keep away vermin and flies. Washing in anything other than cold water would be a serious undertaking, so most of the campers smelled of sour bodies and dirty clothes. Several bags of rubbish had accumulated, waiting to be carried out to the village. Going to the toilet was a matter of peeing in the bushes or squatting over a stinking hole a couple of hundred metres away.

We asked if we could stay the night – in Mikey's tent if necessary. No need to pitch the tent, said the campers. In any case, sleeping on the ground wasn't a very good idea because of the rats that infested the camp – the high tree-houses helped the campers to escape rodents as well as bailiffs. A protestor pointed out a spare hut. I liked the look of it but it was high in the upper branches of a huge horse chestnut. The bare trunk had few hand- and foot-holds. Some chunks of wood had been tied onto the trunk to make the climb slightly easier but they were wet and slippery from the rain. I had a go, and with a leg-up from Mikey I made it up about three metres, but then I was frozen, clinging to the trunk, afraid to use any of my limbs to grope for the next step as one of the tied-on pieces of wood wobbled under my feet. As my knees started trembling with fear and effort, the wobbling got worse. From where I was I could probably jump back down onto the soft, damp forest floor safely, but I couldn't make myself go any higher. I was fairly sure climbing all the way to the top was beyond me, and certain I wouldn't be able to do it at bedtime once darkness had fallen.

Mikey shinned up without any problems. But I had to go back to the circle of campers and admit that I was going to need a lower-down hut. I was pointed towards another one whose normal occupant was away. The two-metre climb up the side of the hut to the hatch in the roof was much more my level. Inside was bedding on a platform, a few items of clothing and, on little shelves around the room, the accumulation of photos, ornaments and mementos of its long-term resident.

Mikey and I returned to the campfire but since so little was happening in the camp and the drizzle had cleared we decided to head off for a walk. The small wood was lovely as the leaves turned autumn red, with small streams cutting through it and bushes laden with blackberries and wild raspberries. We passed the afternoon by putting in a bit of work at the camp in return for the food we'd eaten and the beds we were about to sleep in, doing a huge heap of washing-up and carting some rubbish to the village and water back.

Night fell and most of the campers were finally breaking away from the fire to go to a party. Mikey and I turned down an invitation to join them; we were exhausted from two early starts and long days. We got our bags from the communal area and clambered into our huts. I unrolled my sleeping bag on the bed, put on my pyjamas and tried to ignore the smell that was coming from the bedding, of unwashed bodies and grimy fabric.

I'd brought some skipped chocolate and now seemed a good time for some comfort food. I had been sharing it around earlier, but when I reached into my bag there was none left. That's odd, I thought to myself. The campers had probably seen where I'd put it, got hungry and helped themselves. Fair enough. But there had been five bars there – a bit greedy to take the whole lot. I really fancied some. I felt in the pocket again, and pulled out one corner of a bar, still in a bit of wrapper. I looked at it in the candlelight. The toothmarks in it were rodents', not human. I looked at my bag again. The side pocket where I'd been keeping the chocolate had a hole gnawed in it. Rats. Rats had eaten all five bars of chocolate while my bag had been in the communal hut all day.

I tried not to think about it, blowing out the candle and closing my eyes. I succeeded in drifting off into sleep for perhaps half an hour but woke, my arm numb from lying on the hard bed, to the sound of scrabbling. I sat up hastily and shone the weak light of my mobile phone down on to the floor where I'd put my bag. The noise stopped. I lay back down. It started again. Rats. It couldn't be anything but. I still had some food in my bag from the stash I'd brought for the long journey. However well I had wrapped it up, they were bound to find it, and better if they didn't have to gnaw their way through my bag and spare clothes to do so. I took the food out and put it in a carrier bag on the floor, bringing my rucksack onto the sleeping platform. I tried to close my eyes, but minutes later I heard the sound of plastic being crumpled and pulled at. I lit a candle. The faint light put them off, but it seemed stupidly dangerous to go to sleep with a candle alight in a flammable wooden hut.

And even if I did, the rats would get used to the light or the candle would burn out. Even if all the food was on the floor my bag was bound to still smell of chocolate and biscuit crumbs. There was no way, if the rats were on the floor, they wouldn't get on the bed. I shivered at idea of being woken by a rat running across me. The choice was between sharing my bed with rats or staying awake all night. However tired I was, there was no contest.

If I was going to be awake, I didn't want to be in the hut any more. Despair didn't lend me the strength to climb into Mikey's tree house. I picked my way through the undergrowth to the centre of the camp in the pitch dark and drizzle. No one was around. I'd had enough. Even though I knew it was hardly the most sensible course of action – better to wait for the partying campers to get home and in the meantime get the embers of the fire going again – I couldn't bear it. I hated the smell of the camp – old food and dirty clothes – and I only wanted to get out. I left a note for Mikey and a goodbye note for the campers and went into the village, slipping and sliding along the paths in the rain and the dark, since I didn't own a torch, arriving back at the road muddy and bruised down one leg where I'd fallen over. The bus shelter I found was pretty miserable, but at least there weren't any rats. In all my clothes – pyjamas under trousers and jumpers, with coat and hat on top, I wasn't too cold, and thanks to that amazing leather sofa I had the few pounds for the bus back into Edinburgh, which ran intermittently all night. In the city I wandered the streets to stay awake until dawn broke and as soon as the bus station opened I went inside to lie down on one of the benches, hoping to blend in with the revellers catching buses home after a long night out. I was so exhausted that even on that hard seat I managed to sleep for several hours, with my rucksack under my head and my woolly hat pulled down over my eyes to block out the neon light.

When I woke, I washed my face, brushed my teeth and cleaned the mud off my trousers as best I could in the station toilets. Mikey came to find me. He'd had a rough night as well. He suspected that his hut was infested with bed bugs, which had left him with itchy red bites along his arms and ankles. But he had money in his pocket and didn't feel like going back to London just yet. He wanted to check into a backpacker's hostel or campsite and spend a few days in Edinburgh. I simply didn't have the cash or the inclination. My skull seemed to be squeezing my brain, fuzzy as an untuned radio. I couldn't even face the effort of talking to whoever might pick me up if I tried to hitch, let alone the stress of making my first attempt at hitching alone. All I wanted was to be teleported home.

So thank heavens for money. The little fold of notes in my pocket was my get-out-of-jail card. I queued up, paid my £20, and got a coach ticket back to London. For all my hitch-hiking evangelism, I felt relief to my core when I got on that bus. I'd found my limit. Others might have had the endurance and willpower to carry on without simply paying up for a convenient solution, trusting to fate rather than buying control, but the challenge of getting myself out of that situation without money was too much for me. I was sorry to admit it, but not at all sorry to sink into the fuzzy coach seat, ball up my jumper as a pillow against the window and sleep all the way home.

chapter ten

Glad as I was to get back to a vermin-free bed, getting home also meant getting back to the effort and stress of finding a new place to live. The days were growing shorter so that it was often dark by the time we went out to look through the sacks of rubbish for food and equipment. In the papers, the news was bad and getting worse, with bank bailouts, cutbacks and repossessions.

The judge took minutes to dismiss our legal argument and issue the council with a possession order so they could send the bailiffs. We went back to noting down addresses of obviously empty buildings without enthusiasm. Before we had really got anywhere, we heard that friends of friends had just got back to the UK after being away for months and had a fully formed plan to open a building. They only needed more people to help them occupy it. Did the three of us who were staying in London want in?

None of us knew Stevie or Max very well. I'd met Max once when he was very drunk late one night at a friend's squat. He was in his early twenties, with bleach-blond dreadlocks and half-black, half-coloured stars, an anarchist symbol, tattooed down his arm. But his punk get-up didn't hide the fact that he was utterly unintimidating, with a childish, slightly chubby face and few carefully thought-out convictions, proven by a tendency to shift his views according to what he thought people around him wanted to hear. Stevie, though, had been described by the friend who had put us in touch as the perfect squatmate – thoughtful, cheerful, enthusiastic and phenomenally good at skipping. An Australian in his mid-thirties with a huge smile, he had worked with disabled children before deciding he had served his time and fancied spending a while living cheaply in order to work as little as possible. That had been about five years ago.

The building Stevie and Max had their eye on was big – disused solicitors' offices with plate-glass windows at the front painted with old-fashioned gold letters. Peering through the window we could see that the faded calendars on the walls hadn't had their pages turned since the April before last. There was a window at the back that wasn't locked properly, and although it had bars over it, they could be removed with the tools you'd find in an ordinary toolbox without damaging them. All Stevie and Max needed was one or two people to wait in the street as lookouts then more people to stay inside every day and night to make sure that the owners couldn't legally break the door down. The main drawback was that the new owners, a property development company, had been granted planning permission to turn the building into flats. We decided to take our chances, particularly since the building seemed to have been ignored for almost two years so far.

Viktor and I sat at a bus stop opposite the office while Stevie and Max slipped round the back. We waited, their numbers ready on our phones to call if there was any sign of trouble. Nothing happened – no alarms, no police sirens, no sound from the back of the building where Stevie and Max were working. Once they were inside, Stevie replaced the bars on the back window while Max went round screwing bolts on to the doors to secure them, then sticking squatters' legal warning notices unostentatiously in the windows beside the doors. Seasoned squatters, they'd done it all before, and seemed to find the whole business more exciting than scary.

The worst thing that could happen was the police turning up, and even if they got arrested, it was rare for would-be squatters to be charged with anything. They couldn't be accused of stealing as there was nothing in the deserted building and, as long as no one witnessed him actually doing it, trying to prosecute Max for carefully taking off the bars would probably be considered a waste of time and money by the Crown Prosecution Service, which decides whether to proceed with trials if it ever came to that. I knew their reasoning made sense but I was still nervous even though all I was doing that night was sitting at a bus stop.

The boys were finished in less than an hour. The tour of our new home would have to wait for the morning, when there would be natural light and less risk of attracting the neighbours' attention by flashing torches around. Stevie and Max took their sleeping bags inside to curl up on the floor. Viktor and I went home to our beds.

It was difficult to work up much enthusiasm for choosing our rooms the next day, although Stevie hammed it up playing the estate agent. The building itself was elegant and old, but inside everything was drab, a series of offices all completely stripped of furniture, with dents in the carpet where desks, chairs and filing cabinets must once have stood. 'The minimal look,' said Stevie. The walls were painted functional shades of mushroom and beige, with brighter patches where noticeboards had protected them from grime. I picked one of the smaller rooms, choosing it because it had lots of windows and a nice view over a playing field. We designated the biggest room at the front as the living room and settled in to sit it out, waiting in case the owner visited to see what was happening or tried to evict us if we left the building empty.

We tried to make sure that there were always two people at home but that meant a lot of time sitting on the floor in the furniture-free room. Bringing over a kettle, a radio and a few cushions from the mansion made it slightly more comfortable. Stevie invited a couple of other friends to move in and share the task of keeping the place inhabited but it was still tedious. The drivers working from the mini-cab office opposite noticed us and stopped parking their cars in the yard at the back of our offices. After a day or two, they seemed to have spent enough time staring at us as we went in and out to use the car park again. There was no sign of the owners. We sat inside, missing out on the sunny days of late autumn, waiting for trouble or for enough time to pass to be more confident that trouble wasn't coming, and getting bored.

All except Stevie, who was incapable of sitting still. When he was out he would constantly be collecting useful things and when he was in he'd be using them to cheer us up or improve our home. I enjoyed skipping and thought I'd got fairly good at it but Stevie was in a different league. I got some pleasure from searching for new skips offering different food, but mostly relied on the places I already knew. Just as my mum had a route she took around the supermarket in order to pick up the family's regular shopping list, I had a habitual bike ride I could make every evening to find things I knew I would enjoy eating in the minimum length of time, picking out a few salads from a stack in this bin, a bit of fruit from the hoard in that, some bread from another pile. Usually, in less than an hour, I'd come home with bike panniers full of a decent selection of food for all of us, but the items on offer might be a bit over-familiar.

For Stevie, finding new bins was a hobby. He started to bring home a wheelie suitcase full of organic fruit, live yoghurts and other nutritious treats almost every day from a health-food shop a mile or so away, which he had discovered while on a scouting trip to find the best skips near our new home. As I saw whenever I went along to keep him company and to have an excuse to get out of the house, the heaps of apples, hummus, crackers and bread he rescued still left piles in the bins, even though he would take enough to deliver food parcels to Jamie's library and a couple of other friends' squats nearby.

Also unlike the rest of us, Stevie didn't mind going

through domestic rubbish. He got into the habit of visiting a couple of communal bins at blocks of expensive flats not far from our house. Most of the bags were, of course, full of tea bags, old newspapers and food packaging, but he also brought home the most implausible findings, showing off with a 'Ta-da!' as he pulled out a £20 note, a medium-sized bag of marijuana, a seemingly brand-new portable PlayStation, worth about £100, which he gave to Jozsef, or a sack of designer clothes, from which he gave me a Marc Jacobs top.

We all had hypotheses about how this stuff got in the bins – drugs dumped when trouble seemed to be on the way, a child's computer console binned by an irate parent. Stevie would sell most of the findings he didn't give away on Brick Lane or on the Internet. He was less acquisitive than most of us, pitching up at the solicitors' offices with a small backpack of possessions, all he owned and bothered to hang on to. He decorated his room with quirky but unsaleable findings, such as a discarded architectural model with little working lights inside and an old-fashioned radio built into a table. He had a gift for happiness and would probably have made the best of any situation, but seemed to be in his element while skipping, scavenging and squatting – he enjoyed having places to explore, new things to tinker with, lots of people around and the excitement of the slight risk-taking it all involved.

On the second day Stevie came home to ask for help to carry a bath tub he'd found in a skip not far away. The offices didn't have any bathrooms, just two rooms with toilets and sinks. By the morning of the third day Stevie had used scraps of wood to make a sturdy frame for the bath tub in the larger of the two toilets, removing the sink, plumbing the bath into the sewage outflow, and adding a hose taken from an abandoned washing machine to the electric water-heater that had served the washbasin. Hot baths were back. The next day he'd found some lilac paint and decorated the bathroom, and the day after he'd got started on the kitchen, putting up scavenged shelves for food and making a surface for our kettle and a small oven donated by Jamie from his and his housemates' huge stock of skipped equipment.

Stevie's liveliness was infectious and although it was tempting to just sit around and see what happened with the building before putting in a lot of effort, his energy made the rest of us feel guilty for our relative sloth. We all got on with sorting out our rooms, washing windows, sweeping floors and searching for furniture and mattresses, but even with all the work to do, being confined to the house waiting for your turn to go out made the days creep by.

That problem didn't last long. Other friends of friends had squatted a pub around the corner from us which had been empty for three years. They had moved in at around the same time as us and had poured work into patching up smashed windows, painting walls and finding furniture and mattresses. One morning there had been a hammering at the door. They looked down to see five blokes gathered in front of the pub. 'You'd better fucking get out,' one had shouted. 'Or we're going to fuck you up.' A couple more kicks and the door had started splintering.

The squatters phoned our household, the squatters' network and all their friends who might be nearby. Max had run over straight away leaving me in the solicitors' offices to hold the fort. He had arrived before anyone else and had started shouting at the heavies that they were breaking the law. They had showed him how little they cared by grabbing him and starting to bundle him towards their van, threatening him with a saw, the closest tool to hand, while shouting at the squatters to get the hell out of the pub or it would be worse for Max. Police sirens screamed into earshot and the thugs dropped Max but their boots had already got the door open and one of them was inside.

The police arrived to a cacophony of accusations from the squatters and counter-accusations from the blokes who had kicked the door down. The police weren't very interested in getting to the bottom of who had done what to whom in what order. As far as they could see, the squatters had to get out, and the men who said they were working for the former landlord had to give them a chance to fetch their stuff. That would be the end of it, even if the men had broken the law when breaking the door down. The squatters noted down police badge numbers and the thugs' number plates in order to make a complaint later, but could do little but form a sorry parade between the pub and our place, carrying belongings bundled in blankets.

The dozen of them, all graduated from university that summer, had nowhere to go. We told them to make themselves at home at the solicitors' offices until they found somewhere else. There were enough rooms to go round and with so many people staying in the house it would be easy to make sure there was always someone at home. But confining 20-odd people who don't know each other in an uncomfortable and ill-equipped house without much to do to pass the time is, as reality TV has taught us, a good way to bring out the worst in them. Those of us who had moved into the offices first grew increasingly irritated by the fact that the recent graduates were delighted to eat the food we skipped but not so keen on going foraging themselves. They bought food instead – but usually only enough for themselves. Those who didn't work started to resent those who did, for the fact that they were out all day and didn't make enough effort with DIY in the evenings. Max started to get annoyed that the graduates didn't show any signs of opening another home for themselves, endlessly turning over the pros and cons of half a dozen empty buildings without actually doing anything about it, and no one liked the drunk boys Max had brought home in the early hours one morning after a party, when they woke everyone up with music and shouting, then started a fight in the kitchen. Jozsef more or less disappeared, staying in his room with his tattoo gun and his computer games, and even Stevie's cheerfulness began to slip.

The weather grew miserably cold and I began to realise that I'd made a mistake when choosing a room. I had made it look fairly nice, I thought, with postcards on the walls and my few portable luxuries – my vase, my mini MP3 player and the little computer speakers I'd found to play it through – on a mantelpiece. But lots of big, single-glazed sash windows meant a lot of draughts and, since the room faced north, it received no direct sunlight. From October onwards almost every out-breath was misty and visible. In the middle of the day it often seemed warmer outside the building than in my room.

All of us clustered in the living room around an electric heater. Despite the tensions beneath the household's surface, the atmosphere was usually relaxed, with a pot of tea on the coffee table Stevie had found, a game of chess in progress, and a handful of people sitting on the sofas and armchairs we had quickly accumulated. The graduates had not yet had their student idealism and eagerness to debate abstract political ideas knocked out of them by office drudgery. It was partly their ambition to use the free time and space squatting offered to do something – to house failed asylum seekers, or to run a squatted building for political events – that seemed to hold them back from getting on with opening a building that would simply suffice to live in. It made them good company, though. It was too cold to open the window to air out the room, so it developed a musty, human smell. But during evenings spent chatting or reading in the warmth and the companionable atmosphere, I was happy.

Going to bed, though, became increasingly painful. I Freecycled some thick woollen blankets and put one over the windows of my freezing room and two more on my mattress on the floor. Under them I had my duvet and the hot-water bottle I'd rescued back in the warmth of spring, and underneath my mattress were layers of cardboard to stop the cold floor from leaching the heat out of my bed. I had found a pair of jogging trousers and a sweatshirt printed with the name of a scaffolding company in a skip full of builders' rubbish, which I washed and wore at night. But getting into my pyjamas meant getting out of the warm layers I wore every day, and between the two a moment of shivering nudity. Then it would be a matter of extending my feet, in socks, down under the blankets and duvet, the bed feeling almost damp with coldness. I'd drape my sleeping bag over my head, only my face showing while I read to distract myself during the fifteen minutes or so it would take for the cocoon to warm up enough to be able to fall asleep, balled up in a foetal position with the hot-water bottle on my belly.

Even during the day, I had to bundle myself up in order to stay at least warmish. It would take time to steel myself to get out of my bed, fairly cosy by the morning, with only my exposed nose feeling chilly. Getting dressed would entail another moment of icy nakedness while I scrambled into vest, T-shirt, cardigan, jumper, woolly shawl and laddered tights, their feet cut off, under a pair of trousers. A few of the clothes were things I'd brought with me when I set out, but most had been found at the back of charity shops or had been sticking out of bin bags on the pavement outside houses. Almost all my clothes were black and plain, since it was hard enough to find clothes that fitted, let alone things that made you look the way you wanted to. On the coldest days I'd pull on my woollen hat even if I wasn't leaving the house. Whenever I visited a normal home or office, I'd have to spend minutes stripping off all my layers down to a vest top, aware of the unfamiliar sensation of exposing my skin to air. Temperatures most people found pleasant began to feel a bit too warm, but I was a long way from joining Henry Thoreau in hymning the benefits of life without heating. In *Walden*, the American writer's paean to the simpler life, describing the two years, two months and two days he spent living in a shanty in the woods next to Walden Pond, he wrote: 'The luxuriously rich are not simply kept comfortably warm, but unnaturally hot...they are cooked, of course *à la mode*.' Personally, without heating, I felt chilled most of the time and I didn't like it.

It was almost a relief when the court papers arrived. We'd have to find a new place sooner than we had hoped when we moved in, but none of us could have tolerated our current home for much longer. The winter wasn't going well for us, but things were getting harder for the rest of the country too. When I'd opted out, it had seemed likely that the downturn would be a minor blip. Now, it had become the worst recession since the Second World War, and several friends who were working were being made to take unpaid leave while some faced redundancy. We were all in our mid-twenties so those who had taken the plunge into home ownership had done so only recently, just before the property crash, and were now facing negative equity and serious mortgage repayment worries.

An increasing number of calls to the ASS office, where I

was now volunteering once or twice a week, began to come from homeowners at risk of having their property repossessed and tenants struggling to pay the rent, wondering if they could claim 'squatters' rights' to stop their flats or houses from being taken away. Unfortunately not, we had to tell them. The legal warnings most squatters stick on their doors don't bring any extra security, merely stating the most basic right that anyone has in their home – not to be booted out except through court. Court proceedings to evict homeowners who default on their mortgages and tenants who are in rent arrears take much longer than those for squatters. The only way to go from being a homeowner or tenant to being a squatter is to be evicted through the courts and then, after the landlord or the bank has taken possession of the house by moving you out, to get back inside the building again.

A handful of former owners did exactly that when their homes were repossessed. In August 2008, 68-year-old Terry Armstrong and his wife Kim were evicted from the mill-keeper's cottage they had renovated and lived in for almost 30 years. Terry's business had collapsed and they were unable to keep up with the mortgage. They spent months moving between friends' houses, occasionally going back to look at their old home, which was still empty. In December, they decided to look for the key to the house's French doors that they had always left under a rock in the garden. It was still there. They tried it in the door. The lock hadn't been changed. They moved back in as squatters and celebrated Christmas in their old home but they were evicted again at the end of January. When Terry tried to resist the bailiffs' attempts to remove him from the house he was arrested.

Forty-six-year-old interior designer Samantha von Däniken was also evicted from a £1.6 million home in King's Lynn at the end of August 2008. When the bailiffs let her back into the house to collect some possessions in October, she locked the doors behind her and announced that she was taking up residence again. She stayed until the beginning of January 2009 when the bank sent bailiffs for the second time.

But recently repossessed homes were unlikely to make decent squats unless the object was to make a protest and be an irritation to the company that called for the eviction. It is a rubber-stamping exercise to re-evict someone from a building they have already been evicted from and have got back into, with the courts handing out so-called warrants of restitution if the owner says that there is a 'nexus or connection' between the previously evicted occupants and the new ones – particularly easy to prove if they freely acknowledge that they are actually the same people, of course, as the Armstrongs and von Däniken did. Such warrants also make it risky for squatters to move back into a building they or their friends have once been evicted from, even if it is left empty afterwards. The first you hear of them is a letter telling you when the bailiffs are due for the second time.

Also, the bank or landlord is likely to want to put the reclaimed property to money-making use as soon as possible, so an IPO or a speedy possession order is far more likely than in a run-down property that has been empty for years. Some repossessed homes and flats sit idle for months but they are more likely to be sold or relet immediately. When tenants or owners at risk of eviction contacted the ASS we explained to them that long-term empties – ideally buildings which would be knocked down or substantially altered before being put back into use, and where there is no sign of building work starting any time soon – are much more likely to offer long-term homes to squatters. There is a chance that the owner will tolerate squatters' presence since it doesn't impede their plans for the building, or will at least be a little less efficient in evicting them. Owners will also be less concerned about the decorative state of the house since the whole thing is going to be bulldozed, making accusations of criminal damage less likely. A recently repossessed house is a much riskier bet. Some squatters joked about moving into an abandoned Woolworth's store, but stopped taking the idea at all seriously after some art-school graduates got into the Camden branch but were evicted with an IPO within days.

We tried to encourage the people who contacted the ASS office to give squatting a go. I remembered how much better Greg had made me feel by speaking to me kindly and reassuringly when I turned up at the office on my first day and I wanted to pass on the favour. We also wanted those who phoned us or called into the office to know that they didn't have to be too afraid of toppling out of mainstream life – despite the many obvious downsides to squatting, life on the margins, with less money, less security and fewer belongings, wasn't as dangerous or as squalid as they might imagine. It might sometimes be cold and scary but it could help them with their financial problems and they might even find that they enjoyed some aspects of it.

But squatting did seem a worse solution to people with kids, a demanding job or a lot of possessions as we told them more about it. The media often gives the impression that squatters are impossible to get rid of once inside a property, so we had to explain the likelihood of frequent house moves and swift evictions as well as the need to live in a group and have someone constantly at home to keep the house safe. The shift of attitudes and lifestyle was too much for most unless they were utterly desperate or already looking for an alternative to the status quo as I had been. Many squatters hoped that hardship and anger would coalesce into a widespread squatting movement, as it did after the Second World War and during the sixties, but nothing of the sort materialised. Neither the Armstrongs nor von Däniken moved into a new squat, instead going back to staying with friends while trying to rebuild their former lives.

In the absence of any reliable way to gather data about who was squatting and why, we reckoned from what we saw in the ASS office that very few respectable types were forced off the middle rungs of the property ladder to become squatters, although there is no doubt that some people who hadn't been doing very well even during the boom did start squatting, or return to it, when the recession hit them – groups of building-site labourers whose contracts hadn't been renewed, for instance, became more familiar in the ASS office.

If anything, the recession might have decreased the number of squatters as swathes of economic migrants from the rest of Europe jumped ship. No solid statistics on the number of migrants from other European countries exist, as they are allowed to cross the UK's borders without a visa whenever they like and can live here indefinitely. But the Minister for Borders and Immigration Phil Woolas estimated that 100,000 Polish workers left the UK during 2008, and the number of people joining the Worker Registration Scheme, which is compulsory for citizens of Eastern European countries if they want to take jobs, halved as the recession hit. It seems likely that those already near the bottom of the pile left first. With no state benefits as a fallback and with the pound losing its value, putting up with a life of squatting and skipping while slogging it out for low wages in order to save up made less and less sense, as many of my squatmates – Polish Eric and Italians Fabio, Roberto and Massimo – had already decided.

In most ways, though, the economic storm made little difference to those who were already living for free, and possibly helped us in some ways. The collapse in house prices delayed building projects across the country, whether planned by councils or private property developers. Bad news for construction workers, architects and estate agents, but good news for us, as buildings slated for demolition, like Jamie's library and the nursing home, gained reprieves, and government and local authority plans to sell off places like Chris's little house and the mansion were put on hold until potential profits went back up. The buildings were already emptied out so they would now stay that way for even longer, and it was possible that the financial benefits of letting squatters stay rather than paying to evict them immediately began to make more sense to owners.

The recession did shrink the quantity of rubbish being produced, but not in ways that made skippers' lives significantly more difficult. Environmental charity Waste Watch estimated that households would produce almost 2.5 million tonnes less waste in 2009 than in 2008, a drop of almost 10 per cent, which the charity ascribed largely to people economising by doing less building work on their homes and replacing their white goods less frequently. Fewer accurate figures were available for commercial waste, which we skippers mostly relied on. Several companies, such as Cory Environmental, Viridor and Grundon, which collect rubbish from businesses as well as households across the UK, were hit by a slump in waste production, seeing their profitability tumble as they had less work to do, but Cory Environmental CEO Malcolm Ward ascribed the fall-off largely to a decline in household and construction waste rather than commercial waste.

If there was less food being thrown away, it was hard to tell. Sacks of fresh, high-quality meals were still being dumped by all the supermarkets and cafés we had relied on before the recession really bit. Every cache of sandwiches or ready-meals was so huge that it was impossible to say whether there was slightly less these days, enough to feed only 45 people, perhaps, where before there had been enough for 50. It would have taken a fundamental change to business models to make the cafés and shops underestimate rather than over-estimate demand to be sure of selling out and not wasting any food – and the recession clearly hadn't got bad enough for that to be necessary.

For the first time Marks and Spencer started reducing prices at the end of the day, and estimated that this would cut the quantity of food wasted by 10 per cent – although they still refused to reveal figures for how much food was wasted before and after the decision. Loads of food still appeared in their bins, some of it bearing brightly coloured stickers announcing that it was 'now £3', for instance. Marking the food down to real bargain prices might have undermined its perceived value. Perhaps, if shoppers had seen those expensive sandwiches and cakes reduced to, say, 10p, every single one might have sold, but the store might have earned less and customers might have begun to doubt whether they were really worth their original prices, just as I had after seeing them piled in the bins every day.

Offers of free goodies on Freecycle did shrink away, and my inbox began to be dominated by messages from people asking for items they needed rather than things they wanted to get rid of. The quantity and quality of charity shop cast-offs seemed to slide, too, as people hoarded or sold stuff they might previously have given away. Cancer Research spokeswoman Jessica Borton said the charity's chain of more than 600 shops were having a difficult time, pinched between higher demand from customers looking for a bargain and fewer donations as people replaced their possessions less frequently. But it was still only a matter of searching the streets or looking online to find useful bric-a-brac being given away or thrown away.

The cycle of searching for new homes continued. I'd spotted a former NHS clinic while hunting for empties before we were invited to join Stevie and Max and it was beginning to look like the best bet for my gang. The graduates who had been evicted from the pub were making a separate plan and Max had also got the message that he should find a different set of people to live with after falling out with everyone in the house over the rowdy after-party he had held.

Getting into the clinic was, once again, almost absurdly easy. None of us were cat-burglars and we rejected many long-empty houses, flats and offices as being far too difficult to get into. But, implausible as it may seem, windows really are left unlocked on empty buildings sometimes. Even if you need a ladder to get in through them, passers-by rarely turn a hair if you do it in the middle of the day wearing a yellow workman's jacket, as the DA! art squatters discovered when they used that trick on a £6 million Mayfair mansion.

Even if there isn't an open window, panes get broken, alarms stop working and ironmongery rusts when a place is left empty and ignored for long enough. And when a place is in a tired state and you know it is going to be demolished or significantly renovated before it will be put back into use, drilling a lock, for instance, following instructions from videos posted on YouTube, or giving a rusty bolt a bit of encouragement with a crowbar is not the same thing – practically or morally – as breaking into a suburban home to steal a family's belongings. If squatting is wrong, it's still wrong if you climb in through an open window. But if squatting is not only legal but morally acceptable as a short-term solution to the twin problems of empty houses and housing need, then the slight and cheaply repaired damage that is sometimes necessary to get inside a long-term empty, while still not right, isn't a great crime.

Inside the clinic, though, we found little hazard-warning stickers on all the pipework. Danger. Asbestos. As soon as I saw them, I wanted to hold my breath, remembering my grandfather who had died when I was seven, killed by vicious lung cancer caused by the asbestos fibres he had inhaled while working as a plumber. The thought of the way he faded in a matter of months from being a healthy, active, recently retired man into a weak, drawn shadow barely clinging to life in a hospice bed was something I couldn't think about without tears in my eyes. And the idea of inhaling something now that would fester undetected in my lungs for decades before bringing me down was horrifying.

I knew that I wasn't being completely rational. Asbestos is only dangerous when disturbed, and as Stevie pointed out we weren't going to be chiselling into the insulation or scratching and sniffing it. We also knew from the Internet that the clinic had only been out of use for a couple of years. If the asbestos risk was small enough for the NHS to expose its staff to the danger and itself to the possibility of expensive litigation, it couldn't be too serious. Stevie, Viktor, Jozsef and the rest decided to stay in the building. All were used to living with more dangers than people with conventional lives would tolerate, accepting that trespassing in unknown buildings carries serious risks – rickety floors, dodgy electrical wiring, damaged staircases or too few fire exits. Perhaps I was more cosseted than them or perhaps death by asbestos was closer to home for me. But I knew I couldn't stay in that building.

I told Suzy, who I had helped in the community garden, about the asbestos situation. She thought I could probably have a bed at the place she had moved to when the garden was closed down by the council, a big building in an increasingly fashionable part of town that Suzy's group had been living in for almost a year. The building had been used as photographic studios and recording rooms until its current owners, property developers registered in the Channel Islands, bought it as part of a bundle of properties several years before. They had ejected the artists and musicians who had used the space and left it empty as the area became increasingly gentrified. The squatters assumed that they were waiting to turn it into flats when the most lucrative time came, although they hadn't yet applied for planning permission. A small, triangular room with just enough space for a single mattress along its longest wall – a cupboard, really, though it had a window – was spare because the girl who normally slept in it had more or less moved in with her boyfriend at another squat, so I could sleep in it as long as she didn't want it, Suzy said.

I had often hung out at the studios. Most of the residents were political activists who were, usually, not very active. They occasionally went out to protest against weapons manufacturers, wars, poverty or the fur trade. Usually, though, they woke up in the afternoons then rolled out of bed to the living room, where they lounged on the sofas having endless political debates where ideas would be lobbed as slowly as shuttlecocks, since there was little else that needed doing all day except smoking joints and watching films.

The question of whether squatting and living for free was a revolutionary act in itself was a common topic. Many of the protestors believed it wasn't. Legally using long-term empty buildings, as squatters do, did not challenge the underlying system of property ownership. It was merely a loophole that was part of the current system, like tax havens and bankers' bonuses. Some people might benefit from it, others might not think it is right, but for now it's just the way things are. Our way of getting by couldn't really be called autonomous. It was entirely dependent on the current system, not a workable social alternative in itself, and relied on at least a modicum of toleration from the normal world. Owners could quickly and easily evict squatters, so squatters only ever managed to stay anywhere for long because owners decided not to act or couldn't be bothered. 'If anyone thinks that they're bringing on the anarchist or communist revolution just by soaking up some of society's waste, they're fooling themselves,' said one of the protestors, from his skipped sofa.

Squatting and scavenging remained the most logical way for the anti-capitalist protestors to live, though, they agreed. At least by getting by on waste they were not contributing to the system they were opposed to by shopping, renting or claiming benefits from the state, and it gave them a way of drawing attention to the flaws in the system as it stood. It let them show that it was possible for people to organise themselves without official hierarchies and clear property rules, relying on mutual aid rather than earnings or state handouts, and that anarchy, within the squatting scene at least, did not have to mean chaos. It also freed up their time for other projects, such as disrupting arms fairs, campaigning against the BNP, and obstructing police cameramen trying to photograph those who turned up at protests and meetings.

I agreed that squatting was not in itself a revolutionary act but we differed on whether a revolution was necessary or desirable. Much as I appreciated the kindness I had received while living for free, and glad as I was to help others freely when they needed assistance of a kind I enjoyed and was good at giving, I wasn't convinced that it could work as the basis for organising an entire society. It worked for us squatters because we were operating on the scale of a village, so if one person wronged another or if someone tended to take without giving in return, everyone would know about it – which also had the downside that if you fell out with a well-connected person within the circle, it would be easy for them to poison a large section of the network you relied on against you.

Trying to expand such a system up to the scale of a modern society sounded impossible. Without personal bonds between all the members it would be impossible to ensure decent behaviour without laws and without police, prisons and a court system to make decisions that were as fair as possible and to enforce them. I did not want to have to rely on my friends and family to help me if I was ill – I was glad that professional doctors and nurses existed, trained and motivated to do a good job by money as well as kindness.

But if mutual aid and the free exchange of skills and goods couldn't be expanded to replace capitalism and the state, it is also to be regretted if relationships based on trust and generosity today rarely extend beyond the small circle of our close friends and family. The sense of community I had gained by living for free had been largely absent from my previous life, where most interactions with people I didn't know had involved me paying them for something or vice versa. If prosperity squeezes out the need to rely on neighbours and if small shopkeepers who recognise you are replaced first by anonymous supermarket assistants and then by self-service checkout machines, it is perhaps unsurprising if we live atomised lives and fear those around us. My own life had been poorer for not even knowing my neighbours' names, still less what they were good at or what they might find useful from me. It felt great to know that people like Suzy, who was far from being a close friend, would offer me a place to stay without a second thought if she had a room and I needed it.

chapter **eleven**

As welcome as the activists made me feel, I was aware that I was a guest and not a full member of their household. They were a close group who had lived together in a series of squats for more than two years. Kim, whose room I was sleeping in, often popped in to pick up or drop off possessions. When she and her boyfriend had a row I had to sleep on a mattress on a platform above someone else's bedroom, a spot usually saved for very temporary visitors.

I'd had several invitations along the lines of 'if you're ever in town, look me up' while working at the ASS so I thought I might as well cash them in by going to Bristol and Leeds, the two cities with the largest numbers of people living for free apart from the capital. But no one else fancied getting out of London. If I wanted to get away I was going to have to go back on my resolution not to hitch-hike alone.

Many of the female squatters hitched solo but some had tales of male drivers' hands straying onto their knee when he surely meant to go for the gearstick. They had tips for staying safe, though, as did the hitch-hiking websites. Take a small bag and keep it on your lap rather than letting it go into the boot so that you can bail out quickly and without a second thought for your belongings if you need to, and so that the driver can't be sure you aren't carrying something that could be used as a weapon. Don't use a sign, so you can ask the driver where they're going and they can't simply say that they're going your way to get you into the car. Trust your gut instinct and don't feel bad about saying 'no' to lifts or pleading car sickness or diarrhoea if you want to get out. Best of all, text someone the car's number plate and make sure the driver knows you've done it.

Waiting for a ride to Bristol I didn't have time to get scared enough to make my mind up to go home. I had only waited by the side of the road for five minutes before I heard a honk from a car that had just passed me and I was on my way, running along the hard shoulder to hop in with a software engineer who was heading home from a few days' work in the capital. I had scribbled down his number plate and once I was inside I mentioned that I was going to text it to Colin. We chatted inconsequentially until he dropped me off at Maidenhead where the pattern was repeated with another driver within minutes. Hitching in a pair had always been a fairly efficient way to travel but as a woman on my own I couldn't have gone much faster if I'd been driving myself, never waiting more than ten minutes for a lift.

Down in Bristol, I stayed in a rickety four-storey building inhabited by half a dozen dance music obsessives in their early twenties who tended to wake up around mid-afternoon, fry up some breakfast, recuperate for a while, then gear up for another night of partying or settle in to chat or watch DVDs until the early hours, unless they had to drag themselves along to their part-time jobs in bars and clubs. Their rooms were nicely sorted out, painted and furnished with books, records and DVDs on shelves, but the communal rooms were a cheerful shambles with footprints all over the ceilings where Mimi, a tiny, hyperactive girl with fluorescent-coloured dreadlocks, had been held upside down with paint on her feet while the squatters had been doing up and decorating the house, which had been almost derelict.

Turning up in a new city meant learning a whole new set of decent skipping haunts, though staying in a house full of people who ate almost exclusively from the bins meant I had plenty of tips. The usual suspects – supermarkets, bakeries and cafés – remained reliable. Their kitchen cupboards were bursting with hundreds of jars of Polish tomato sauce and beans that, Mimi said, had been a staple of Bristolian squatters' diets for the past few weeks since a warehouse on an industrial estate not too far away had dumped several pallets loaded with thousands of the jars whose best before dates had just expired. Texts had been sent round and everyone had stocked up with as much as they could carry.

Many squats in Bristol seemed to last reasonable lengths of time, giving some of the squatters time to work on their homes and put them to use as more than a place to sleep, a fantasy many London squatters entertained but only sometimes had a chance to get round to before being kicked out.

A neglected building that was squatted in 1995 has become a community centre and housing co-op called Kebele after the occupants were given the chance to buy it. They managed to raise the funds to put down a deposit and get a mortgage, which they paid off in 2006 using money paid by members in return for affordable, secure accommodation in the building and by running cafés, yoga classes and other events, paid for by donation. Staffed by volunteers, their weekend vegan breakfasts now attract a wide range of their neighbours – parents and children, yuppies with hippie tendencies as well as squatters.

A long-standing squat known as the Magpie, a disused petrol station, contained a well-equipped metal workshop and had been painted a rainbow of colours on the outside by the inhabitants. A huge squatted warehouse was used for a weekend of workshops aimed at people who were not yet squatting but who might want to start, with workshops on plumbing, electricity and housing politics. I gave a talk on the law, and free lunches and dinners cooked from skipped produce were dished out to the crowd of 100-odd attendees, although most of those who came to the event were already part of the squatting scene, not the middle-of-the-road people the organisers had hoped to attract and win over.

I had been offered a place to sleep up in Leeds by a squatter called Ed. Hitching up there from Bristol, a man in his forties, an estate agent hit hard by the recession, started sharing his mid-life crisis with me while giving me a lift as far Birmingham, explaining exactly how much he hated the wife he had recently divorced. 'I'd like to really hurt her, the money-grabbing bitch,' he said.

'Right. Hmmm. Still, Christmas holidays soon, huh?' I'd replied.

A slightly twitchy lorry driver said, just before we got to Nottingham, where he was meant to drop me: 'Bet you're glad you got picked up by a nice guy like me rather than a psychopath.'

'Yes! Thanks very much!'

'Well, I haven't let you out yet, have I?'

Hilarious. My laugh was strained and I reached for my phone.

But it was just a tasteless joke and I got to Leeds unscathed. Ed's home was a sad place, an end-of-terrace house neglected on the inside even though it had been squatted for more than two years. The occupants, most of whom worked in cafés and bars, didn't seem to have had the inclination to make it any nicer. It was a bit damp so it was freezing all the time. The living room exuded gloom with its stale smell, muddy-coloured furniture and a few tatty posters for punk gigs on the walls. Even the residents' dog, an elderly mongrel, seemed to lack *joie de vivre*, barely even getting excited about food or walks. I resorted to wearing my pyjamas as an extra layer under my normal daytime clothes for warmth. Still, Ed was interesting if morose company, thinking too hard about things and paralysing himself by seeing the downsides to every choice; he had not got on with anything very much since graduating from university a few years before. We mooched around town with the glum dog, popping into his friends' squats for cups of tea and into the odd supermarket bin for a quick skip.

The popularity of squatting in each city doesn't depend on the supply of empty houses. In Liverpool, almost 15,000 houses are vacant, most of them two-up, two-down Victorian terraces emptied as part of the Blair government's 'Housing Market Renewal' project which began in nine northern areas in 2003. With a budget of £1.2 billion, the plan was to demolish existing properties to make way for newer homes along with large supermarket developments and shopping districts intended to draw buyers back into neglected and unpopular neighbourhoods. The scheme has proved hugely controversial, with long-running debates about whether it would have been cheaper, greener and more historically sensitive to give the residents refurbishment grants to bring the existing Victorian properties back to a decent standard, rather than razing the lot to start again. So far all that has happened in most areas of Liverpool is that street after street of houses has been compulsorily purchased and ignored for more than five years, allowing them to grow so derelict that refurbishment is barely an option any more.

Near Anfield stadium and around the Welsh streets where Ringo Starr grew up it is easy to walk for quarter of an hour without passing an inhabited building, seeing only row after row of abandoned homes, doors and windows blinded with metal sheets. The boarded-up windows along main routes through the city were painted with cheery murals in an attempt to make them look less depressing while the city was European Capital of Culture in 2008, but the acres of empty houses, many with shrubs starting to grow out of the guttering and through the roof-tiles, are like patches of bleached-out deadness in a coral reef. The occasional group of children plays football in streets that no cars have reason to go down, but mostly they are silent and deserted.

Despite the many empty houses, though, the city does not have the combination of desirability and high rents that encourages squatting elsewhere. With little work available there are fewer economic migrants than in more prosperous cities and it is easier to find a flat to rent that is affordable on housing benefit than in areas with more housing demand. The population of the city has halved since the 1930s when changes in the shipping industry made the docks less viable. Suburbanisation sucked people out of the centre and the lack of industry meant that few incomers arrived to replace them. It's just conceivable that there really isn't any demand for these houses, although it's hard to believe that no better use could be made of them than simply leaving them empty year after year, even if the decision to knock them down eventually is the right one. I was told by a group who had tried to open a building to use as a centre for meetings and gatherings, but had found it impossible, that the council cracks down immediately on anyone who tries to make a home in one of the thousands of empties they own. There are very few squats and nothing approaching a community of squatters, they told me.

In Bristol, Leeds and London, however, there are plenty of people who can't afford rent but still want to stay – for work, family, art, politics, music or the million other reasons to want to live in a big, exciting city. All three have plenty of empty homes – 5.4 per cent in Leeds, 3.8 per cent in Bristol and 2.5 per cent in London, compared with the national average of 3.1 per cent, according to EHA figures. That combination, plus police, councils and landlords with bigger problems than squatters to worry about – or, perhaps, authorities that have had enough contact with squatters to know the law and realise that squatters are not always so evil that they have to be moved on immediately – has been enough to allow a community of squatters to grow up, sharing information, helping each other and organising events, and perhaps also attracting more squatters to get started or move to those cities.

You can safely bet that if you look hard enough in any city in England you will find people sleeping in buildings they don't own. But away from networks of squatting neighbours and friends like the ones I found in Bristol, Leeds and London, there are fewer people asserting their rights to live in empty buildings, putting in work to make them homely and comfortable and using squatting as a long-term way of living reasonably stable, secure lives. In Oxford, I knew of a handful of Eastern Europeans who managed to squat without much of a local scene. In Bradford, the one household of squatters I met had been in their building for almost three years but seemed fairly sure that theirs was the only squat in town. Although they guessed that a few homeless people sheltered in derelict buildings they knew of, all the other would-be squatters had gone the nine miles to Leeds. A small group of twenty-somethings from Cambridge squatted a series of buildings – a bingo hall and an empty shop due to be turned into a Tesco – to use as meeting spaces, for art exhibitions and roller discos, though they didn't get to stay in them for very long. Calls to the ASS sometimes came from people in Manchester and Birmingham where a few groups managed to find a string of reasonably long-term homes. Brighton had a handful of punks who seemed to bounce from one building to another, getting in then getting kicked out so regularly that many gave up or left town.

Back in London, Mikey had finished another month or so of freelance work and was keen to go on another adventure. Getting to Scotland hadn't been a problem so we decided to see whether we could manage a free trip to Europe. We had been looking at couchsurfing.com, the biggest of several websites that have sprung up over the past decade which encourage people to welcome others to stay in their houses as non-paying guests. It sounded too good to be true, with people offering free places to sleep from Kuala Lumpur to Kazakhstan. The site was launched in 2004, and the millionth member joined in March 2009.

The idea of creating a network to host guests free of charge is not a new one. Servas Open Doors, set up in Norway in 1949, is often thought of as the first formal organisation with that goal. It was founded to promote peace by helping people build personal connections with foreigners by allowing them into their homes, and takes its name from the Esperanto word for 'serve'. It still exists today with 20,000 members. But the Internet, a perfect environment for creating a network across geographical boundaries, revolutionised the concept. Now, rather than sending off for a brochure and relying on an organisation to vet would-be hosts and guests as Servas Open Doors still does, all you do on couchsurfing.com or on similar web-based organisations such as hospitalityclub.org is set up a profile page. The pages are similar to those on other kinds of social networking websites such as Facebook and MySpace, including your name, location, personal description and photo plus a few hippie touches such as an invitation to state your mission in life and to describe an amazing thing you have seen or done. You then fill in boxes saying whether you're able to host visitors and if so how many.

Anyone you have visited or who has visited you can leave a reference which is visible to everyone who views your profile, as with feedback on eBay, so nervous couchsurfers can decide to stay only with people who have many references vouching for their safety. It would conceivably be possible, by setting up dozens of profiles, to fake such references but it would be a long process and there must be easier ways to trap vulnerable people if that were your goal. The particularly worried surfer could rely only on 'verified' hosts and visitors, people who have used an option offered by the site to confirm their name and address using their credit card details – but although you didn't have to pay for the service, most surfers seemed to be trusting enough to do without it.

Mikey and I had set up profiles before going to Scotland. Mikey had already hosted a Canadian boy who had left a very enthusiastic reference praising Mikey's hospitality and slightly grimy home. Now we started sending messages through the site asking if we could be guests at other people's places. We didn't mind too much where we ended up going so decided to aim for Belgium then Holland, the country with the most liberal laws on squatting in Europe.

We were astonished when around half the people we contacted got back to us within a day or two to say that yes, we'd be welcome to stay with them. We had mostly targeted interesting-looking people who lived an easy day's hitch apart, which probably helped us to find people who didn't get swamped with couchsurfing requests since they didn't live in tourist hotspots. We had also picked people whose profiles we genuinely liked the look of, so it was easy to write emails explaining why we'd like to go and stay at their house rather than in a youth hostel for reasons other than a desire to economise. Both Mikey and I had quickly found ourselves inundated with requests to stay at our places in London, often from people who had copied and pasted one message to dozens of people, usually without seeming to have read our profiles and without having hosted anyone themselves. I was in no position to resent anyone who was looking for a cheap way to stay in an expensive city, but as with most aspects of living for free, if you weren't paying with money you had to pay with effort – in this case by making yourself an interesting guest and by passing the favour on.

We had our trip planned out within a week. The first destination was Ostend in Belgium, across the Channel from Ramsgate. We had hitched to Ramsgate by mid-afternoon so we had a couple of hours before the next ferry, the last one of the day, in which to cadge a free lift on the boat. We knew that cars didn't have to pay extra for additional passengers on this crossing, but so far there weren't any cars waiting, only lorries, and as their tickets specify how many passengers may ride in the cab they couldn't help us out. The first car driver to arrive to catch the boat flatly refused to let us join him. How was he supposed to know that we weren't carrying drugs or something else that might get him into trouble when crossing the border? The second screwed up his face in apology but gestured to his car – he already had a brood of three children taking up the back seat. The lads who arrived in the third car didn't react when Mikey and I went over to ask for a ride as they walked to the ticket desk, looking through us when we tried to explain ourselves. There were only 15 minutes before the ferry was due to sail. Foot passengers were not allowed, so even if we'd had pockets full of cash paying up was not a fall-back option. What could we do? Hitch round to Calais and hope to hitch a later sailing from there? Abort the entire mission and just hitch home? Try to persuade the first driver of our innocence again? Then a little hatchback screeched up onto the forecourt of the ticket office. Our chance! But the car was packed with furniture. Still, desperate now, we breathlessly waylaid the couple as they headed to the ticket desk to confirm their booking, talking both at the same time as fast as possible to explain the situation and insist that we could squeeze up as small as necessary, but that we really did need to get across to Belgium tonight. 'Sure, why not?' said the husband, a bearded, corduroy-wearing geography teacher-type.

'You'll only have to fit into the car until we're on board anyway,' his wife agreed.

The chairs, destined for the pair's holiday home, were unloaded and we breathed in while they were piled back in on top of us, one of them on the wife's lap. But we fitted all our limbs inside, the husband slammed the door and we were the last vehicle up the ramp onto the boat.

We arrived at our host Junior's house cold, damp from the drizzly rain but pleased with ourselves. There was only time for a quick shower and some bread, sausage and cheese because Junior wanted to take us out into town, to drink some Belgian beer, meet his friends and maybe end up at a party. We were his first couchsurfing guests ever and he wanted to show us a good time. He tried to buy the drinks, but Mikey had money from his last spell of work and I still had cash from selling the sofa, so we didn't let him. Junior had recently used his earnings as a dock worker to buy the house and thoroughly pimp it, with a white leather sofa, futuristic lamps and his huge collection of records and skateboards displayed on the walls. We put our bags in his spare room, which he usually used to store his collection of designer T-shirts, and headed out.

The next morning, slightly the worse for wear, we got back onto the road, aiming for Harelbeke, where our next hosts lived. Hitching in the UK may be fairly straightforward but on mainland Europe it is easier than finding a taxi at closing time. If we found ourselves waiting more than quarter of an hour we'd start wondering what we were doing wrong. At home, the majority of lifts seemed to come from bored men, usually slightly eccentric and very keen to chat. On the continent the people who picked us up tended to be very normal – families on outings who would squish you in the back between the kids, couples who might carry on a row that had started before they picked you up and young people going to or from work. Most were less interested in striking up conversation and less intrigued by the fact that we were hitching, simply leaving us alone to sit quietly in the back. It wasn't the language barrier – Mikey speaks fluent French and most of the drivers spoke perfect English. It was simply that the whole business was less exceptional and less worthy of comment.

We arrived at the tiny village where our second hosts lived by lunchtime. Florian and Uli, in their fifties, welcomed us into their beautiful house that they had built to live in with their three children. Since the kids had left home they had been rattling around in it and were glad to have guests to make it feel a bit more bustling, they said. They were planning a couchsurfing trip to Japan, and had used the site to travel through France the previous year. Uli showed us our rooms – one for each of us, with beds already made up – then sat us down on the sofa, brought us cups of tea and sandwiches and asked what we fancied doing while we were in Harelbeke.

We were thinking of going to look at some of the nearby Second World War cemeteries, we said. 'That's a good idea,' she replied. 'Would you like to borrow the car?'

Borrow her car? Was she seriously going to hand over her car keys to us, a pair of complete strangers? We were speechless. 'Or perhaps some bikes?' Bikes seemed a better idea, and Mikey and I rode off.

When we got back, dinner was in the oven – sausages and potatoes, cabbage from their garden, home-made apple cake and some kind of spirit, home-distilled by Florian, which tasted of lemons. They described a particularly merry Christmas they had once spent in England and we taught them to make brandy butter, while Florian brought out a couple of other, differently flavoured spirits from his cellar.

The next stop was Antwerp where we had arranged to spend two nights staying with Lut. She was another great host, somewhat easier-going than Junior, Florian and Uli who had been slightly overwhelming in their eagerness to entertain and look after us. Where they had pressed us with tea and biscuits, Lut just pointed out where the tea bags and kettle were and told us to sort ourselves out whenever we liked, and didn't try to stop us from doing the washing-up so we could feel at least a slight sense of paying her back for her generosity. We spent a happy day exploring the town, following Lut's tips for places to go, then met up with her in the evening for chips and beer.

Then we headed for Holland, where we had arranged to stay in several squats. Along with famously liberal laws on drugs and prostitution, the Dutch system permitted squatting, making it entirely legal to take over a building that had been empty for more than a year as long as no damage was done while getting in. Once inside, Dutch squatters would invite the police to come round to check that they really were living there by showing that they had brought in a 'squat set' – a bed, a table and a chair. They then called the fire brigade to check that the place was safe to live in. After passing those tests, the squat was legitimate and there was no need for the squatters to leave someone indoors constantly as in England. The place was officially their home so they are protected from sneak evictions.

Dutch owners could take squatters to court to get possession orders swiftly if they could provide evidence that they were on the verge of putting the building back into use, with a rental contract set to start or builders about to arrive to work on the building. But if they couldn't, and they simply wanted to move the squatters out so that the building could stay empty, it was a far longer process and could take six months or longer.

Our first stop was Den Bosch, a small, bland town with a modernised, characterless town centre. A café owner furiously told me and Mikey off for lingering too long over one beer (Mikey's) and one tap water (mine) while we waited for evening, when we'd agreed to meet the squatters we were staying with. We found Wim, an earnest law student, waiting as promised in the town square to take us to his place, an empty old folks' home that he shared with eight others. It was a relatively ugly one-storey building, but it was clean and comfortable inside. They had already been living there for two years and had no reason to expect a court case to start in the foreseeable future. The biggest room had been turned into a studio for several of the squatters who were studying sculpture at the town's art school, and was criss-crossed with elaborate aerial walkways for the house's cats. They showed us the spare room that we would be staying in but then we retreated to the only pleasantly warm place to be at that time of year – the kitchen-cum-living room, which had a gas heater. Although the squatters had lived there far longer than most British squatters manage, and although they had put in a lot of effort to make it nice, it was still a draughty, neglected building so it was still freezing.

One of the residents was filming a documentary about Dutch squatters. Another was casting a larger-than-life sculpture of a polar bear from concrete. When we arrived, several of the housemates were heading out to an exhibition of art made by people in a homeless day centre they volunteered at. The next day, we joined a few of them who were heading over to another squat across town, a long row of buildings that were once offices but were now used as a social centre for gigs, meetings and meals, with only a few people living there.

Wim was on the rota to staff the 'free shop' kept there –

a room well stocked with clothes, furniture and other oddments that anyone was welcome to help themselves from or contribute to. A few of his housemates had agreed to help prepare that week's communal meal, to be served in exchange for donations later that night. The event was a regular one, and similar shared meals are served weekly or several times a week in squats across Holland. Mikey and I went along to help and found ourselves roasting chestnuts to go with root vegetables in a soup, kneading home-made bread, chopping peppers for a salad and peeling apples to be stewed. The food wasn't skipped, instead bought cheaply at the end of the day from a street market.

That evening, about 30 people arrived at the squat for dinner, sitting down in the dining room around shared tables, seven or so at each. The dinner, prepared under firm instructions from the girl in charge of that day's cooking, was delicious – far better than the vegan slop I had improvised at Food Not Bombs. A sign by the serving table suggested a donation of three euros, though those of us who had cooked didn't have to pay. The people eating were from a wide social spectrum – many were squatters, of course, but Mikey and I shared our table with a middle-aged architect wearing a tidy shirt and little round glasses, who came to have dinner with his daughter at the squat almost every week, plus a group of students from the hall of residence in town.

Despite being rather a dull and conventional town, famous mostly for a distinctive kind of chocolate éclair, the Bosch ball, Den Bosch had several squats hosting weekly meals and a regular *kraakspreekuur*. This translates literally as 'squat conversation hour', and is a meeting of the dozens of local squatters to talk about anything that had happened, make plans for future events, assist anyone who was going through court and help members of the group to open new squats, working as a team – some people to get the door open, others to carry along the table, chair and bed at the right moment, yet others to liaise with the police and speak to the neighbours and, ideally, a big gang of bystanders to get in the way of CCTV cameras and make it less clear who had done any damage that was necessary to get inside.

Mikey and I headed for Amsterdam next, where squatting is so much part of the landscape that tourists are offered walking tours of the most interesting occupied buildings and four separate *kraakspreekuurs* occur every week across the city. We were staying with Marlous, a slightly grumpy-looking Dutch girl who lived in and looked after a typical tall, thin Dutch townhouse. The building had been squatted for almost ten years and had been used for the past five years by a feminist group housing Chinese women who were working in the country without papers. Marlous showed us the draughty attic where we would be sleeping and apologised that there was no hot water as the boiler had just broken. Although she made us feel welcome enough, she clearly wanted us to leave her alone so she could get on with the novel she was trying to write, so we interrupted her once more to get some tips on other squats to visit then headed out.

Marlous had rattled off several communal meals and events we could go to that evening in small squats in her part of town, as well as telling us about a squat that included a sauna on the other side of the city, and several bigger squatted buildings that would be hosting bars, gigs or parties. We went to a music and poetry night at a squat just round the corner, where a crowd of entirely normal-looking people had gathered to listen to a middle-aged man play classical Spanish guitar, then read Dutch poetry. Since Mikey and I understood none of it, we focused on the cherry cake that was being served up in exchange for small donations.

'What's the best way to hitch out of Amsterdam?' we asked Marlous. 'Oh, just go to the *liftplaats*,' she said. There were official hitch-hiking spots in half a dozen Dutch cities, she explained. Amsterdam's one was just a kilometre or so away from her place on the main road heading north. That would be our best bet, although it was perfectly legal to hitch wherever we liked except on the motorways. It was easy to find when we got there, with a blue sign showing a hitch-hiker's thumb and a notice saying '*Liftplaats* 100 metres', then a lay-by and another thumb sign. We were so impressed that we had to take a photo of each of us standing by the sign with a thumb out. I snapped Mikey with his camera, then he walked back to photograph me while I posed. He had only just pressed the shutter when a car pulled into the lay-by to pick us up.

That driver took us all the way to Leiden, our next stop, where we had arranged to stay with a group of squatters who were living in a disused nightclub. When we arrived, they showed us round the beautiful university town with its pretty canals cutting through streets of sixteenth-century houses. They also told us that they and a few friends living in other nearby squats had planned a different kind of sightseeing trip the next day.

They lent us pairs of army boots and we got into one of the gang's car with no idea where we were going. We drove for half an hour, one of the boys packed in the boot so that there was space for us all, then parked in a remote car park and set off across a field until we got to a chain-link fence which we all shunted each other over. They led us through undergrowth until we arrived at a big glass-roofed building. A faded sign announced that we were at a zoo. This used to be the entrance hall. We went inside. The complex had been disused since the late eighties but little had been done to decommission it apart from moving the animals out. The hall still contained faded parasols decorated with adverts for ice cream and in a rack there were still postcards, curly from water and sunlight, but the place was reverting to forest. Small trees had begun to sprout through the floor of the lobby and ivy had clambered in through a broken pane in the glass roof. We had to push our way through weeds and shrubs to get from one animal house to another, guessing at what had lived in each cage. The giraffe house, with its high ceilings and tall doors, was pretty obvious, as was the gorilla enclosure in the middle of a lake, which the boys started to scheme about squatting.

The Leiden boys were the only Dutch squatters we met

who depended on skipping for most of their diet. They made nightly trips to the back of a supermarket, and had a chest freezer packed with rescued bread, cheese, meat and pre-cut chips that they chucked into their deep-fat frier for almost every meal. Most of the other Dutch squatters we had met were less hard up than those in England. Since squatting was less difficult, one had to be less desperate – or less determined to opt out of the mainstream – to get involved, so going to the effort of skipping rather than shopping seemed to be far less integral to their lifestyles.

Being away from home forced me to spend more money, even though transport and accommodation were free. It would have been rude not to have got my round in while staying with such generous hosts and although I had brought plenty of skipped snacks with me, Mikey and I ran out and had to shop for food. My diet got significantly worse – without skipping or much money we had to rely on the cheapest staples to fill ourselves up – pasta and pesto, poor-quality cheese and cheap bread. We were glad to take some of the brie, yoghurt, cakes and crusty loaves the Leiden squatters offered us for the rest of the trip.

Our final destination was a squat in Rotterdam which a group of students had only just moved into. They had already repaired the floors of the five-bedroom townhouse and had spent quite a lot of money on fixing the plumbing. Now they were saving up to fix the electricity properly then to replaster some of the walls, a degree of effort and level of expense which would be crazy in England, where the chances of staying for longer than a few months in a squat, even if the building was set to stay empty for years, were slim.

The benefits or otherwise of all Holland's liberal rules are open to debate but squatting – like prostitution and dope smoking – is probably impossible to stamp out completely. Even in America, where the laws on squatting are among the most draconian, tramps still secretively take up residence in empty buildings and build shacks on patches of wasteland. Scores of vagrants live in disused railway tunnels under New York. By allowing an inevitability to come out into the open, the Dutch rules made squatting in Holland a less risky, marginalised way to live. The laws protected buildings which have not been empty long and buildings which are about to come back into use, but didn't give owners the tools to get rid of squatters quickly if the squatters were causing no trouble and the building had no prospect of being returned to use.

The fact that squatting was so much easier in Holland than in England seemed to mean that many conventional people with professional jobs were doing it – enough, perhaps, to moderate the extreme views and antisocial tendencies of some. There were also enough motivated, well-organised squatters to build up a system of *kraak-spreekuurs* across the country and a degree of rapport with neighbours and police which must have made it easier for people who were in desperate need of housing to get a safe, stable roof over their heads. No doubt some Dutch squats were disruptive, terrifying places, just as some in England are, but far more visible than noisy, dangerous drug dens were squats that had been turned into something of use to the whole community, opened up as cafés, restaurants, free shops and gig venues where there might otherwise have been a shell of a building falling into disrepair, attracting vandalism and arson and dragging down the value of neighbouring properties.

The Dutch laws on squatting, like many of the country's liberal rules, have come under attack in recent years. MPs from three right-wing parties have joined forces to draft a bill to outlaw squatting altogether, which would introduce a prison sentence of up to 32 months for anyone trying to live in buildings they didn't own. Officials from Amsterdam, Utrecht, Rotterdam and The Hague city councils, the four areas with the most squatters, wrote to the parliament telling MPs they did not support a ban. They added that they would prefer to see more powers to tackle property speculation, such as taxes and fines for leaving property empty. The Dutch parliament is still considering the new laws and is set to come to a decision in 2010. The squatters we met expected their way of living to become illegal, but most – particularly the Leiden gang – insisted that they would carry on squatting whatever the politicians decided.

Heading home from Rotterdam, we made a sign that said 'London', just to see what happened. We hadn't made a very early start and it didn't matter if we only got as far as Belgium since Junior had told us we could stay with him or his friends in Ostend whenever we needed to. But we were both exhausted from a fortnight of intensive socialising and travelling, and nice as it was to be on the receiving end of hospitality we were desperate to get home for a rest. The first driver to pick us up was heading for Belgium on his way to visit his elderly mother in Dunkirk, so we hopped in and listened to his Simply Red and Dire Straits CDs for a few hours as we whizzed along the motorway. When we got to the turning to Ostend, he decided to make the detour to drop us at the ferry port – and because it was chucking down cold November sleet we didn't try very hard to dissuade him. One of the drivers waiting for the last ferry crossing of the day agreed to give us a lift on and off, and once we were on board, we got chatting to a lorry driver who agreed to drive us to the M25.

By the time we got off the boat it was ten. We stood out on the wind-whipped forecourt of the ferry terminal waiting for Mick, our lorry driver, to roll off the boat. After about an hour, Mick's truck appeared but it felt as if we had only just begun to warm up when he dropped us at an M25 petrol station and we set about pestering people as they went from their cars to pay in the little shop. It was gone midnight, and I couldn't blame anyone for avoiding talking to a pair of scarecrows like us, let alone welcoming us into their car.

Finally, a kind lorry driver agreed to detour inside the M25 on his way round London to drop us at the first night-bus stop he could find. One long bus ride took us from Croydon to Trafalgar Square, then another to Colin's house. I didn't have the key to the studios and although I could have woken the squatters to let me in, Colin was still the only person I could rely on not to mind being disturbed at nearly five in the morning by his exhausted girlfriend, dressed in an ugly raincoat and battered trainers, with only a faded postcard from the zoo to offer as a 'hi-honey-I'm-back-from-holidays' gift.

chapter twelve

We had skipped our first mince pies while at the solicitors' offices in October. By late November when I was back from Holland and staying at the activists' studios again we were finding them almost every day in café and supermarket bins. Someone brought home three huge Christmas cakes with marzipan and icing, rescued from Iceland's rubbish, which we got through in less than a week. Advent began and we started to find brandy butter, turkey sandwiches with cranberry sauce and bag after bag of Brussels sprouts.

I checked a luxury chocolate shop's bins several weeks before Christmas. Their rubbish bag was usually full of cardboard and bubble-wrap but on a good day there might be a few boxes of chocolates. Today it was almost too heavy to lift. I peeped inside. It was full of bars. Hoiking it onto the handlebars of my bike, I took it to a nearby alley for a proper look. There were about 40 100-gram bars of chocolate – some white, some milk, some dark. Some swirled with fruit, some embedded with nuts, some flavoured with ginger and lemon. I had another dozen bars of even more special dark chocolate with packaging describing the single estate where the cocoa beans that had gone into them had been grown. I had ten sticks of pure cocoa the size of fat cigars, each packaged in its own tin, and I had half a dozen jars of chocolate shavings – some plain, some flavoured with Aztec spices – for making hot chocolate. I also had a broken Father Christmas-shaped chocolate lolly. None of it went out of date before New Year. I could only assume they had cleared the shelves of ordinary, year-round stock to fit in the specially shaped and flavoured Christmas chocolate, and hadn't had the space to store all this nor the inclination to price it cheap to get rid of it. I couldn't fit the whole lot into my pannier.

Without the need to trudge round the shops being barraged by adverts for festive indulgences while trying to imagine what my friends and family could possibly want as presents, and without craving a few days off from work, Christmas sneaked up rather than dominating the season. The chocolate would do the trick as Christmas presents for my family and friends, I decided, along with the jars of wild blackberry jam I'd made in the autumn and the flowers I'd been knitting out of my Freecycled scraps of wool. Many of the British squatters I knew were going home to their families for Christmas Day. The studio was going to be empty so since my mum, a midwife, had to work on Christmas Day itself, I was happy to take the job no one else wanted and stay there to keep it safe.

I'd been talking to Stevie, Viktor and Jozsef about their Christmas plans. Since none had family in the UK they were all at a loose end. We decided to gather any other squatters we knew who were stuck in London on 25 December to celebrate Skipmas together at the studio. Anita and a couple of the vegans were still around, as were a handful of other friends. Everyone agreed to collect as much food as they could from their favourite skipping haunts on Christmas Eve then come round to the studios in the afternoon to make dinner.

The scenes at the bins that night were beyond anything I had seen before. The Christmas bank holidays joined up with the weekend that year so many shops in the parts of town dominated by offices were to be closed for a full four days. Their bins were overflowing and much of the food had several days of shelf life left. I took my big hiking back-pack as well as my bike pannier and could have filled them both again and again with great food. As it was, I was picky. Our Skipmas dinner was to be strictly vegetarian and as vegan as possible so I passed over four whole turkeys and several pre-prepared turkey breasts as well as scores of less festive ready-meals at the back of one branch of Marks and Spencer's. I found Christmas puddings and mince pies but a rarer treat was all the cheese and milk that was being thrown away. One small branch of Sainsbury's had got rid of at least a hundred pints of milk – full-fat, semi-skimmed and skimmed, whichever you preferred. The vegans wouldn't be interested but I could freeze it for another time. There were packets of smoked salmon, pots of hummus and tzatziki, dozens of apples, packaged in cardboard and plastic to protect them from bruising, and bag after bag of ready-prepared vegetables and salads. I passed seven Christmas trees – five bare and two with tinsel – dumped on the pavement outside businesses which would be closed until the New Year so had no more need for festive trappings. I could barely cycle home under the load I already had so decided we could do without a tree.

When I had thought about it at the end of summer I had expected Christmas to be slightly sad. When the day came I ate a mince pie for breakfast in the quiet studios then headed out on my bike to take advantage of the silent roads – no buses, no taxis, hardly any cars. I deliberately took a route thorough the centre of London via all the junctions that are usually the most lethal – jumping the lights at Oxford Circus, whizzing round Piccadilly Circus and Trafalgar Square, down the Mall to Buckingham Palace then to the Serpentine in Hyde Park to watch hardy types jumping in for the annual Christmas Day swimming race.

Back at the studios, people began to arrive weighed down with food. Viktor brought bread and cake, the vegans had found bags of nuts in their shells and Luke, the PhD student, had a vegan fruitcake his mother had cooked for him even though he wasn't going home for Christmas. Stevie had, of course, done best of all, hunting down tofu and soya milk yoghurts to please the vegans as well as bringing a huge haul of root vegetables and eggs.

Anita, who worked as a chef in a vegan café and was a natural organiser, put everyone to task. She used flour Stevie had found to make dough for pizza bases. I roasted vegetables. Viktor stewed apples. Luke shelled nuts. A couple of hours later a dozen of us sat down to a huge and delicious dinner. We pulled crackers Stevie had found, then dug into bread and dips, home-made salads with roasted red peppers and aubergine as well as half a dozen different kinds of shop-made salads, stuffed vine leaves and falafel. We had home-made pizzas – cheese for the vegetarians, tofu for the vegans – and roast potatoes. Then apple pie with custard and Christmas cake. As is traditional, we were stuffed.

No one had thought of giving each other presents but everyone wanted to play games. Stevie taught us an elaborate and hilarious version of wink murder and we played charades. Looking around the group as the evening wore on and we sat back on the sofas picking at a bit more cake and drinking yet another cup of tea, I felt as full of goodwill and well-being as I ever have at Christmas.

The days after Christmas were, according to Stevie and Viktor, among the best times for finding stuff abandoned outside people's houses as they cleared out old stereos, clothes and other possessions to make way for their new gifts. The only other time as good was the end of the academic year in early summer when students going home from university jettisoned things they couldn't be bothered to take with them. The trip to Holland had used up the last of my sofa money so I was very glad to find a DVD player and some speakers to sell on the Internet.

January 2009 was the coldest month for twelve years but I was far less chilly then than I had been in October at the solicitors' offices. I had found a big black padded jacket with a thick hood, a pair of waterproof shoes and several pairs of gloves, all left in piles of rubbish or dropped in the street. My sisters had given me thermal leggings and long-sleeved thermal vests as Christmas presents. Padded out with layers and a puffy coat I looked as bulky as a bouncer but I was warm. I Freecycled an electric heater which, though I didn't like to leave it on all night because of how much energy it used and the risk of fire, at least eliminated the chilly moments of nakedness when changing from pyjamas to daytime clothes and back again.

As I was cycling to the supermarket bins in the rain one night a taxi hit my back wheel going round a big round-about, throwing me into another lane of traffic. The cars screeched to a halt while the driver, rather than giving me a hand up, started screaming at me that it was my fault. Another driver had to get out of his car and help me off the road. My right leg was in agony. The taxi driver only stopped hectoring me when the police arrived and pointed out that as he'd hit me from behind, it was probably his fault. Once I wasn't being shouted at I realised that I was just badly bruised and shaken but my bike was a write-off, the back wheel run over and the rear fork bent out of shape. I was put in the back of a police van for the first and only time in my squatting and scavenging career for a lift home with my crushed bike.

It was far worse to be injured or ill while living for free – no Lucozade, no Hobnobs, no daytime telly and only economy loo roll to blow your nose on. But during previous winters I had seemed to get ill every month or so. That winter, despite not finding any vitamin pills to dose myself up on, I caught far fewer colds and the week I spent unable to walk or sit without pain after the bike accident was the only time I was confined to my bed. My healthiness probably had a lot to do with not sharing an office or cramming myself on buses and tubes with hundreds of other contagious people. But I don't doubt that, like my improved sleeping patterns, it had a lot to do with the fact that I was eating healthily, I got plenty of exercise and my life was far less stressful than it had been while I was earning and spending.

Walking down the street, everyone looked braced as they rushed from tube to work to lunch to gym to tube to home to bed, foreheads furrowed and mouths set as they visibly fretted – perhaps, as I had before, about the tasks still undone, their place in the office hierarchy, whether they were going to be able to afford the things they wanted. I certainly had worries these days – how I was going to transport myself now my bike was knackered, where I was going to live when the studio got evicted, how long a new place might last, whether it would have violent owners, or whether it would be full of asbestos or worse. But from day to day I didn't have much to fuss about or decisions to worry over. I had everything I really needed, I'd already dealt with worse problems and I knew I had people around me who would help me if things went wrong. I had resigned myself to making the most of what came my way rather than striving for perfection, so if things fell short of what others had it wasn't such a reflection on me.

Because I wasn't going into an office or out to clubs,

gigs and restaurants, I didn't have to upset myself over what I looked like or whether I was dressed right in my black clothes. My hair was cut by students at a nearby hair salon who did a good job on their training days when it was free to go and get a trim, but didn't give you as much choice as a paying customer. To test whether I looked too shabby I tried sauntering past doormen into expensive hotels. They never stopped me, so I could take a seat in the lobby to read the papers or maybe eat some scones left behind on a tiered plate, an unwanted part of someone's afternoon tea. George Orwell, when down and out, was marked out as a tramp as soon as he'd pawned his smart suit. But relaxed dress codes today mean it's not always easy to tell whether someone looks grungy because they can't help it or because they've paid for shabby-chic clothes, and I found that I could still go anywhere I wanted. Everyone else in the street seemed far too pre-occupied to pay me much attention anyway. As long as I was reasonably clean, it seemed, I'd do.

Jamie phoned. 'I heard your bike got wrecked. I've just found a spare one – do you want it?' Once my bruising had healed enough to go out I'd been forced to acknowledge that I couldn't walk everywhere I wanted to go. Using public transport when I was used to living without relying on money would have forced me to find a more reliable source of income than selling the odd bit of tat I happened to find. I hiked up to the library to check Jamie's bike out. It was a perfectly serviceable, bog-standard commuter's bike, pale blue and in need of nothing but a new set of brake pads, which were available at trade price down at the free bike workshop in south London. Jamie had been walking past a house people were moving out of and, seeing the bike left against a wall, had asked whether it was wanted any more. It wasn't. It took a while to get my nerve back but it was good to be on two wheels again.

After the activists had spent a year in the studios the court papers had finally arrived. The owners hadn't decided to tolerate the squatters, their witness statement said – they simply hadn't visited the building for the past year. If they had they couldn't have failed to notice the curtains, the lights inside, and the window boxes Suzy's boyfriend had built, which Suzy had filled with flowers and vegetables as a substitute for her previous garden.

The squatters had won a couple of adjournments over minor technicalities but the owners got their possession order in January. When the activists suggested a deal to stay in the building, the company's representative admitted that it would stay empty since the property price crash made it pointless to work on it but still refused to let them carry on living there. The countdown of a month or so to the arrival of the bailiffs started and everyone went back to house hunting.

I liked the activists but, since I didn't want a revolution, I wasn't really part of their gang and I found their inertia frustrating. I started asking around to see if anyone else was on the move or had a spare room for me. No luck. When Stevie, Viktor, Jozsef and the rest had been evicted from the

NHS clinic with an IPO, Stevie had gone to Barcelona, and Viktor and Jozsef had moved to two flats on a council estate in Tower Hamlets, east London. I went round to visit, and if I didn't exactly ask whether I could move in, I heavily hinted that I'd like to. Jozsef's three-bedroom flat was already fully occupied so there was no space for me there. Viktor had a two-bedroom flat to himself but uncomfortably admitted that he didn't want a flatmate at the moment. The flats were small, he doubted that the council would carry out evictions if squats were left empty, and he was enjoying his privacy after living with lots of people at the offices and the clinic. I had to swallow down my hurt and disappointment. Now I'd have to find a new gang and a new house on my own.

chapter **thirteen**

Two days later I got a text. 'Hey Kath, opened a flat for u today. Come around tonigh or tomoro morning to see it if u can – V.'

Viktor had sorted me out a flat? Really? I texted him straight back. I was doing a shift in the ASS office but I'd cycle round as soon as we closed at 6 p.m. It was impossible to fit enough gratitude into the brief message.

The flat was on the Ocean Estate, a sprawling complex of 85 high- and low-rise blocks and strips of terraced houses, built between the forties and seventies in a mish-mash of architectural styles. Several of the buildings were scheduled for demolition and redevelopment so the council had started to move tenants out, leaving the flats vacant until the buildings were completely empty and plans and money were in place to knock them down and replace them. Some squatters, spotting what was going on, had moved in. A few had already been there for a couple of years. The local council didn't seem to be making any effort to get rid of them at the moment.

The flat that was to be mine was sandwiched between the blocks that contained Jozsef's and Viktor's flats, they'd told me. The long, red-brick buildings in that part of the estate all had four storeys, with festoons of clothes on washing lines strung along the open corridors from the central stairwells, similar to many council blocks across the city. Light came from most of the flats' windows along with the smell of cooking and the noise of TVs, kids playing and babies crying. Looking up to the top-right corner flat, which Viktor had told me could be mine, I could see that the flats next door and below it had already been sealed up with sheets of perforated steel, like half a dozen others in the block of 24, while mine still had doors and windows. I went upstairs and knocked on the door. Victor opened it, shrugging as if it was nothing when I tried to thank him, while Jozef stood behind him in the hall, smiling his usual half-grin and shyly looking at the floor.

But the inside of the flat was in a wretched state. A team of council contractors had spent several hours working methodically to make it as uninhabitable as possible short of actually knocking it down. There was no furniture. Every internal door had been ripped out, along with the carpets and light fittings. The possessions the previous tenants had left behind – a greasy cooking pot, some children's toys, a broken radio and other junk – had been thrown to the floor. The toilet, bath and sinks had been pulled off the walls, and concrete had been poured down the sewage outflows to block them. Someone with a hammer had gone round the flat smashing every plug socket and light switch and had shattered the toilet and basin, leaving shards of ceramic all over the floor. The water stopcock had been turned off, the tap had been sawn away so it couldn't be turned back on, then all the water pipes had been hacked out. The fuse box had been pulled out of its cupboard and taken away, and the cables that should have led from the mains to the fuse box then to the various circuits around the flat had been cut off right up inside the metal tubes which took them through the walls. Finally, a workman had taken a tin of anti-climb paint, black-brown and so oily it would never dry, and slathered it on to the window ledges, door frames and walls so that anyone inside the flat, and certainly anyone climbing into it, would get smeared.

While I carried on thanking Jozsef and Viktor as they showed me round, I couldn't imagine how I would ever make such a bombsite into a nice place to live. I'd known before I'd arrived that the council would have smashed it up – it's standard practice, done by most councils to most properties set to stay empty until they are demolished to stop squatters and scrap-metal thieves. I'd peered through the perforated steel placed over the windows of dozens of other flats and maisonettes to see the wreckage council workmen had left.

Viktor had watched the tenants leaving, handing the keys over to a council worker who had let the flat-smashers in. The contractors had got to work, throwing sofas, cupboards, carpets and doors from the third floor into the back of a rubbish van, most of them fracturing as they landed, and carrying out the fridge and all the pipes, radiators and other metal. The boys had watched the workmen get back into the van and drive away.

They knew, from watching the same thing happen to flat after flat, that the next team of council contractors would be along soon to smash every pane of glass in the windows facing the corridors and remove the front door, then to drive thick bolts into the window and door frames to attach steel sheets over the gaps. The boys had picked up a spare lock and gone over. A firm shove had been all it had taken to open the front door, which had been closed only with the previous tenant's cheap latch. They'd gone inside, changed the lock barrel and stuck a legal warning on the door. They had told the team who were supposed to put metal over the windows to go away since the flat was now squatted. Then they had texted me.

In the time it had taken me to arrive they had made a start on sorting out the mess, sweeping the rubbish into piles. It really wasn't too bad, they said. The smashers often did a more thorough job, slapping anti-climb paint all over the walls and removing or destroying the kitchen sink, bath tub and oven. Viktor's flat had been in a similar state when he'd moved in and I'd seen that he'd managed to make it nice. It was too dark to do much now, they said, but tomorrow we'd all start work to undo the council's efforts to wreck their own property.

Alone in the dark flat that evening, staying in to keep it safe, I had plenty of time for thinking. If it made sense to the council to smash perfectly habitable flats then leave them empty, it made no sense to me. I'd squatted publicly owned empty buildings before, at Chris's place and the mansion, but being confronted by the sheer number of wasted houses on the estate and their deliberately ruined state was like a punch in the guts. Why had I slogged away in jobs I disliked to cover the rent while homes like this one were sitting empty? Why had I paid council tax while living in the borough a few years before when the local authority seemed happy to fritter its resources away?

I had heard the story of Ocean from other squatters who had looked up old newspaper articles and council minutes to get an idea of how long the flats on the estate would stay empty – a clue to how long they might be able to live in them, though no guarantee that the council would not evict them much sooner. When first built, the Ocean Estate had been considered a success, a good place to live. Eighties pop star Billy Ocean grew up there and liked it enough to adopt its title as his stage name. But by the nineties, the estate was in bad shape and had become one of the most deprived areas of Tower Hamlets, itself the third most deprived borough in the country, despite encompassing the executive flats and financial head offices of Canary Wharf and fashionable, gentrified areas like Hoxton and Shoreditch. On Ocean, and on many estates between those two islands of prosperity, flats were leaky and damp after cuts in local authority housing investment during the Thatcher years, and the estate was a hotspot for drugs and crime as well as unemployment, poverty and poor educational achievement. Most of the flats were occupied by Bangladeshi families, often in severely overcrowded conditions, with grandparents, parents and young children sharing the two- and three-bedroom flats.

Tony Blair had visited the estate in 2001 to promise £56 million of investment, and the organisation set up to spend the money, the Ocean New Deal for Communities (NDC), announced that by 2010, 'The Ocean will be a beautiful place to live in the heart of London, rich in its culture, education and employment.' As I sat in the dark flat, that plan seemed to have failed. In fact, within three years of Blair's visit, the promise had begun to look hollow, according to the newspaper cuttings found by the squatters who had done the research. By 2004, three of the five organisations funded by the NDC had their payments suspended because of police investigations into fraud or allegations of mismanagement. An ex Labour councillor and his brother were eventually convicted of the theft of some £40,000 of NDC funds. Under the project's original master plan, created with the input of the tenants, 25 of the blocks on the estate were to be replaced with new housing. But a lack of funds forced the NDC to draw up a 'minimum sustainable option' – demolishing and rebuilding as few as ten of the worst buildings.

To raise the £200 million needed to carry out even that scaled-back scheme, the council had wanted to transfer the estate to a privately run housing association which could borrow from the private sector to carry out the work then claw the money back afterwards in rent and by building more densely on the site in order to sell off a proportion of the new homes for private ownership. But housing association tenancies are less secure than those enjoyed by council tenants and many suspected that rents would rise once the flats were transferred. The Ocean residents voted no. That meant no new money and therefore no revamped Ocean Estate.

The council had carried on 'decanting' tenants from the blocks that were earmarked for redevelopment, still hoping to carry out the project without transferring the homes to the private sector. By the time I arrived, eight years after the regeneraton was first promised, there was still no money and no firm plans. Until there were – the bit of the story we squatters were really interested in – the flats would sit empty.

As I lay that night on cushions borrowed from Jozsef with Viktor's sleeping bag pulled over me, sleep didn't come easily. Every noise had to be identified before it could be dismissed. I woke several times and struggled to fall back to sleep. But the boys kept their promise, turning up at the door soon after nine in the morning with bags of tools and some skipped cakes for breakfast. Two of Jozsef's friends who were visiting him also offered to help. Viktor started on the sewage pipes first, chiselling out the concrete that had been poured into them. After he had got rid of the first five centimetres of blockage, he called me over. The workmen had shoved carrier bags into the pipes, he showed me, so that the concrete didn't go right down the drains and clog up the entire sewage system of the block. Once you'd broken up the first bit, you could just pull it all out. Jozsef had brought along some tile adhesive, which he used to patch up the toilet – the workmen hadn't made a very thorough job of smashing it, so he managed to fit it back together then fix it well enough to be watertight and then attached it to the cleared sewage outflow.

Jozsef's friends got to work in the kitchen, using wood rescued from a skip to build a stand for the sink that had been pulled from the wall but left on the floor. Viktor had brought a spare tap from the stash of scavenged bits of plumbing and electrical equipment that filled the spare room in his flat. He attached it before turning the stop-cock back on, gripping the stub of the old tap the workmen had sawn off with a pair of long-nosed pliers. We had running water.

Then Viktor set up a plug socket. It was powered straight from the mains without a fuse and without being earthed, but while it was a long way from being safe it let us plug in a lamp and a kettle. The electricity meter had been left in the flat so I set up an account straight away. I went round sweeping the floors and filling bags with the rubble and junk then tackled the anti-climb paint with a rag. It is designed not to dry so it doesn't, but as long as it was on non-absorbent surfaces, like the gloss paint on the door frames and windowsills that the workmen had concentrated on, I could wipe it off with a rag and a bit of effort.

By evening the flat had all the basic components of a habitable home – a toilet, running water, legal electricity and walls you could touch without dirtying your hands or clothes. I couldn't believe how easily Viktor and Jozsef had managed to sort out what had looked to me like a hopeless situation. I'd found a clean mattress a couple of hundred metres away and Jozsef had housesat while I cycled up to the activists' studios to fetch some of my possessions.

I dare say I could have counted on my non-squatting

friends to help me out if I'd needed it and had asked for it, but, quite apart from the fact that most of them were as hopelessly inexperienced as me at DIY, it hadn't been built into our relationships when we had all been successful and independent, getting on with our own lives and meeting up for company not cooperation. I probably understood most of my work and university friends better than I did Jozsef, with his home-made tattoos and patchy English. But I had spent months living companionably with him, drinking tea and sharing food. I knew I could work alongside him and rely on him when times were difficult, and I could judge his mood and make him smile. He had put himself at risk to rescue the others when the police arrived at the row of little houses, I had written a legal argument for him, Viktor and Stevie in an attempt to delay their eviction from the clinic, and he was helping me now. We weren't like family, with a deep, long-standing emotional involvement. For now we were simply in this together and the camaraderie felt good.

Night in the flat alone was still freezing cold and unsettling. I watched through my uncurtained window as a soft-topped car arrived at the block of flats opposite just before midnight. Several people shuffled out of the shadows to meet it then I watched them go up the stairs and climb underneath the panel of steel on one of the windows. Junkies, Viktor had told me, being visited by their dealer. The estate had a long-standing drug problem and during the nineties was said to be the cheapest place in the UK to buy heroin. The council had made efforts to help addicts living on the estate and eliminate dealers over the past decade but this group of users still crept in to shoot up most nights. The flat wasn't a place they slept in or lived in during the day – they had just pulled away the metal over the window with a crowbar and crawled in, making no efforts to turn it into a home. If council staff closed it up they just opened it again or used the stairwell to take their drugs. Viktor had climbed over their legs on his way to his flat more than once, seeing them injecting into their groins. The car drove away.

Perhaps leaving flats empty for a couple of years wasn't a big deal to the council in the context of a complicated redevelopment scheme that had already stretched to nearly a decade and looked set to drag on for much longer. But there had to be a better solution than letting the buildings become a playground for junkies and pigeons. Temporarily empty buildings which can't be used to house long- or medium-term tenants are not a new problem and scores of 'short-life' housing organisations exist to fill buildings that will only be empty for a short period with people who are thoroughly grateful to live in them and willing to contribute money or effort in return.

Many of these groups, such as Westminster Housing Co-op, which accommodates key workers such as teachers and firemen, and Phoenix Housing Co-op, which takes people from council waiting lists, grew out of communities of people who were squatting in the seventies. The owners of the buildings the squatters were living in, seeing that it was better for them to be used than left empty, made deals with the squatters. When the squatters fulfilled their side of the bargain, proving that they caused no disruption and gave the buildings back to the owners when needed, the landlords allowed them to use other empty buildings to continue to house themselves. From that start, some have grown into large bodies too respectable to mention their squatting roots; some even use the fact that they keep squatters out as a key selling point. Many still run as co-ops, with everyone they house becoming a member and being given a say in their organisation's decisions.

Because redevelopment projects can be lengthy and delayed, short-life housing isn't always so short. Jim, a cantankerous but incredibly knowledgeable Scot now in his sixties, a recipient of the ASS's Golden Crowbar award for long service to the group, joined a short-life housing group which was looking after Gray's Inn Buildings on Rosebery Avenue in central London after having spent several years as a squatter. He arrived there in 1978 and was told he would only be able to stay for a year or two. In 2003 the council got round to redeveloping the block and Jim finally moved out.

Most short-life housing organisations are clamouring for empty buildings to borrow. Many pay the owners a fee for the use of the properties as well as keeping them maintained and handing them back on time, all usually paid for with the rents they charge to the people they accommodate. Rent is usually between £40 and £70 a week per person, far lower than private sector rent for a similar property. If the object of regenerating the Ocean Estate was to create more mixed communities, perhaps the council could have started straight away by opening the flats up to members of a co-op that housed a different group of people from those already living on the estate – artists prepared to do work with the community in exchange for their accommodation, for instance. Or perhaps the flats could simply have been used to house some of the thousands of people in the borough living in overcrowded accommodation.

The council could have employed a company focused less on housing people and more on securing properties. Businesses including Camelot and Ad Hoc place so-called 'property guardians' in empty buildings to prevent squatting and vandalism and to guard against the decay that often occurs naturally in buildings that are left empty. The guardians are not tenants and therefore have few rights. They pay fees, not rent, of around £50 a week. Fierce notices are placed around houses looked after by Camelot warning the occupants that if they have guests to stay they risk instant eviction, and that the company's staff may come in without warning at any time of day or night to check up. This serves to police the occupants and prevents them from claiming 'exclusive occupation' of the building, one of the defining aspects of being a tenant. Guardians must have a regular income, no children and be prepared to move out with a fortnight's notice. Despite the lack of freedom, security and privacy offered by the property guardian companies to those they house, they have more people wanting accommodation than they have empty buildings to look after.

Many squatters loathe the property guardian companies, considering them to be self-interested money-grabbers. They say that guardian companies do not use the buildings to accommodate as many people as possible, have rules that exclude those who need housing the most and drum up business by playing up the problems of squatting. Those who live as property guardians are widely thought of as blacklegs, crossing an ideological picket line by accepting poor living conditions, few rights and relatively high fees when they could hold out for better. Also, to many squatters' minds, it isn't clear that being a property guardian is any more safe and comfortable than squatting – both involve fairly regular house moves without much notice and living in makeshift conditions. If squatting is slightly less secure, at least you can have your boyfriend to stay over without worrying that the company is going to send someone round to do a check-up, you can choose who you live with and you don't have to pay £50 a week.

I was glad to be reclaiming at least one of the flats the council had chosen to leave empty. But to turn my cold little flat in the desolate estate into a good home, first of all I needed flatmates to help with fixing the place up and for the comfort of having companionship in a scary place. An Irish girl called Jo was house hunting, I heard from the vegans. She had just broken up with her boyfriend whose rented flat she had been sharing and wanted to come back to squatting. She was working as a bike courier, they told me, but needed to live on as little as possible to save money to cycle to India. She came round the next day, a skinny, ginger-haired explosion of energy, with tattoos all over her hands, arms, chest and back. Despite having already cycled 60-odd miles delivering packages and letters across the city, she was almost dancing with excitement at the prospect of a new place to live. Her huge smile didn't slip when I showed her how basic the place was at the moment. 'No problem! We'll fix it all up in days. It'll be awesome!'

chapter fourteen

Jo moved in that weekend, carting all her possessions in a
toolbox, a wheelie suitcase and a backpack. As soon as
she'd dropped them in her room, the biggest one so that she
could have space to work on her various bikes, she wanted
to go out and hunt for stuff to improve the flat. I'd been
working on it gradually, cleaning the filthy kitchen and
bathroom floors and painting the carpetless concrete of my
bedroom floor white. But the living room was still bare, the
kitchen didn't even have shelves to put food on and the
electricity supply was a single risky plug socket. Jo wanted
to get it all sorted out right away. We should borrow a bike
trailer from a friend, she said, then wander the streets gathering everything that could possibly be useful.

First we found the carcass of an Ikea wardrobe, then a
couple of cans of paint, sky blue and crimson, then a bead
curtain for the kitchen doorway. Next, a clean double
mattress for Jo's room, a couple of doors then, best of all,
an undamaged toilet, half buried in a skip full of building
rubble. 'Awesome!' Jo cried. We spent most of the afternoon giggling as we packed it all onto the trailer, stacking it
up and wheeling it as gently as possible to stop the stuff

tumbling off. The more junk we gathered the more of a spectacle we became. Kids hanging around on a corner pointed and jeered, and a passer-by stopped to take a photo of us on his mobile phone.

With a chisel and hammer borrowed from our squatting neighbours, Jo bashed away until she got through the concrete wall to the solid metal pipes that enclosed the electricity cables, which she cheerfully spent hours sawing through with a hacksaw until she had freed the ends of the cut-off cables coming in from the mains and out to the flat's circuits. Happiest with tasks that used her unstoppable energy for quick results without too much strategic thinking or multi-tasking, she also painted everything in the kitchen sky blue – leaving drips and smears on the sink, floor and some of the plates and saucepans that I had Freecycled. She made a start on painting one wall in the living room crimson – although she hadn't washed the paintbrush very well, so when the wall started to come out toilet-paper pink because of the white that had still been on the brush she abandoned the job.

Meanwhile, I didn't mind taking on the fiddlier tasks. I went round with a tiny screwdriver, using little plastic tubes for splicing cables to extend the wires that the workmen had cut off and that Jo had freed from the wall. I worked out how to install new plug sockets, light switches and fittings, some of them donated by squatting friends and a few bought in a hardware shop. I washed all the brushes to go over the partially pink wall in solid crimson.

Then it was a matter of installing the fuse box, which

one of Jo's friends had rescued from a skip months ago and saved in case it came in handy. I didn't want to do it and neither did Jo. The main fuse box for the building was in the corridor so we could turn off all power to the cables in our flat without trouble but the dangers of getting it wrong seemed too great. We wanted Phil, one of my fellow ASS volunteers, to come round and put it in. But he wouldn't, he said, for the same reasons that the ASS tried to teach people how to start squatting rather than just installing them in squats. It wasn't very difficult or dangerous and if we worked out how to do it this time we'd be more confident about sorting out a similar problem in future. In any case, he didn't have time to come and fix everybody's fuses. He drew me a diagram and pointed me towards the relevant chapter in the DIY manual kept in the ASS office. 'You'll be happier if you do it yourself than if I come and do it for you.'

I didn't agree. I added a fuse between the mains wire and our one plug socket, making it marginally safer, but that was as far as our fear of electrocution let us get. Finally, after almost two weeks, I got sick of having to move our one lamp from room to room and shivering without a heater. I put on rubber-soled shoes and rubber gloves in case of shocks, turned off the power and got to work linking the mains cables from the meter to the fuse box, then linking 30 smaller cables through the fuses and out to the flat's circuits. It took me several minutes to work up the courage to switch the power back on. The fuse box didn't crackle or start to melt. Sparks didn't fly out of the spaghetti tangle of cables. I went into the living room and gingerly flicked the light switch. The lights went on. I flicked it off. They went off. On. Off. On. There was light. It felt like a miracle. I plugged in my phone charger to check the plugs. They worked. I turned on the oven, which had been pulled out from the wall but left in the kitchen by the workmen. There was a pop as the trip switch in the fuse box blew. I turned the oven off, reset the trip switch and tried turning the oven back on. It started heating up. I did a little victory dance. Phil had been right. I was really pleased with myself. I texted Jo. 'Awesome!' came the reply.

Life in the flat grew increasingly civilised. The doors we had found in the street turned out to be the wrong size for any of the door frames in the flat. But we put the wardrobe on its side with one of the doors on top and called it a kitchen table, plumbed in the new, undamaged toilet, another task I had imagined would call for technical knowledge I lacked but which turned out to be surprisingly easy once I got started, and hung the bead curtain. We found a sofa in the street and Jozsef lent some of his Gothic paintings to hang in the living room. The things we'd had to buy to replace the locks and fix up the electricity and the plumbing had set us back about £15 each but everything else – the kettle, the set of shelves for the kitchen, the chairs – was scavenged.

In Viktor's block, visible from my window and with far more empty flats than my own, the junkies continued to come to meet their dealer during the night, trying to attract as little attention as possible. Lynn, a mouthy woman in her forties who had been living between squats and barely canal-worthy houseboats for more than a decade and whose squat on the Ocean Estate had already lasted two years, gave the drug-users lip every time she walked past them. One night one of the addicts challenged her and threatened to punch her. She screamed for help. Two squatters and one tenant, her long-term neighbours, came running. They chased the man out, rugby-tackled him to the ground and warned him not to come back. He never did, and the other junkies also melted away, presumably to find a more peaceful place to feed their addictions. The flat they had used as a shooting gallery was squatted by a group of art students.

The main sources of unpleasantness once the junkies had gone were a gang of Bangladeshi lads who turned up in cars or on foot most nights, lounging around a children's playground, shouting or playing music until the early hours. They rarely came past the block where I lived but if I had to pass near them, they would sometimes mutter offers of skunk and, when I turned that down, jeeringly ask me to give them oral sex. One night they started setting fire to rubbish in the playground. 'It's just like Belfast!' said Jo as she, acting on gut instinct rather than thinking about things for long enough to get scared, went down to tell them to stop it. They didn't stop it and offered to sell her crack. But it wasn't easy to tell whether they were serious dealers or just bored boys imagining they were living the hip-hop dream. I never saw drug paraphernalia abandoned around their playground and there was no sign of knife crime or turf wars. Their presence was threatening but that was probably the idea and usually it was left at that.

The security guards employed by the council to patrol the estate didn't seem inclined to ask the youths to turn the volume down or to stop touting drugs and shouting abuse at passers-by. Instead, the guards, most of them Polish, spent their time sitting in their cars watching films on portable DVD players, occasionally letting their huge Alsatians out of their cages in the cars' boots to foul the grassy patches around the blocks and to bark endlessly.

The security guards' job appeared to be primarily to prevent more squatters from moving in but they failed at that task too. The corners of the metal sheets could be prised away from the doorways quickly and fairly quietly with a crowbar, making enough of a gap to crawl through and put up a new door inside before removing the metal covering completely. It could usually be done before the security guards noticed – although when they did spot anyone at it they called the police. A couple of groups of would-be squatters were caught with crowbars in hand and arrested for – though not eventually charged with – criminal damage. But squats were still being opened at a rate of one every week or two in the seven blocks due for demolition.

Making the flats habitable was a lot of work and most of the squatters had to put up with smashed and boarded-up windows on the sides of their flat facing into the corridor. But group after group still made the calculation that trying to move in was their best option. The council didn't seem to be putting much energy into evicting squatters, so the likelihood of being able to stay in the flat for several months compensated for the effort it took to make a place habitable. Rag-tag groups of squatters carrying carpets, doors or furniture through the yards around the blocks to fix up their flats became a frequent sight.

More flats were emptying all the time. A couple of times a week we would watch as a family loaded their belongings into a removal van then listen to the workmen hammering, sawing, ripping and throwing things out of the flat to the ground and shattering every pane of glass. We knew that the flat would be disused for at least another year and – judging by the failure of attempts to revitalise the estate so far – probably much longer. We usually watched out to see if there was a chance to get into the flat before it was steeled up or, better still, before it was smashed, but the workers began to make sure the flats were constantly watched to stop people like Viktor pulling the same trick twice. They became increasingly thorough in their destruction, removing kitchen sinks, baths and ovens rather than just pulling them out of the wall and writing all over the walls with anti-climb paint: 'Everton FC', 'I love Nicky' and painting smiley faces.

One morning when I heard the sound of breaking glass I stuck my head out of the door to see which flat was being destroyed this time. The foreman of the smashers saw me and beckoned me over. 'Do you want a sofa?' he asked when I got close enough.

'Yes, please! But we'd like some doors even better...'

The foreman spoke to his team, and instead of chucking the internal doors off the balcony, they started to carry them along to my flat, letting me and Jo replace the blankets we'd hung over our doorways with something genuinely sound- and draughtproof. When a council employee with a clipboard came over to check the progress, the foreman shooed me away. When she'd gone, I came out again to help them move the carpet they were in the process of ripping out of the flat into my own. Since the flats all had identical layouts it fitted perfectly. The foreman, a stocky bloke with a blond crew cut, didn't want to chat and turned down my offer of a cup of tea but gave me a wink. 'I was there once,' he said. 'Squatted up in Hackney back in the eighties before I got my council flat. Good luck to you.'

March came and the weather got warmer. It was a relief in many ways, allowing me to sleep under slightly fewer blankets and stop hiding a hot-water bottle under my jumper if I wanted to sit still for longer than half an hour. But it also made our lack of a fridge more of a problem. Since we were living in such a poor area, far less seemed to get dumped in the street than in better-off parts of town and anything that did get put out was rescued almost immediately by tenants or, more often, squatters. Once while out for a walk I saw a fridge on the pavement, but by the time I had rushed home and fetched Jo to help me carry it, it had been whisked away. We had to go skipping for food every day since there was no way to store anything. Meat was risky and milk or cheese went off disappointingly quickly. Then I remembered that back when we were living at the mansion I'd found a fridge-freezer that we didn't need since the building had already contained three of them. I'd helped the vegans take it back to their new place. Perhaps it was going spare? It was, said Anita, and my fellow ASS volunteer, Josh, who had a van, helped me to fetch it in return for petrol money.

I gradually got used to the atmosphere on the impoverished estate with its decaying blocks. The group of primary-school age kids who often played in the tarmac yards around the buildings, supposed to be parking spaces but empty of cars because few around here had the money to run them, gradually got to know my name and usually wanted to chat when I was passing by. My neighbours guardedly returned smiles and 'hello's, but many in the block, particularly the women, spoke little English so the conversation rarely went beyond that. The other squatters – two more households in my block, plus maybe a hundred people scattered across the other seven condemned blocks – were mostly friendly. Knocking on one another's doors, most of us would tap out a cheerful rat-tat-te-tat-tat so that whoever we were visiting would know it was a friend, not a threat, waiting outside. I still tended to jump when the letterbox snapped, wondering what the noise was – though it was always the postman. One morning I heard a heavy knock at the door and saw, through the frosted glass, a workman's yellow hard hat. 'Oh no,' I thought. 'What now?' I peered through the letterbox to see Jozsef in a child's toy builder's hat laughing at me.

To anyone unfamiliar with the estate it must have looked like a textbook example of grim urban deprivation – poor families of recent immigrants mingling with squatters in old, tired buildings, the kind of place you would avoid walking through at night. A group of would-be guests who had contacted Viktor through couchsurfing.com managed to find his flat but refused to stay, preferring to pay up and go to a backpacker's hostel than risk spending a night on the estate. It's always hard to know how dangerous a place is – maybe I avoided trouble because I was lucky rather than safe. But it didn't feel like a place where threats lurked around every corner.

Jo and I cleared out the third and smallest bedroom of the flat, which we'd used to stash bits of wood and other findings that might come in handy, so that one of Jo's friends, another bike courier, could move in. Sam made almost no effort to decorate the room, slinging down a mattress, sticking a poster over a smear of anti-climb paint on the wall and unpacking his few belongings onto the floor, turning it into a sea of junk and unwashed crockery. But he brought his harmonica, his set of boxing gloves and pads with which he taught me to throw a punch, and an electric shower, which meant an end to washing ourselves from a bucket, the chill taken off the cold water with a kettle-full of hot. He sang in his deep, bluesy voice almost constantly, messing around with versions of Rolling Stones or Bob Dylan songs while cooking, or reinterpreting J-Lo and Destiny's Child as blues numbers in the shower every morning. Although he earned reasonable pay, Sam was trying to send money home to his mother, who was ill and trying to get by on incapacity benefit, so lived as cheaply as possible himself, saving on rent and food but paying for a steady supply of marijuana. He quickly proved himself to be a great housemate, easy-going, funny and good at keeping his messiness confined to his own room.

A girl who had been squatting in a flat on the estate for more than two years set up an emergency phone number so that texts could be sent out if any of us were getting hassled by the youths, junkies or security guards. We called a couple of squatters' meetings which always started late, lasted too long and tended to be dominated by Lynn passing on every smidgen of gossip going. They did give us a chance to meet each other and make plans, though. Lots of people wanted to open a flat as a social centre, housing a free shop and a skipping exchange, where people could bring spare scavenged food and junk for others – squatters and, we hoped, neighbours – to help themselves. But when the man who had volunteered to do the actual opening got his crowbar confiscated by the security guards and narrowly avoided arrest, the plan was shelved and we tried to deal with our immediate problems instead. When the boys started throwing stones at one squat's window about two dozen squatters materialised in five minutes, simply standing and watching until they gave up, while the security guards stayed in their cars. When the security guards tried to kick down the door of a recently opened squat, about 30 people turned up to stand in the corridor until the police arrived, who backed up what we had been telling the security guards: that what they were doing broke the law, because the flat was now someone's home and they were inside it.

By the end of April my floor, which when I first moved in had been made up of four families of tenants, one empty flat and mine, was a full house of six squats in a row. A group of Hungarians plus a Spaniard and a couple of English twenty-somethings moved into three of the flats. They had been living together for a while and mostly worked in bars or shops, spending most evenings sitting outside chatting, eating or watching films. We joined them now and then, shared our food when we had skipped too much of one thing and borrowed each other's tools when we needed them but didn't really become part of their crew.

There was a downside, of course. Every time a new squat was opened we'd watch the people carefully in case they were going to bring us trouble. A middle-aged Romanian couple moved into one of the flats on my floor. We barely saw them, but whenever they did emerge from the flat they looked skinny, haggard and unhealthy, and did not meet anyone's eye. Drug or alcohol problems, we suspected, though we had no evidence. They kept themselves to themselves and seemed to be looking for a quiet life. They didn't bring dealers or fellow addicts to our building, so as far as we were concerned it was better that they were under a roof than on the street. Everyone in the corridor kept an eye on them but left them alone.

With only three of us living in the flat, and Jo and Sam working full-time, we didn't keep it inhabited all the time. Every time I came home after leaving it empty I'd look up to my doorway on the top floor, and when the door was still in place, not removed and replaced with metal sheets by council staff or kicked in by a thief so desperate that burgling a squat made sense, I'd feel the same faint sense of relief I felt whenever I left my bike locked up somewhere dodgy but found it still there when I returned. More neighbours were a reassurance, especially the easy-going guys on our corridor, sitting outside on their scavenged garden furniture. I gradually stopped worrying about leaving the flat empty.

The Ocean Estate empties had been declared permanently void by the council so were no longer classified as homes. I gathered from talking to EHA's David Ireland that they simply didn't exist in government audits of empty council housing or the statistics gathered by the Empty Homes Agency. Those figures only included flats which were, officially speaking, flats – places that were still part of the letting stock that had been left empty between tenants, or while waiting for minor repairs or renovations – the kinds of places squatters tend to avoid, since they probably wouldn't get to stay long. The Department for Communities and Local Government admits that no central record is kept of how many long-term void council properties there are up and down the country. Councils do not have to publish the figures. Tower Hamlets council eventually revealed that more than 4 per cent of its total stock of council housing was either void or squatted, but gaining the information required a Freedom of Information Act request and two appeals against their refusal to release the statistics. The EHA, extrapolating from the data they have managed to collect, estimates that there are between 80,000 and 100,000 long-term void council homes in the UK.

Within a 20-minute bike ride of the Ocean Estate, I knew of two huge blocks of empty maisonettes containing almost a hundred disused homes each, as well as half a dozen smaller buildings with about half the flats emptied out, waiting for other stalled redevelopment projects. They were ugly buildings, which probably did deserve to be levelled, but no uglier than the still-inhabited council blocks they stood next door to, and they seemed equally capable of providing homes until they were knocked down.

Flats on the Ferrier Estate in Greenwich began to be emptied out in 2004, ready for redevelopment which still hadn't started five years later and will take 20 years to complete. The hulking, uniform blocks of flats and maisonettes made up 1,900 homes, built from yellow-grey concrete panels in the late sixties. When I visited, all the low-rise buildings, three or four maisonettes piled up in tiers like square amphitheatres around scrubby grass, were scattered with boarded-up empties. In several buildings, occupied homes were the exception, with two or three families remaining among swathes of deserted flats. One large block comprising more than a hundred homes had been emptied out completely, surrounded by three-metre-high fences topped with vicious spikes. Inside the fences was a post-apocalyptic scene. Doors had been removed and the flats' big windows had been smashed so that you could see into the buildings and look at the décor chosen by whoever used to consider them home, though the wallpaper was streaked with damp and bird droppings, and saplings had sprouted through the concrete yards and paths.

In another part of the estate an elderly tenant, a life-long Londoner, leaned out of his window to talk to me as I wandered around. The flats are plagued by mosquitoes these days, he said. They breed in pools of stagnant water in the leaky empties. Mice too. But the local schools are brilliant, because they now only have about half the number of pupils they were designed for, since swathes of tenants have been moved away. The grandchildren are loving it. Himself, he isn't leaving until they drag him out. It's home. He's lived here for decades. 'I'm not an old wine,' he said. 'They're not going to decant me.'

'Any squatters here?' I asked.

'Not many.' But just supposing one did want to get into the flats – hypothetically speaking, of course – the best way would be from the roof. You can get up there from the fire escapes, he added, giving me a knowing half-grin. 'That's how I'd do it, if I was doing it. Enough said.' And he pulled his head back inside.

But squatting would hardly be the best way to fill the empties even if Greenwich Council had been prepared to tolerate it, which, from what I heard anecdotally, they were not, preferring to evict squatters as soon as possible. It would be hard to argue that we squatters were the most needy and deserving of housing. We had simply decided to move in. No one had vetted us to determine whether we had earned a free house and although some of us were vulnerable and others were doing socially useful things, some just used the freedom from rent to spend more time relaxing or partying. The families staying in grim bed and breakfast accommodation paid for by the council while waiting for a flat, or the nurses and charity workers struggling on tiny wages while doing indispensable work would probably have made more worthwhile use of my flat than me, Jo and Sam. But the risk and effort of squatting was prohibitive for those with children or a tough job unless they were absolutely desperate. If we hadn't moved ourselves in, no more worthy candidate would have been housed in our place.

I never had reason to fear my squatting neighbours but I could understand why non-squatters might have been afraid of us. If we squatters were watchful every time a new household moved in it must have been far worse for the tenants, most of them families with small children, to have troops of scruffy neighbours arriving without really knowing who we were or what we were up to. We were young, we watched out for each other and we clearly didn't have the same attitudes to private property that others did. Most non-squatters weren't aware of the laws that made it illegal to squat in a building that was someone else's home, so they may have been afraid that we could occupy their flats if they went away for a few days. And if we were capable of living in houses that didn't belong to us, perhaps we would be just as ready to steal from our neighbours. In fact, most of us saw a clear distinction between squatting and thieving, just as there is a difference between skipping and shoplifting or hitch-hiking and fare-dodging. But anyone reading the newspapers could be excused for imagining that we were all a bunch of dangerous, amoral 'crusties', 'dossers', 'anarchists' and 'lazy, scrounging soap dodgers', as the *Sun* referred to squatters in the first six months of 2009.

We didn't get many opportunities to shatter people's prejudices against us. One of the tenants from my block knocked on my door to ask if he could have the previous tenant's satellite dish because his own had broken. When I invited him in to help himself to it he looked slightly uncomfortable, glancing over his shoulder at his wife who was down on the ground floor looking up at us. Once he was inside he admitted he was surprised to see that we had furniture and books, a fully functioning kitchen and a working toilet. 'What do you sleep on?' he asked.

Beds, I showed him, resisting the urge to tell him, 'On torn-up newspaper in the corner, like rats.'

I remembered how terrified I'd been of what I was letting myself in for when I walked out of my rented flat almost a year ago. If all you knew was that we squatters lived in shattered flats and if you had never tried to find the things you needed to turn a wreck into a home you might well imagine that we lived in squalor, pissing in a bucket and sleeping on the floor, and that the only people who could put up with that kind of life were addicts and sociopaths.

No doubt some of the remaining tenants did hate and fear us but most seemed to mind our presence less than one might have expected. Perhaps it wasn't so hard for those left in our blocks, most placed in there temporarily while waiting for the council to make a decision about whether or not to house them permanently, to understand why people might find it necessary to squat. They shared our frustration at the decision by the council to leave flats empty while they lived crammed into their tiny, overcrowded apartments and competed with others on the housing waiting list for a flat of their own, and could see that the flats would have been empty had we not moved into them. We encouraged some of the families to squat flats themselves to create more space. Most held back, afraid of jeopardising their relationship with the council, but one middle-aged Bangladeshi man, turned down for permanent housing by the council at the end of his spell of temporary accommodation, did accept the help of some of the squatters to open a place to live in with his three-year-old son.

We were an unaccountable presence on the estate. We knew there was a reasonable chance that we would be forced out within a few months. The circumstances didn't inspire commitment to the area or gratitude and respect for the council. We squatters asked Westminster Housing Co-op to approach Tower Hamlets council to ask if they could take on the flats as they emptied out, but they were turned down. Letting a housing co-op use the properties might have sent out the signal that the redevelopment had been delayed yet again, said Simon Thurstan, of Westminster Housing Co-op, who was clearly resigned to hearing regular refusals from councils and other owners.

Through the ASS, I tried to get some kind of dialogue going between the squatters and the council bureaucrats. Maybe they didn't like our presence and they'd prefer it if we just packed up and left tomorrow. But since that wasn't going to happen, perhaps we could come to some kind of agreement to deal with the situation better? The council could have negotiated 'Orders by Consent' with the squatters, to be formalised in court. We could have promised to be quiet and tidy and to move out when the council genuinely needed to knock the flats down if they let us stay until then. Such an agreement would have saved the council the cost of fighting us. It would also have given them a way to regulate the situation – if squatters made trouble they would have been breaking their side of the bargain so could have been evicted easily – if not arrested for contempt of court. For those not causing problems it would have given them a stake in the area, a reason beyond their own natural decency to contribute and behave well.

Emails, faxes and phone calls to the council's legal department and head of regeneration went unanswered. Eventually, when the head of the council's legal department answered my call, I was told that no one was interested in any kind of communication with squatters under any circumstances. As far as the council bureaucrats were concerned, it seemed, it was us versus them with no possibility of negotiating a ceasefire.

It was agreed at a meeting that half a dozen of us squatters should go to speak to the Tower Hamlets cabinet meeting, using a brief slot where locals could address the elected councillors to explain why we were squatting and suggest possibilities for moving forward. 'But what about the families living in overcrowded flats?' one of the councillors asked us.

'You may be decent people,' said another councillor to the handful of us in the meeting – the maximum number allowed to attend. 'But what about all the others?'

The prejudices against squatters seemed too deep-rooted to do anything about. It wasn't our fault that the tenants were overcrowded. If the council wanted to give them more space, perhaps they could stop smashing perfectly good flats.

Every squatted flat I went into had been fixed up comfortably and I'd often feel ashamed that we had stuck with a door balanced on a wardrobe as a kitchen table, for instance, while others had found a proper work surface in a skip, cut it to shape and fixed it up properly. From the outside the estate looked grim. But Jo, Sam and I would spend cheerful evenings in our living room, eating and chatting. My squatmates had phenomenal appetites from cycling for a living, particularly Jo who, though she was whippet-thin, could happily eat four slices of toast, butter and chocolate spread as an after-dinner snack. Because they were working they tended to buy food as often as skipping it, and could easily get through a whole tub of luxury ice cream at a sitting. I would try not to listen while they compared stories of that day's near-misses on the road.

I had no responsibilities – no job, no rent and only tiny phone and utility bills. If I found myself worrying occasionally about how long we'd live there, where we'd go next and how safe it was to leave the flat empty, that lack of security also meant I was free to stay or leave as I liked. We might get kicked out in a few weeks, but I might simply get sick of it and decide to pack up and go somewhere else before then. If I wanted, like Jo, to cycle across the world, there was nothing to stop me. If I wanted to hitch to Europe, to one of the other cities with plenty of squatters such as Berlin or Barcelona, I could.

Maybe we did live in a terrifying ghetto, the kind of place sensible people avoid. But it was probably us squatters they would have been most afraid of, and we knew each other well enough to know who we could trust. Nothing was keeping us here if we didn't like it – there were plenty more empties in the city. But there was satisfaction in having carved out a comfortable place to live where otherwise there would have been sheets of steel and a population of pigeons, and in banding together into a friendly and reasonably stable community. Perhaps our kitchen plumbing did leak enough to fill an ice-cream tub with drips of water every few days but it did the trick. It wasn't a perfect solution, for the council, our neighbours or for us, but it was home.

chapter fifteen

Weeks could go by without me having to open my purse but I had grown so used to it that the fact barely registered. Our flat was comfortable. Spring had arrived so I was rarely cold. Finding food was no hassle, a matter of cycling to any of a couple of dozen reliable skipping spots and filling my pannier. I slept as much as I liked, read as much as I liked and went out whenever I felt like it. My parents had stopped worrying about me, and I met up with my old friends in much the same way as I did before, eating meals at their homes or my squat, or walking in the park and wandering around free art galleries.

Text alerts would sometimes come from the squat networks I was part of, calling me and everyone else to help someone who was in trouble and reminding me that difficulty – an unexpected eviction or hassle from owners or police – was far closer than it would have been if I were living more conventionally. But life usually continued without panic and alarm. Squatting neighbours who knew that I worked at the ASS would knock on the door now and then for advice or just to borrow some salt and I'd do the same, going round to Viktor's to get help with some DIY, or pinching a tea bag from the guys down the corridor. I had lived alongside the security guards and youths for long enough to feel little threat from them, and living with Jo and Sam was a pleasure.

I still had barely any money, just a few pounds left from a morning of selling scavenged clothes and other junk on Brick Lane. But it wasn't a source of anxiety any more. My purse would stay buried at the bottom of my bag until there was something I needed to buy – some gaffer tape, toilet roll or new batteries for my bike lights, perhaps. Living for free had become a habit, no longer something I really had to think about except when I met up with earning, spending friends and had to drink tap water and switch off when they were discussing work, or when I met strangers and felt status anxiety prodding me to prove that I wasn't inferior to them because of the way I lived, or answering questions about my lifestyle again and again. Yes, we did have water and electricity. No, none of my housemates were addicts. Yes, squatting was legal, yes, I had enough to eat, yes, I did enjoy my life and no, I didn't feel guilty about it. I didn't mind discussing it – it gave me a chance to vent my anger at the swathes of empty homes, and to challenge prejudices against my and my squatting friends' way of getting by. But I did sometimes wish that, when people asked me what I did, I had an answer I could give them that would be met with a bored nod and a change of subject, rather than curiosity or fury.

Colin and I had muddled through. We couldn't do some of the things that had been habits in the past – watching bands, going out for dinner, catching the train to interesting-sounding places at the weekend. I'd been jealous when he'd gone to gigs with friends – particularly female friends – or had decided to spend weekends at music festivals rather than stopping in London with me. He'd felt left out when I'd gone off on adventures with Mikey, Jamie or Viktor, coming back from hitch-hiking or exploring empty buildings brimming with stories. He'd been busy with work when I wanted company and I'd been full of energy, not worn out from a week in the office, when he wanted to rest at the weekends.

Although we'd had seismic rows, worse than any we'd had when I was working and renting, it still seemed worth sticking together. We'd managed to keep our relationship more or less fair. I'd kept his freezer full of ready-meals and bread and provided the makings of lazy weekend breakfasts from the bins of coffee shops and cafés – yoghurts, fruit, pains aux chocolat, bottles of juice. I'd waited in at his place for deliveries and workmen. In return, he'd treated me to a glass of wine and the use of his washing machine now and again. I'd never had to fall back on his support to cope with danger or unpleasantness and he had stayed at my places – which had usually been closer to the centre of London and to his office than his rented home – at least as often as the other way round. In the end, the really important thing seemed to be that we still managed to have a good time together even if we were just sitting in a squat or trying to hitch-hike in the rain.

I'd only promised myself that I'd try to live this way for

12 months, and as the days lengthened and April ended, the time was nearly up. I totted up how much it had cost me to survive. It averaged out at less than a pound a day, even including the trips to Holland, Belgium, Bristol and Leeds, and splashing out on that bus ride back from Scotland.

I had rarely felt this healthy and calm, sleeping properly and eating well, but the circumstances that made it possible for me to live this way also made me angry. Even if the shops, businesses and homeowners couldn't reduce the amount of waste being produced, they did not have to dispose of their surplus as rubbish. FareShare, the food redistribution charity, believes that it would be possible to collect and redistribute up to 15 times more surplus food than they currently do. Dozens of small schemes to redistribute white goods and furniture exist up and down the country. Short-life housing schemes have waiting lists hundreds of names long.

Instead many organisations are doing the opposite, putting huge amounts of effort into stopping people who want their rubbish from taking it. Food is being pulled out of its packaging or deliberately soiled with coffee grounds and blue dye. Bins are locked up behind tall fences, unclimbable by any but the most determined and agile. Flats and houses are boarded up like fortresses or comprehensively destroyed on the inside. Anyone who tries to move in can expect to be evicted within months if not weeks, only for the building, once emptied again, to stay empty.

Of the houses I'd lived in, all but one of them was still disused by their owners. Builders had arrived a couple of months after our eviction from the solicitors' office to get on with converting the building into flats. But the squatters in the nursing home were still there, paying their small rent to the owners. Pete was making electronic music and running occasional club nights. Monica had a job at the Tate and had bought a gym membership for the showering facilities. Tom was still busking and still dominating the house. They had vegetables growing in the nursing home garden. Chris's little house was occupied by the Russian bailiff's security company who had kicked us out, but there were no signs of habitation when I cycled past that spring. The mansion was boarded up again, more securely this time. The studios, the clinic and the row of little houses were still sitting empty. And I was still in the Ocean Estate flat.

Several skipping spots that had been reliable sources of meals at the beginning of the year have become impossible. A large branch of EAT in the Square Mile used to throw away three or four black plastic sacks of sandwiches, wraps, salads, yoghurts and fruit. It still does. It's just that today you can watch through the window as the shop assistants open every single packet before putting it in the bag, emptying yoghurt over salads and sandwiches.

The security guards at New Covent Garden now chuck people out far more enthusiastically than when I first went there. First you began to have to arrive in the very early hours if you wanted to get a decent load of fruit and vegetables before being forced to leave. The activists were often still up at 3 a.m. when the market opened, so they simply cycled over before going to bed when they wanted green-groceries. At the beginning of the summer of 2009, would-be skippers at the market began to be handed fliers carrying the Metropolitan Police's logo telling them that taking waste produce would be considered theft and that they risked prosecution if they continued to take it. Many scavengers have stopped going to the market.

Rules could change to make it less cost-effective to deliberately produce excess food and throw it away or to let homes sit empty. A first step would be to get definitive facts about what is happening. The government could collect and publish accurate figures showing how much food and other waste is generated by shops and manufacturers; quangos already do this for household waste. This would give customers solid facts upon which to judge businesses' claims that they disposed of their rubbish in an environmentally friendly way, and use their purchasing power to make a difference.

The tax on landfill could be increased still further, making reusing or recycling waste more appealing. Tristram Stuart, a food-waste activist whose book *Waste: Uncovering the Global Food Scandal* was published in 2009, suggests enforcing the separation of food waste from other kinds of waste in order to tax those who waste food and divert food that continues to be dumped away from land-fill. Such a law has existed in South Korea since 2005.

Councils could be compelled to reveal how many empty

homes they own rather than shunting those that have been declared permanently void off the balance sheet, as my home had been along with 80,000 to 100,000 others according to EHA estimates. The EHA has a raft of suggestions for changes to the tax system that would make it more expensive to leave houses empty for long periods and easier and cheaper to bring them back into use. The charity is contributing to training events for local authorities to teach them to make better use of the powers they already have to turn empty privately owned houses back into homes.

Changes to the law always sound tedious and invasive. But perhaps a more cheerful thought is that spending less and consuming less – particularly if that allows you to work less or choose your work more freely – may actually improve your quality of life as well as being greener. Having no more possessions than I could carry made far less difference to my life than I had expected. Being forced to live more communally and socially and to interact with strangers more often made me encounter a wider range of opinions, made my life more interesting and exciting, and even though I was sometimes scared and uncomfortable, made me much less afraid of the world than I had been a year before.

Although government action might reduce the volume of waste produced it would take an almost inconceivable shake-up of the way we live to eliminate it. As long as there is inequality there will be those rich enough to consider items valueless when others would scrabble in the gutter for them. It may be possible to imagine a future in which absolute poverty is history and a time when shipments of waste to the developing world would not be met by armies of people so desperate that they are prepared to risk their health by clambering over it to scavenge from it. But if poverty is relative the poor really will always be with us. For every person replacing a two-year-old laptop, there will be someone without one. For every person buying food in expensive supermarkets and paying for their surpluses, there will be a pensioner struggling to buy decent food to get through the week.

Leaving aside the social problems caused by empty buildings and the environmental problems caused by wasting food, electronic equipment and other goods, it is a matter of simple human decency to let other people have or borrow the things you don't want. It's great that there are campaigns against homes being left empty and food being wasted but until and unless they are successful, squatting and scavenging are better solutions for the poor, hungry or badly housed than simply sitting by and passively waiting for someone else to solve the problems. If property owners don't like their empty buildings being squatted then they should put them into use, rather than smashing up the insides. If businesses do not want their surplus food to be scavenged they should waste less rather than destroying good food with dye.

Perhaps public opinion has turned against squatters as home ownership has risen, making people fearful of squatters hijacking their own homes rather than resenting landlords who choose to leave their buildings empty. The risk is largely a fantasy since squatters can be evicted immediately from homes which are in use and very quickly from places which are empty only temporarily, and damaging other people's property is as much of a crime for squatters as anyone else. The fact that most squatters keep their way of life private also makes it less likely that the prejudices against them will be shattered. No one who bought a sandwich from Viktor, who placed an order at the Ivy with Fabio or asked Monica for directions to a particular artwork in the Tate would have known how they lived, or thought of them the next time they read about squatters in the *Sun* or the *Daily Mail*, but they were far more typical of the squatters I met than the feckless, filthy scroungers of stereotype.

Even if some squatters and skippers are an inconvenience it would still be better to let the practices continue and not only because it's a shame to let the resources go to waste. Those who cause trouble – by behaving antisocially while squatting or by tearing open bin bags rather than untying them – are the minority and are also likely to be the most desperate. They are the people least likely to be able to stop skipping and squatting if it is made even more difficult or unpleasant. Having a higher proportion of squatters and scavengers who are ethical, well organised and still engaged with normal society is probably the best way of moderating the bad behaviour of a minority.

The idea that squatters and scavengers should just be left to their own devices where they are harmlessly using up resources that would otherwise be ignored is not so fanciful. It was almost as easy to evict squatters in the seventies and the eighties as it is today but most squats then lasted far longer than they do now. Squatters turned buildings that would otherwise have been empty into homes and created functioning communities – probably more peaceful and less troublesome precisely because their homes were more stable than they are now. The squatters were not constantly locked in a battle with the authorities, and it was worth it for squatters to invest the effort to make things work.

In Barcelona, possibly the skipping capital of Europe, people can frequently be seen carrying crooked sticks made out of wood and bent wire used for rescuing bags from the communal skips that are on every street corner, like hooking a duck at a fairground. The bins are often full of food from shops and supermarkets nearby, and no one in the city – not shop assistants, not bin men, not police – seems to think it so extraordinary that people might want to rescue it, still less that they should be stopped.

Barcelona and Berlin could both compete with London for numbers of squats. In Spain and Germany, however, the laws on squatting are far more ambiguous than in England. If squats continue to exist in both cities, it is often due to owners accepting that there is no point in evicting squatters when the building will stay empty. Scores of long-lived squats in both places function as art galleries and meeting spaces, places for gigs and communal meals, just as those in Holland and some of the squats in the UK that last for more than a couple of months try to do. It may be too much to hope that England's laws on squatting could be liberalised to match Holland's sensible ones, which protect buildings empty only in the short term as well as squatters who choose their homes with care. Such laws may not even survive in Holland. But property owners could rethink their hatred of squatters and just leave them alone as long as they are causing no trouble and the building would otherwise lie unused. Even better would be to negotiate contracts so that both sides know what they can expect from each other.

In a handful of spots along the roads into Washington DC people queue up at rush hour, waiting for cars to pull over and let the people at the front of the line hop in. It's hitch-hiking for commuters, known to locals as slugging, a practice that started in the seventies in response to the introduction of 'High Occupancy Vehicle' (HOV) lanes on the roads from the suburbs into the city. At certain times of day cars must be carrying at least three people to use the lanes. Casual car-pooling began as solo drivers picked up passengers from bus stops, offering to drive them into the city for free. The drivers could dodge the jams by using the HOV lanes, the passengers saved the bus fare or their own petrol money and congestion was cut for everyone. The story goes that the word 'slug' – both a noun and a verb – was coined by bus drivers struggling to tell whether people standing at bus stops were waiting for a bus or a free lift in the same way that they had to keep an eye out for fake coins – or 'slugs' – being handed over as fares. Since then slugging has become so established that there is now a range of routes, each with specific pick-up and drop-off points for both the morning and the evening commute, as well as a website setting out the accepted rules and etiquette for drivers and passengers – no smoking, never leave a woman standing alone in the slug line and slugs don't touch the car stereo. Slugging sprang up without official help, but local authorities in other cities could step in to facilitate a similar economical, environmentally friendly and practical idea, perhaps by opting for HOV lanes rather than tolls to encourage car sharing. Even signs for hitching spots like those in Holland might help.

Across the developing world, an estimated 15 million people scrape out a living by combing huge rubbish dumps for waste – rags, aluminium cans, cardboard – that can be sold to recycling businesses for a tiny sum. Most policy-makers saw them as a problem to be got rid of until a decade ago, says Martin Medina, who has written a book on waste-pickers in Asia, Africa and Latin America called *The World's Scavengers: Salvaging for Sustainable Consumption and Production*. Today, he says, some authorities are realising that when waste-pickers receive support they can be 'a perfect example of sustainable development'. Brazil's labour ministry has recognised informal waste collection as a legitimate trade. In Colombia, cooperatives of waste-pickers are being allowed to bid for waste-management contracts in Bogota and the third largest city, Cali, in an acknowledgement that they are often more efficient sorters of rubbish than higher-tech methods and that sifting through the rubbish, though unpleasant and unhealthy, provides vulnerable people with a source of income without which they would be in an even worse situation. The situation of most urban scavengers in England is of course far more comfortable but perhaps authorities and businesses could accept that by rescuing consumer goods and food from bins they are helping to divert some of the waste from the landfill.

In England today, as a scavenger, skipper and squatter, I had been treated as a pest to be kept out with anti-climb paint and security guards, a social pariah in most people's eyes. But by living like that, I got a glimpse of what was being thrown away. I had been eating it, wearing it and living in it, and I had been happy while doing so.

As spring arrived so did a letter from the insurance company of the taxi driver who had knocked me off my bike in the winter, offering me money to make up for my wrecked bike and injured bum. It wasn't a fortune but it was enough, after a year of living on next to nothing, to feel rich. I bought Colin a few drinks to celebrate the end of a year. We went out to the cinema and ate ice cream but then we went home to the squat. I saw no reason to return to what most people would consider a normal way of life. My insurance payout would have lasted only a month or so if I'd had to pay rent and buy all my food – less if I had tried to feed myself in the manner to which I'd become accustomed, on sushi, bread from artisan bakeries and air-freighted summer fruit all winter. Besides, I had a happy home shared with friends in a community where we knew each other and looked out for each other. It was improvised and temporary but I liked it and I didn't have to pay for it. Why would I move out?

There was food I craved from the shops but what I wanted most turned out to be the cheapest on offer. I saw croissants in the bins every night but I had never found any porridge oats, which I missed having for breakfast. I would turn away several hundred shrink-wrapped blinis from the Waitrose bins but I prized the rare find of crackers or bog-standard digestive biscuits.

Walking into a supermarket for the first time after a year to buy the basics I couldn't find in the bins was a nasty shock. Among the aisles, every shelf-edge was trying to distract me from what I had planned to buy with notices pointing out what good value this packet of crisps was, what a bargain those ready-meals were, how much cheaper these loaves of bread were than those in other shops. When I queued among the other shoppers for the checkout the assistant didn't meet my eye. Going skipping might have been an effort, having to be in the right place at the right time and having to put up with an occasional bit of spilt food and aggravation, but I'd become inured to that just as I'd previously been used to the grimness of supermarkets. When I had to pay, I couldn't believe how much it came to. More than £5 for a bag of oats, coffee, milk and some fruit? I could have lived for a week on that.

I had been missing some aspects of moneyed life.

Although I had found, borrowed or learned to do without most things, it was nice to buy some antihistamines for my hay fever that spring. I got some new underwear to replace my old that was going into holes and a colourful dress and a skirt to break up my black uniform. It was a luxury to buy a snack – an apple or a packet of crisps – on the spur of the moment if I got hungry when out. I'd tried to get into the habit of slipping something to eat into my bag before leaving the squat but had often forgotten or stayed out longer than I expected and found myself waiting, famished, for skipping time.

I had badly missed going to the cinema, to gigs and the theatre. I wanted to buy music. It wasn't that I had been getting bored but I had known I was missing out on good things. Before, after years of taking the privileges of being reasonably prosperous in London for granted, I had begun to feel jaded and uninterested in the choices available to me. It was great to be so excited about it all again. I felt good about the idea of spending money on it, too. Handing over cash to the National Theatre or to the Rough Trade record shop was nothing like going into Tesco. I feel good about being a paying audience if my money helps organisations I value to exist.

I was surprised by how much I missed sport. I'd seen it primarily as a necessary evil before, prescribing myself a dose of lengths in the swimming pool or a distance to run in order to compensate for other indulgences. But health and vanity aside I wanted to go back to it far more than I had imagined, missing the cool relief of diving into a pool or the satisfaction of a really good workout. I happily paid up for a monthly pass to the local pool and joined a kick-boxing gym.

I decided to stop cycling. Fifteen cyclists died on London's roads in 2008 and 430 were seriously injured. I remain convinced that going everywhere by bike was the most dangerous aspect of my year without money, far more dangerous than hitching, eating food out of bins or being surrounded by my fellow squatters. It was certainly the only time I got physically hurt. Now I had cash I decided to take buses and tubes everywhere. So I did. For about two days. Sitting on the buses made me travel-sick. The tubes were so much hotter and more crowded than I remembered and you had to walk such a long way to get to the platforms. Not like getting on your bike to cruise at a comfortable pace from door to door. And it was so slow! Even when I cycled unhurriedly I tended to arrive more quickly than I would by bus if not by tube. At least I was always able to make a sensible estimate of how long the trip would take before setting off rather than leaving myself vulnerable to the vagaries of the public transport system.

I was racing through my money far faster than I had expected, with one £10 note after another seeming to evaporate from my purse on food and transport, leaving nothing to show for it. Paying the bus fare to go and look for free food felt a bit silly, too. Except when it was raining, I went back to cycling almost everywhere.

In many ways, with a little money I had the best of both

worlds. While living on nothing I had found it very comforting when I had £20 to hand as insurance against things going wrong. Now I had more I could enjoy the freedom of not having to go to work to pay the rent or buy food but I could also pay for things I needed or wanted without having to think about how to get the money.

But if you squat you can't have possessions you couldn't bear to lose. As soon as I had picked up my laptop and some nice clothes from my mum's house, I began to fret about what would happen to them while no one was in our flat – it remained perfectly possible that we would get home one day to find that the council had closed it up. We would probably have to move house again before long so it would be silly to have more stuff than I could easily carry. Getting my record player and vinyl collection back from my sister would have been stupid, however much I missed it.

Going back to working full-time would be difficult though not impossible while squatting. It would have been fine as long as we were stable in the flat but when we needed to move – and therefore needed to spend nights scouting around and opening places then house-sitting for weeks before feeling safe again – it would be hopelessly disruptive. Viktor had struggled with exhaustion when he'd had to go to his sandwich-making job after a late and anxious night of opening a squat and trying to be fully alert in a more demanding job would have been even tougher.

Sam and Jo seemed to have found a good compromise, spending some of the money they earned on food, entertainment and possessions while saving most of it for other things. If they had to take a day off to sort out house business or just to have a rest, it didn't matter – they wouldn't get paid and another bike courier would do their work. Everyone would understand because many couriers lived in squats, and in a job that requires daily battles with taxis and HGVs, punk attitudes and a relaxed approach to risk are a given.

I had realised I would go back to working for money sooner or later so would be able to – and might have to – give up squatting. A year without working had taught me that I preferred being busy. I felt happier and more satisfied if I got up before mid-morning and arrived at the end of the day feeling as if I'd achieved something, whether I was working on the house, doing a shift in the ASS office or writing. I'd even gone back to setting an alarm clock, finding that if I slept too much for a couple of days it would then become impossible to rest for a night or two. Others might reach a natural equilibrium but after months of trying I hadn't. I loved being able to flip the alarm off and sleep in when I felt like it but the pleasure of idleness wore thin for me. I didn't want to forget that and slip back into resenting work. Working like you don't need the money may be a tired old cliché, but I now know that, as long as I am prepared to squat and scavenge, I really don't need it. On the other hand, having cash for security and convenience as well as entertainment would be no bad thing as long as I don't forget that most possessions are luxuries, not necessities.

At the time of writing, at the beginning of September 2009, I am still in my little Ocean Estate flat, eight months after moving in. The freezer is still full of skipped food but my shelf also has shop-bought porridge oats, a jar of Vegemite, coffee and milk. Jo and her new boyfriend Sean have cycled off towards India. The casualness with which they sold or gave away all of their few possessions before leaving made me think back to the hours I'd spent stashing my stuff in my mum's garage. It had been liberating to learn to care less about my belongings and to be more confident that I would be OK even if I had next to nothing, but I was still a long way from being as free from worry about stuff and security as Jo and Sean. They left nothing in storage. They sold their laptops and spare bikes for extra travelling money, and dumped a bag of clothes in the middle of our living room labelled 'clean and free'. I got Jo's woolly hat and Sam got a T-shirt Sean had won in a bike couriers' race. With only what fitted into their panniers – a tent, sleeping bags, a few changes of clothes – they cycled to Dover on the first day, hitching the ferry to Calais with a lorry driver on the second, their bikes in the back of his huge empty truck.

Viktor has gone home to Hungary, but Jozsef is still my neighbour. I can see the paintings he has hung on his living-room wall from my kitchen window. Stevie has left Barcelona for Canada and Jamie and his housemates are just about to move out of their library now the owner has planning permission to turn it into flats almost two years after they moved in. The nursing home squatters are still going strong and Sam and I are today tidying the flat before one of Sam's friends arrives to move into Jo's old room.

Squatters have stopped opening flats on the estate and some of the better-organised ones have already moved out, suspecting that it can't be long until we get taken to court and then evicted, now that almost all the tenants have been moved out and council surveyors have started digging boreholes so that structural engineers can design foundations for the new buildings. But just a couple of hundred metres away, the three blocks of flats that will be levelled only when my block has been completely rebuilt have already started to be emptied. One option Sam and I are considering when we get evicted from this flat is to move across the road.

I keep my eyes open for empty buildings, and when I spot a promising-looking one I feel a faint swell of excitement at the idea of moving in, and curiosity about what would happen if I did. Perhaps it would turn out to be a happy, long-term home, like the activists' studios or my Ocean flat. Perhaps we would get kicked out quickly or even brutally. I can understand why so many of my squatting friends live this way year after year – it would be easy to carry on now I know how to do it, what it's like when the worst happens and that I have a network of fellow squatters who will help me if I need it. Paying rent would be galling now I know there are hundreds of thousands of long-term empties crying out to be turned back into homes. I would miss living with the friends I have made and the sense of community I gain as a squatter. On the other hand, it would be lovely to have a place where I knew I could stay indefinitely, where I could unpack some of my things from my mum's garage and spend the winter without going to bed freezing cold every night.

I am more optimistic today than I was when I walked away from my old life. For all its flaws, the world is not the hostile and dangerous place I imagined, and I feel a greater sense of its possibilities. Stevie felt like going to Spain, so he packed up his bag and hitched south, finding a squat to live in when he arrived. Jo felt like cycling across the world, so she built a touring bike and headed off. Mikey decided to make a pilgrimage to Jerusalem, aiming to walk all the way without a penny in his pocket and depending on the kindness of strangers to see him through. I gave up everything I used to think I couldn't do without, and if anything I am happier today than I was before. No doubt Jo, Stevie and Mikey will face difficulty, fear and discomfort but despite that – or perhaps, partly, because of it – they'll probably end up having a good time.

Wherever I live in future, whether it's free or a place I pay money for, I hope I will manage to remember that I can get by without possessions but not without friends and allies. Stuff – a record collection, a wardrobe of clothes, a leather sofa – is nice, but the material props that seemingly support a safe and secure existence can turn to dust as mine did when I lost my job and had to give up my flat. I didn't survive without money or possessions just because of the empty houses and wasted food and consumer goods. I got by because squatters and scavengers band together to help each other. Websites like Freecycle and couchsurfing thrive thanks to the goodwill and generosity of their users. Drivers will give you a lift if you stand by the side of the road with your thumb out. I got by because of the people I relied on and who relied on me, strangers and friends.